More Equal Than Others

More Equal Than Others

Humans and the Rights of Other Animals

RAFFAEL N FASEL

College Assistant Professor and Affiliated Lecturer,
University of Cambridge, UK

OXFORD
UNIVERSITY PRESS

OXFORD
UNIVERSITY PRESS

Great Clarendon Street, Oxford, OX2 6DP,
United Kingdom

Oxford University Press is a department of the University of Oxford.
It furthers the University's objective of excellence in research, scholarship,
and education by publishing worldwide. Oxford is a registered trade mark of
Oxford University Press in the UK and in certain other countries

Published in the United States of America by Oxford University Press
198 Madison Avenue, New York, NY 10016, United States of America

British Library Cataloguing in Publication Data
Data available

Library of Congress Control Number: 2023948641

ISBN 978–0–19–890740–4

DOI: 10.1093/oso/9780198907435.001.0001

For Giordana

Acknowledgements

The seed for this book was planted fifteen years ago when, as a law student at the University of Fribourg, I was confronted for the first time with the legal abyss that separates humans from nonhuman animals. At least on paper, all 8 billion humans have fundamental legal rights. By contrast, the 70 billion land animals and the 0.9 to 2.7 trillion fishes that we kill and use in one year alone possess no such rights. The idea of analysing this state of affairs began to take shape eight years ago, on 27 May 2015. A freshly minted graduate of Yale Law School, I was sitting in a packed courtroom in the New York State Supreme Court Building in Lower Manhattan and witnessed the first-ever court hearing in the Western world on whether two nonhuman animals—the chimpanzees Leo and Hercules—should be recognized as legal persons with the fundamental right to bodily liberty. The hearing was a memorable one not only for its historic subject matter, but also because of the story it was telling about the changing nature of society and law. The courtroom wall behind the judge was adorned with a large painting that depicted the way justice had been administered for centuries: by men in wigs. Sitting before that scene was a female judge, Judge Barbara Jaffe, and that judge was considering whether nonhuman beings should be granted a legal status and rights akin to those possessed by human beings. Law evolves, like the humans and animals in this story, and it is the aim of this book to expound when and how facts about the nature of an animal should induce change in the law.

I have received a great deal of help along the way. My foremost thanks go to my PhD supervisor Nigel Simmonds whose masterly guidance and exemplary approach to legal scholarship influenced the thesis on which this book is based in more ways than he believes. I am also grateful to Jeff Skopek for having stood by my side as an advisor. Alasdair Cochrane and Antara Haldar put the thesis through its paces in the final viva. I would like to thank them both for the challenging but stimulating discussion, and Alasdair for having been such an unwavering champion of the book project. To Sean Butler I am grateful for his collegiality and his enthusiasm for the topic; to Matthew Kramer for allowing me to test some of my ideas in the Cambridge Forum for Legal and Political Philosophy; to Trevor Allan for his insightful observations on my work; and to Don Broom and Peter Fordyce for helping me better understand the science of animal sentience. Over the course of my doctoral studies, I was fortunate enough to be able to moor at a number of other academic institutions and I am thankful to the people I have met there. At the University of Oxford, Pavlos Eleftheriadis gave me helpful feedback in the formative stages of my dissertation. At Harvard Law School, Kristen Stilt and Chris Green provided me with a warm research community; and Gerald Neuman was kind enough to take the time to discuss my ideas on human rights. At other institutions I have never docked but still found sympathetic ears for my work. I am particularly thankful to Will Kymlicka, Ann Thomson, and Federico Zuolo for their comments and their generous help with my research.

I have also had the opportunity to expose others to my ideas at several conferences and workshops. At Cambridge, I presented my work in the first-year seminar for PhD in Law students and in the Cambridge Legal Theory Discussion Group. I am indebted to the Group's convenors Tom Adams and Haris Psarras. At Yale, I received valuable feedback from Leora Dahan Katz and Beth Henzel in the Law School's Doctoral Conference. At Oxford, I had the opportunity to present a paper at the Oxford Human Rights Hub's Workshop in Human Rights. I am grateful to the organizers and to Tarunabh Khaitan for commenting on my paper. More of my work was presented at the European University Institute. I would like to thank Elena Brodeală and the members of the Constitutionalism and Politics Working Group for hosting me in Florence, and Manès Weisskircher for his comments on my paper. I am furthermore grateful to Erwin Lengauer at the University of Vienna for inviting me to discuss my research. I would also like to thank Kristen Stilt and Chris Green for letting me present a chapter in the Harvard Animal Law and Policy Program Workshop. At the World Congress of the International Association for Philosophy of Law and Social Philosophy (IVR) in Lucerne, I presented the Species Membership Approach in a stimulating workshop organized by Visa Kurki, Saskia Stucki, and Thomas Sparks. Finally, I am grateful to Jesse Tomalty and Alasdair Cochrane for giving me the chance to discuss my work on sentient equality at the University of Bergen. On all these occasions, I have received perceptive comments from members of the audience to whom I would like to express my gratitude.

I am furthermore grateful for the generous financial support from the Vincent Merkle Foundation, the Swiss National Science Foundation, the Haldimann Foundation, Sidney Sussex College, and the Cambridge Law Faculty, which enabled me to undertake my PhD journey. Alex Flach and Brian Stone at Oxford University Press have helped me get the project across the finishing line, and I remain thankful to them as well as to my wonderful Project

Editor Charlotte Kershaw. Further down in the pecking order, but not in my appreciation, are the following human and nonhuman animals: John Adenitire, Amadeus, Pablo Marcello Bacquero, Basil, Charlotte Blattner, Lucius Caviola, Ya Lan Chang, Kelly Dhru, Max Harris, Runze He, Yukinori Iwaki, Visa Kurki, Jyr-Jong Lin, Lucky, Lucas MacClure, Maayan Menashe, Crescente Molina, Ben Mylius, Joshua Neoh, Jay Shooster, Tvisha Shroff, Christoph Stritt, Saskia Stucki, and Joe Wills. Particular thanks go to John, Joe, and Saskia who read and commented on the manuscript. Michael Gold did a sterling job as my research assistant, and Sam Kharabanda Groom expertly proofread the final manuscript with a particular view to eradicating any remaining German turns of phrase. Finally, I would like to thank my wife, Giordana Campagna, for her love and commitment, and my parents, Ursula Birbaum and Walter Fasel. Without their support, this book would have never seen the light of day.

Raffael N Fasel
New Haven
June 2023

Contents

1

Introduction

1 A trend to grant rights to animals and its discontents

In 2013, a group of animal rights lawyers known as the Nonhuman Rights Project (NhRP) made international headlines when they filed a lawsuit on behalf of Leo and Hercules, two chimpanzees used for research at Stony Brook University in New York. The NhRP argued that the chimpanzees are legal persons with a right to bodily liberty, and that they should therefore be released from Stony Brook and transferred to a sanctuary.[1] The case has raised fundamental questions not only about the current legal status of animals, but also concerning the relationship between animal rights and human rights. As the BBC asked in its reporting on the case: 'Should animals have the same rights as humans?'[2] Or would the conferral of rights on animals undermine the rights of humans,[3] especially those who may lack relevant capacities such as autonomy and thus an interest in bodily liberty?

In this book, I will explain that both those arguing for an extension of legal rights to animals as well as those worried about how such extensions might undermine the equality and rights of human beings have a point. Failing to extend legal rights to some animals means withholding vital protections from them that they deserve based on their capacities and interests. But granting them rights based on these capacities and interests threatens to undermine the status and rights of human beings who lack the relevant capacities and interests, or possess them to a lesser degree. I propose a practical yet unorthodox

[1] *Nonhuman Rights Project, Inc v Samuel L Stanley et al*, Verified Petition (2 December 2013) Supreme Court of the State of New York, County of Suffolk <https://archive.nonhumanrights.org/content/uploads/Suffolk-Verified-Petition-of-E.Stein-and-S.Wise_.pdf> accessed 11 June 2023.

[2] Owen Bennett-Jones, 'Should Animals Be given Human Rights?' *BBC News* (26 May 2015) <https://www.bbc.com/news/world-32854504> accessed 11 June 2023.

[3] Biologically speaking, humans are animals, and I will sometimes indicate this by speaking of 'humans and other animals'. However, in contexts in which the conceptual division between the two is considered important, I will refrain from including humans in the category of animals. Sometimes, I will also separate the two for stylistic reasons. I will apply the pronouns 'he/she' and 'who' to animals in contexts that are favourable to their rights, and 'it' in contexts that are not. See on terminology also David Nibert, *Animal Rights/Human Rights: Entanglements of Oppression and Liberation* (Rowman & Littlefield 2002) 153.

More Equal Than Others. Raffael N Fasel, Oxford University Press. © Raffael N Fasel 2024.
DOI: 10.1093/oso/9780198907435.003.0001

solution to this conundrum: in law, rights and other legal entitlements should be granted to animals on the basis of the species to which they belong, and not based on the capacities or interests that individual animals have. I call this position the Species Membership Approach (SMA).

To understand this proposal and why it is unorthodox, it is helpful to consider the trend that has emerged to grant animals legal rights, and the resistance this trend has faced. While most of the attention has been on the NhRP's litigation in the United States, legal developments around the world have given rise to debates about whether only humans should possess fundamental rights or whether some nonhuman beings should have similar protections. In 2016, a court in Mendoza, Argentina, ruled that Cecilia, a chimpanzee held at the local zoo, was a 'non-human legal person[]'[4] with fundamental rights and should be moved from captivity to a great ape sanctuary. In 2017, the Supreme Court of Colombia followed suit when deciding that Chucho, an Andean bear kept at a zoo in Barranquilla, was a legal person and had to be transferred to a nature reserve.[5] In 2020, the citizens of the Swiss Canton of Basel-Stadt voted on a ballot initiative which proposed to amend the canton's bill of rights by including a right of nonhuman primates to life and bodily and mental integrity.[6] In 2022, the Constitutional Court of Ecuador ruled that the country's constitutional protection of the rights of nature also guaranteed the rights of individual animals like the woolly monkey Estrellita, who was declared a subject of rights with, among others, the rights to life, bodily and mental integrity, and to food.[7] These developments are just the tip of the iceberg of a broader trend towards recognizing nonhuman animals as creatures with highly developed

[4] *'Cecilia'* [2016] Tercer Juzgado de Garantías Mendoza P-72.254/15 (Ana María Hernández tr <https://www.nonhumanrights.org/content/uploads/2016/12/Chimpanzee-Cecilia_translation-FINAL-for-website.pdf> accessed 11 June 2023) 25. See also Gabriel Samuels, 'Chimpanzees Have Rights, Says Argentine Judge as She Orders Cecilia Be Released from Zoo' *The Independent* (7 November 2016) <https://www.independent.co.uk/news/world/americas/argentina-judge-says-chimpanzee-poor-conditions-has-rights-and-should-be-freed-from-zoo-a7402606.html> accessed 11 June 2023.

[5] *'Chucho'* [2017] Supreme Court of Justice of Colombia, Chamber of Civil Cassation AHC4806-2017; Semana, 'Chucho, el oso de anteojos que triunfó en la Corte Suprema de Justicia' (27 July 2017) <https://www.semana.com/nacion/articulo/chucho-el-oso-que-gano-un-habeas-corpus-en-la-corte-suprema-de-justicia/534034> accessed 11 June 2023. This ruling was recently overturned in *'Chucho'* [2020] Constitutional Court of Colombia, Communication No 3 SU-016/20.

[6] See for an overview Raffael N Fasel and Sean C Butler, *Animal Rights Law* (Hart Publishing 2023) 138, 149–51.

[7] *'Estrellita'* [2022] Constitutional Court of Ecuador, No 253-20-JH, translation available at <animal.law.harvard.edu/wp-content/uploads/Final-Judgment-Estrellita-w-Translation-Certification.pdf> accessed 11 June 2023. See also Macarena Montes Franceschini and Kristen Stilt, 'Estrellita the Woolly Monkey and the Ecuadorian Constitutional Court: Animal Rights Through the Rights of Nature' [2023] ReVista: Harvard Review of Latin America <https://revista.drclas.harvard.edu/estrellita-the-wooly-monkey-and-the-ecuadorian-constitutional-court-animal-rights-through-the-rights-of-nature/> accessed 11 June 2023.

capacities that are worthy of having legally protected rights akin to human rights.[8]

Attempts to legally protect animal welfare have a long history, and nearly 80 per cent of states today have some form of animal protection legislation.[9] In the news and in parts of scholarship, such protections are sometimes even viewed as conferring 'legal rights' on animals.[10] The idea behind such ascriptions tends to be that, if humans have duties regarding animals, such as to not treat them cruelly, then animals have corresponding rights, such as a right not to be treated cruelly.[11] Seen in this light, the above-mentioned developments might appear to be of a piece with such long-standing efforts to improve animal welfare. However, to view these developments as 'more of the same' is to overlook that they mark a more profound shift: animal rights scholars and advocates are increasingly calling for animals not simply to have better protections of their welfare, but to have fundamental rights similar to those of human beings. These animal rights proponents are not just asking for 'thin', 'welfare rights'. Rather, they demand 'thick', 'fundamental rights' for animals.[12] The difference is an important one: in contrast to welfare rights, fundamental rights protect their holder's vital interests, such as their interest in having their bodily integrity protected. Also, in contrast to welfare rights, fundamental rights for animals could not easily be infringed by humans' countervailing interests in using animals for their own purposes.[13] In this new paradigm, the use and killing of animals for purposes such as the production of food, for sports, or for entertainment—all permitted by animal welfare law—would in many instances qualify as

[8] Anne Peters, 'Rights of Human and Nonhuman Animals: Complementing the Universal Declaration of Human Rights' (2018) 112 American Journal of International Law Unbound 355–56; Jessica Eisen, 'Animals in the Constitutional State' (2017) 15 International Journal of Constitutional Law 909, 911–12. See on the 'animal turn' in the social sciences and humanities Harriet Ritvo, 'On the Animal Turn' (2007) 136 Daedalus 118; Anne Peters, Saskia Stucki, and Livia Boscardin, 'The Animal Turn: What Is It and Why Now?' (*Verfassungsblog*, 14 April 2014) <https://verfassungsblog.de/the-animal-turn-what-is-it-and-why-now/> accessed 11 June 2023.

[9] Fasel and Butler, *Animal Rights Law* (n 6) 14–15.

[10] See eg Elizabeth Preston, 'Octopuses Don't Have Backbones—or Rights' *The New York Times* (27 August 2022) <https://www.nytimes.com/2022/08/27/science/octopus-research-animal-rights.html> accessed 11 June 2023. See also Cass R Sunstein, 'The Rights of Animals' (2003) 70 The University of Chicago Law Review 387, 389–90; Alasdair Cochrane, 'Ownership and Justice for Animals' (2009) 21 Utilitas 424, 432; Visa AJ Kurki, 'Why Things Can Hold Rights: Reconceptualizing the Legal Person' in Visa AJ Kurki and Tomasz Pietrzykowski (eds), *Legal Personhood: Animals, Artificial Intelligence and the Unborn* (Springer 2017).

[11] This interpretation is often inspired by Wesley Hohfeld's analysis of rights, according to which every duty necessarily correlates with a claim-right: Wesley Newcomb Hohfeld, 'Some Fundamental Legal Conceptions as Applied in Judicial Reasoning' (1913) 23 Yale Law Journal 16, 30.

[12] See on these terms, respectively, Fasel and Butler, *Animal Rights Law* (n 6) 83–92; Saskia Stucki, 'Towards a Theory of Legal Animal Rights: Simple and Fundamental Rights' (2020) 40 Oxford Journal of Legal Studies 533, 551–52.

[13] Stucki, 'Towards a Theory of Legal Animal Rights: Simple and Fundamental Rights' (n 12) 552; Fasel and Butler, *Animal Rights Law* (n 6) 88.

fundamental rights violations, similar to how the use and killing of humans for the same purposes would be viewed as a violation of their human rights.

The shift from welfare rights to fundamental rights for animals has met with considerable resistance. For instance, when the citizens of Basel-Stadt went to the polls in 2022 to vote on the constitutional amendment proposing to extend the rights to life and mental and bodily integrity to nonhuman primates, the cantonal authorities advised them against its adoption on the ground that '[i]f fundamental rights were also granted to non-human primates, this would blur the line between humans and animals and our fundamental and human rights would be watered down and relativised'.[14] In Idaho, lawmakers even went as far as passing a law 'provid[ing] that environmental elements, artificial intelligence, nonhuman animals, and inanimate objects shall not be granted personhood'.[15] The law's sponsor, the Republican Representative Tammy Nichols, reportedly sponsored the law in an effort to prevent human children from becoming 'equal' or 'inferior' to nonhuman beings.[16] In scholarship, too, the idea of extending fundamental rights or legal personhood to animals has faced opposition. Animal rights sceptics such as Richard Cupp have argued that 'allowing animal legal personhood based on cognitive abilities could unintentionally lead to gradual erosion of protections for . . . especially vulnerable humans'.[17] The shift from welfare rights to fundamental rights for animals, and the challenges this has invited, raise unprecedented questions about the relationship between human rights and animal rights. The most urgent question is: Can animals be granted fundamental rights without putting human rights in jeopardy?

2 The need for a species-based approach in law

Many of those who propose that animals should have fundamental rights follow a relatively straightforward argumentative blueprint. According to them, an individual animal deserves a particular fundamental right if the

[14] Kanton Basel-Stadt, 'Darüber stimmen wir am 13. Februar 2022 ab' <https://www.staatskanzlei.bs.ch/dam/jcr:f489f501-a703-4326-9c28-0b6311eea086/w-a-2022-02-13-abstimmungserlaeuterungen.pdf> accessed 11 June 2023 (my translation).

[15] Idaho State Legislature, 'House Bill 720' <https://legislature.idaho.gov/sessioninfo/2022/legislation/h0720/> accessed 11 June 2023.

[16] Rebecca Boone, 'Bill Would Bar Idaho's Lands and Animals From "Personhood"' (2022) <https://www.usnews.com/news/best-states/idaho/articles/2022-02-15/bill-would-bar-idahos-lands-and-animals-from-personhood> accessed 11 June 2023.

[17] Richard L Cupp, 'Cognitively Impaired Humans, Intelligent Animals, and Legal Personhood', *Pepperdine University Legal Studies Research Paper No 12* (2016) 501 <http://papers.ssrn.com/abstract=2775288> accessed 11 June 2023.

animal can be shown empirically to have the capacities and interests that serve as grounds for the possession of the right.[18] For instance, if it can be demonstrated that an animal has the capacity to feel pain and thus an interest in not being harmed, then, all else being equal, that animal is said to deserve a right to bodily integrity. This approach can be found, for example, in the increasingly popular sentientist rights theories, according to which all sentient animals (ie animals who are able to have subjective experiences) are deserving of some fundamental rights.[19] However, it is also a prominent feature of other animal rights accounts.[20] What characterizes all these theories is their focus on the *individual*. Proponents of this approach argue that only an individual's own interests, and not the species to which the animal belongs, should determine the moral and legal protections the animal receives.[21] Animal rights advocates of all stripes agree that basing protections on species membership and ignoring individual beings' interests is to commit 'speciesism', that is, discriminatory treatment based on an irrelevant criterion. Species, the argument goes, is as arbitrary a standard for granting or withholding rights as sex or race.[22] This principled opposition to discrimination based on species membership has been an important catalyst for the animal rights movement. Peter Singer's forceful critique of speciesism in his seminal 1975 book *Animal Liberation* played a key role in making the rejection of speciesism, and the concomitant emphasis on individual interests, the cornerstone of the movement.[23] The ethical view that judgements about how we ought to treat beings should depend entirely on their individual characteristics is known as 'moral individualism'[24] and has gained a large following, especially among animal ethicists. As the animal rights scholar Alasdair Cochrane has observed, 'at the heart of many traditional theories

[18] See eg Alasdair Cochrane, 'Evaluating "Bioethical Approaches" to Human Rights' (2012) 15 Ethical Theory and Moral Practice 309, 319; Peter Singer and Agata Sagan, 'When Robots Have Feelings' *The Guardian* (14 December 2009) <https://www.theguardian.com/commentisfree/2009/dec/14/rage-against-machines-robots> accessed 11 June 2023.

[19] See eg Alasdair Cochrane, *Sentientist Politics: A Theory of Global Inter-Species Justice* (Oxford University Press 2018). I consider this approach in detail in Chapter 5.

[20] See eg Steven M Wise, 'Hardly a Revolution—The Eligibility of Nonhuman Animals for Dignity-Rights in a Liberal Democracy' (1998) 22 Vermont Law Review 793.

[21] See eg Gary L Francione, *Animals, Property, and the Law* (Temple University Press 1995) 8–11; Wise, 'Hardly a Revolution—The Eligibility of Nonhuman Animals for Dignity-Rights in a Liberal Democracy' (n 20) 798; David Bilchitz, 'Moving Beyond Arbitrariness: The Legal Personhood and Dignity of Non-Human Animals' (2009) 23 South African Journal on Human Rights 38, 64–65.

[22] Richard D Ryder, 'Speciesism' in Mark Bekoff (ed), *Encyclopedia of Animal Rights and Animal Welfare* (2nd edn, Greenwood Press 1998) 527–28.

[23] See, for the latest edition, Peter Singer, *Animal Liberation Now: The Definitive Classic Renewed* (Harper Perennial 2023). See also Richard D Ryder, 'Speciesism Again: The Original Leaflet' [2010] Critical Society. I elaborate on the concept of speciesism in Chapter 4, Section 3.

[24] James Rachels, *Created From Animals: The Moral Implications of Darwinism* (Oxford University Press 1999) 173.

of animal ethics has been a staunch commitment to the individual and their interests, alongside a general scepticism about the moral relevance of group-based distinctions'.[25]

This book challenges this orthodoxy in animal rights scholarship. I argue that while species membership may be an arbitrary criterion for recognizing fundamental moral rights, it is a useful criterion *in law* for the extension of fundamental legal rights and cognate legal entitlements. These entitlements, I propose, should be extended to deserving nonhuman animals based on their species membership and not on their individual capacities. This is the Species Membership Approach, or SMA. The SMA joins other incipient species-based proposals such as Martha Nussbaum's and is attractive because it presents a practical solution to two equally damning problems that the two prevalent fundamental rights conceptions have faced.[26]

The first problem is encountered by those adopting accounts that concentrate entirely on individual capacities and that reject species membership as a relevant criterion for the extension of rights. Because of their focus on what individuals deserve, I call this the *Meritocratic conception of fundamental rights* (or Meritocracy, for short). The issue with this conception is that adopting such a focus puts in jeopardy the idea of equal status and equal rights, which are the centrepiece of contemporary human rights law.[27] The reason why the Meritocracy poses a danger is that its individualistic focus requires giving more and stronger rights to beings who possess a larger set of capacities and more well-developed interests. This risks creating a hierarchy of rights-holders who hold different rights and to different degrees. It is no surprise, then, that many human rights advocates have opposed extensions of fundamental rights to animals based on their capacities, warning that this would imperil the rights of human beings, especially vulnerable humans such as infants or persons with disabilities.[28] The SMA overcomes this problem by protecting the equality of human beings in virtue of their species membership.

Those who have opposed extensions of fundamental rights to animals are facing the second problem: not to allow for any such extensions to animals on the mere ground that they do not belong to the human species is increasingly at

[25] Alasdair Cochrane, *Sentientist Politics: A Theory of Global Inter-Species Justice* (Oxford University Press 2018) 5.

[26] Martha C Nussbaum, *Frontiers of Justice: Disability, Nationality, Species Membership* (Harvard University Press 2006) 347; Martha C Nussbaum, *Justice for Animals: Our Collective Responsibility* (Simon & Schuster 2022) 108, 140. For similar approaches see Chapter 7, Section 2.3.

[27] See, for a definition of these terms and an exploration of the umbrella notion of *Equal Consideration*, Chapter 3, Section 3.

[28] See eg Cupp, 'Cognitively Impaired Humans, Intelligent Animals, and Legal Personhood' (n 17); Jeremy Waldron, *Dignity, Rank, and Rights* (Meir Dan-Cohen ed, Oxford University Press 2012) 69.

odds with scientific findings about the sentience, behavioural complexity, and intelligence of beings such as chimpanzees, pigs, elephants, dolphins, or octopuses. Long believed to be mere 'dumb beasts',[29] these and many other animals have been demonstrated to possess some of the same capacities and interests that humans have. These capacities include not just the ability to feel pain,[30] but also more complex capacities such as the ability to plan for the future,[31] to make and use tools,[32] to mourn the dead,[33] to have intricate social relationships,[34] to use human sign language,[35] or to have a culture.[36] Limiting fundamental rights to human beings might help protect the status and rights of humanity, but it has come at the cost of excluding other beings who, based on their capacities and interests, would deserve similar legal protections. Because of the exclusive status and rights that this view accords to only a small group of beings—the human species—I refer to it as the *Aristocratic conception of fundamental rights* (or Aristocracy, for short). The SMA resolves the problem of the Aristocracy by allowing extensions of fundamental legal rights and cognate legal entitlements to deserving nonhuman beings.

The usefulness of the SMA, this book will argue, can only be fully grasped if we understand the tension-filled relationship between the Meritocratic and the Aristocratic conceptions of fundamental rights. Three important aspects of this relationship have been neglected in human and animal rights scholarship: the common historical roots of these conceptions; their conceptual relationship; and the practical consequences that follow from their relationship.

Consider first the underresearched *history* of the Aristocratic and Meritocratic fundamental rights conceptions. It is commonly believed that the first shoots of modern animal rights thinking appeared in early writing such as Henry Stephens Salt's *Animals' Rights: Considered in Relation to Social*

[29] See on this term Catherine Osborne, *Dumb Beasts and Dead Philosophers: Humanity and the Humane in Ancient Philosophy and Literature* (Oxford University Press 2007) (who argues that a humane attitude towards animals can be traced back to Antiquity).

[30] See eg on fish Lynne U Sneddon, 'Pain Perception in Fish: Indicators and Endpoints' (2009) 50 Institute for Laboratory Animal Research Journal 338.

[31] See eg on jays and primates William A Roberts, 'Mental Time Travel: Animals Anticipate the Future' (2007) 17 Current Biology R418.

[32] Robert W Shumaker, Kristina R Walkup, and Benjamin B Beck, *Animal Tool Behavior: The Use and Manufacture of Tools by Animals* (Johns Hopkins University Press 2011).

[33] See eg on elephants Laura Parker, 'Rare Video Shows Elephants "Mourning" Death' *National Geographic* (31 August 2016) <https://www.nationalgeographic.com/news/2016/08/elephants-mourning-video-animal-grief/> accessed 11 June 2023.

[34] See eg on dolphins Monica F Blasi and Luigi Boitani, 'Complex Social Structure of an Endangered Population of Bottlenose Dolphins (Tursiops Truncatus) in the Aeolian Archipelago (Italy)' (2014) 9 PLoS ONE 1.

[35] See eg on gorillas The Gorilla Foundation, 'Communication' <https://www.koko.org/communication/> accessed 11 June 2023.

[36] See eg on chimpanzees A Whiten and others, 'Cultures in Chimpanzees' (1999) 399 Nature 682.

Progress (1894),[37] and that the movement started to flourish in the late twentieth century with the influential works of philosophers like Singer and Tom Regan.[38] Contrary to this view, this book demonstrates that, in fact, proposals to grant fundamental rights to animals go as far back as the eighteenth century. While it is generally recognized that the idea of human rights traces its roots to that time,[39] few know that animal rights, too, were being discussed in the Enlightenment. This is a problematic gap in our understanding because animal rights were not debated in isolation in this period, but in relation to human rights ideas. Shedding light on these debates therefore not only promises to yield a more complete account of the history of animal rights, but also a deeper understanding of their relationship with human rights.

This book focuses on the French Enlightenment to show that Meritocratic claims to extend fundamental rights to animals emerged as part of a *naturalist* current of thinking that became prominent in the seventeenth and eighteenth centuries. Naturalists believed that the human species is part of a continuum of matter on which beings differ from each other only in degree, not kind. According to naturalism, humans are both characterized by great variation within their species, and are not different in principle from nonhuman animals. Because this raised the question of whether humans deserve a differentiated set of rights, naturalism conflicted with another important current at the time, which would come to form the basis of the Aristocratic rights conception: *egalitarianism*. According to egalitarianism, human beings are fundamentally equal, despite differing from each other physically and mentally (I refer to this as the *Equality Thesis*). This thesis was often backed by the claim that the human species is special and separate from all other species (the *Separateness Thesis*). I will illustrate the tension between the egalitarian and the naturalist currents by drawing on the writings of two French Enlightenment philosophers: the egalitarian Jean-Baptiste Salaville (1755–1832) and the naturalist Jean-Claude Delamétherie (1743–1817). In an essay from 1802, Salaville defended the exclusive rights, dignity, and equality of human beings against the theories of naturalists like Delamétherie who rejected the idea of human equality in favour of a hierarchical conception of humanity, and who

[37] Henry S Salt, *Animals' Rights: Considered in Relation to Social Progress* (MacMillan 1894).

[38] Robert Garner, 'The Contemporary Debate in Animal Ethics' in Peter Adamson and G Fay Edwards (eds), *Animals: A History* (Oxford University Press 2018) 322–23. See also Robert Garner and Yewande Okuleye, *The Oxford Group and the Emergence of Animal Rights: An Intellectual History* (Oxford University Press 2021).

[39] See for the classic account Lynn Hunt, *Inventing Human Rights: A History* (Norton 2007). For a critique see Samuel Moyn, *The Last Utopia: Human Rights in History* (Harvard University Press 2010) 3. For a critique of this critique see Vincenzo Ferrone, 'The Rights of History: Enlightenment and Human Rights' (2017) 39 Human Rights Quarterly 130, 136.

proposed that not only human beings should have fundamental rights, but also animals. I will argue that Delamétherie and Salaville have undeservedly faded into obscurity: to my knowledge, they were the first in modern Western history to develop a comprehensive defence of Meritocratic and Aristocratic positions. And even though Delamétherie and Salaville were too little known to influence modern debates, the naturalist and egalitarian ideas they pioneered remain at the forefront of our thinking today.

To understand the ways in which the naturalist and egalitarian currents have shaped our thinking on human and animal rights, I conduct, in a second step, an *analysis* of the Meritocratic and Aristocratic fundamental rights conceptions that these currents have informed. This book proposes that the two conceptions are best viewed as antithetical ideal-types, meaning that they can be found on opposite ends of what I call the *spectrum of fundamental rights conceptions*.

Take the Aristocratic conception, which is based on egalitarianism. Drawing on the growing literature which points to the numerous parallels that exist between supposedly 'new' ideas like human rights, human equality, and human dignity, and 'old' ideas such as noble[40] status and special privileges, I will show that a good part of current human rights thinking and practice is, in central respects, Aristocratic. To spell out these parallels, I examine two key features of the Aristocratic conception: *Equal Consideration* and *Internalism*. First, according to the feature of *Equal Consideration*, the Aristocracy conceives of human rights-holders as possessing a high and equal rank simply in virtue of being born human (I refer to this as *Heredity*); it provides all humans with equal rights (*Equality*); and it excludes all nonhuman beings from the equal rank and from the equal rights (*Exclusivity*). To coin a phrase, *Equal Consideration* considers humanity to be separate *and* equal. Second, I will show that proponents of the Aristocracy explain the equal status and rights of humanity by adopting *Internalism*. An *Internalist* approach is one that explains human rights, equality, dignity, and other concepts not by pointing to facts about human nature, but by taking normative decisions, or developing normative stories and interpretations that give an account of humanity's special status and rights.[41] I call this approach one that *founds* rather than *grounds* humans' equal status and rights.

[40] I use the terms 'nobility' and 'aristocracy' synonymously.

[41] The terms 'internalism' and 'externalism' have other meanings in other contexts, eg in epistemic justification. See eg George Pappas and Clayton Littlejohn, 'Internalist vs. Externalist Conceptions of Epistemic Justification' in Edward N Zalta and Uri Nodelman (eds), *The Stanford Encyclopedia of Philosophy* (Spring 2023, Metaphysics Research Lab, Stanford University 2023) <https://plato.stanford.edu/archives/spr2023/entries/justep-intext/> accessed 11 June 2023. My use of the terms is independent of such other meanings.

Founding explains these concepts by remaining within the normative domain, whereas *grounding* bases them on empirical facts.

On the other end of the spectrum, there is the Meritocratic conception of fundamental rights, which has taken its cue from the naturalist current. As I noted above, Meritocrats argue that animals deserve to hold the same fundamental rights that human beings possess if they, too, have the capacities that are relevant for these rights. The Meritocracy is in many respects the antithesis of the Aristocracy. For this reason, the two characteristic features of the Meritocracy are the mirror image of the two Aristocratic features. In the case of the Meritocracy, these features are *Differential Consideration* and *Externalism*. First, proponents of the Meritocracy reject *Equal Consideration* in favour of *Differential Consideration*.[42] They do so by taking an individual's possession of certain physical and/or mental capacities, rather than mere birth, as the ground for rights (*Merit*); they reject equality in favour of a gradualist approach to distributing rights (*Gradualism*); and they include any type of being in the category of rights-holders who deserves it (*Inclusivity*). Second, adherents of the Meritocracy adopt an *Externalist* approach to explaining rights. This means that, rather than drawing on normative decisions, stories, or interpretations as *Internalists* do, they build on empirical facts about the capacities and interests of individual beings to explain their rights. In other words, *Externalists* point to nature to explain why someone should have rights. They *ground* rather than *found* rights.

Figure 1.1 The spectrum of fundamental rights conceptions

I propose that the individual fundamental rights accounts that we can find in practice and scholarship (*x* and *y* in Figure 1.1) can be located somewhere on this spectrum of fundamental rights conceptions, between its Aristocratic and Meritocratic ends. None of the accounts we will find are likely to be perfect instantiations of either conception. This is because, as I will elaborate shortly,

[42] Note that, as I explain in Chapter 4, Section 3, Meritocrats adopt what is often called the principle of 'equal consideration of interests'. This principle requires that equal interests should be treated alike. By contrast, the principle of *Equal Consideration* that characterizes the Aristocracy requires that equal interest-*holders* be treated equally.

these conceptions are ideal-types. For the purposes of my analysis, I will therefore assume that all those whom I call Meritocrats or Aristocrats defend accounts whose features come sufficiently close to the ideal conceptions.

Third, and finally, once we acquire an understanding of the conceptual relationship between the Aristocracy and the Meritocracy, we can see the *practical* relevance of the idea of the spectrum of fundamental rights conceptions. Because the Aristocratic and the Meritocratic conceptions have opposing strengths and weaknesses, the most viable path forward, I will propose, is a practical middle ground between these conceptions. This practical middle ground allows us to utilize the strengths of both conceptions, while minimizing their weaknesses. The emphasis here is on the word 'practical'. My proposal—including the SMA—resists the temptation to want to solve the problem on the theoretical level. Hence, it does not side with one or the other fundamental rights conception. Nor does it attempt to construct a compounded theory that combines elements from both conceptions.[43] Rather, it aims to provide a practical way forward that accepts and leverages the tension-filled relationship between the two conceptions.

As I will argue, current legal systems are much closer to the Aristocracy than the Meritocracy. This is because they arbitrarily exclude all nonhuman animals from the high status and the fundamental rights that human beings possess. To move us towards the middle ground, I will make the case for a 'Meritocratization' of the Aristocracy. I will show how such a Meritocratization could be achieved by discussing avenues for changing animals' status as legal property and extending specific fundamental rights to them. However, I will also emphasize that when extending fundamental rights and other legal entitlements to animals, one should not commit the common mistake of ignoring that the more one moves in the direction of *Differential Consideration*, the more one loses out on *Equal Consideration*. In other words, the more protections are granted on the basis of individual capacities, the greater the risk of undermining human equality. This, then, is the basis for the SMA: the practical but radical proposal that, in law, we should break with the orthodox rejection of the species criterion, and extend fundamental rights and cognate entitlements to deserving animals on the basis of species membership rather than individual capacities.

Underlying my call for rehabilitating the species membership criterion is an insight that is as obvious as it is sometimes neglected: law plays by different rules than philosophy. In particular, different strategies are required for

[43] See Section 3.

extending legal rights than are required for extending moral rights. This insight is of great importance today, now that fundamental animal rights are no longer confined to the realm of philosophy but are starting to be cast into legal form. Philosophical arguments have a role to play in this process. But they are more often than not simply copy-pasted into the legal domain. To give just one example, in 2018, a consortium of seventeen philosophers submitted an *amici curiae* brief in support of a *habeas corpus* petition that the NhRP had filed on behalf of the chimpanzees Kiko and Tommy, modelled after its earlier petition in the Hercules and Leo case mentioned above.[44] The philosophers followed in Singer's footsteps in advising the court that 'species membership alone cannot rationally be used to determine who is a person or a rights holder'.[45] In giving this advice, they appeared to assume that what holds true in philosophy must also hold true in law, without reflecting on the reasons that a court might have for deviating from 'the best philosophical standards of rational judgment'.[46] In making my case for the SMA, I will show that there are important pragmatic and political reasons that make it legitimate for judges and other legal officials to work with—rather than around—the idiosyncrasies of law.

3 Definitions, methodology, and focus

Let me say a few words about definitions, methodology, and the focus of this book. First, definitions. By *fundamental rights* I mean entitlements which protect important aspects of a being's existence and well-being, akin to the protection that human rights secure for the central aspects of human existence. Fundamental rights include rights such as the right to life, the right to bodily integrity, the right to free speech, freedom of religion, or the right to vote. In the human case, these rights are generally found in declarations and treaties or in constitutional fundamental rights catalogues.[47] In contrast to human rights,

[44] See Lauren Choplin, 'Chimpanzee Rights: The Philosophers' Brief' (*Nonhuman Rights Project*, 26 September 2018) <https://www.nonhumanrights.org/blog/philosophers-brief-book/> accessed 11 June 2023; Kristin Andrews and others, *Chimpanzee Rights: The Philosophers' Brief* (Routledge 2019).

[45] *Nonhuman Rights Project, Inc v Patrick C Lavery et al and Nonhuman Rights Project, Inc v Carmen Presti et al* (23 February 2018) Proposed Brief by Amici Curiae Philosophers, 8 <https://www.nonhumanrights.org/content/uploads/In-re-Nonhuman-Rights-v.-Lavery-Proposed-Brief-by-PHILOSOPHERS-74435.pdf> accessed 11 June 2023.

[46] ibid 2.

[47] See eg Universal Declaration of Human Rights (1948, UDHR) <http://www.un.org/en/universal-declaration-human-rights/> accessed 11 June 2023; International Covenant on Civil and Political Rights (1966, ICCPR) <http://www.ohchr.org/en/professionalinterest/pages/ccpr.aspx> accessed 11 June 2023; International Covenant on Economic, Social and Cultural Rights (1966, ICESCR) <https://www.ohchr.org/EN/ProfessionalInterest/Pages/CESCR.aspx> accessed 11 June 2023. For a

however, fundamental rights are not limited to human beings. Rather, 'fundamental rights' is an umbrella term that encompasses human rights as well as equivalent nonhuman rights. For reasons of simplicity, I will often simply talk of 'fundamental rights' or 'rights'. For the most part, my focus will be on fundamental *legal* rights: fundamental rights that are recognized and protected through legal processes.

Second, methodology. Regarding my selection of the French Enlightenment, it is worth noting that neither the egalitarian nor the naturalist currents originated in that period. Salaville and Delamétherie were not the first to pursue egalitarian and naturalist approaches to rights and dignity. More basic versions of their positions have surfaced at least since ancient times.[48] Nor have their ideas engendered today's positions on human or animal rights. In fact, their exchange seems to have gone largely unnoticed, even by contemporaries.[49] So why focus on this period and on two relatively obscure thinkers? For two reasons.

First, the French Enlightenment was a formative period for the naturalist and egalitarian intellectual tendencies. In this period, they took on the form that would allow them to serve as the basis for the Aristocratic and Meritocratic conceptions that still dominate our thinking about fundamental rights today. What is more, naturalism and egalitarianism were openly (though, in the case of the former, sometimes clandestinely) debated positions. They were not mere tacit assumptions of established conceptions in the way they often are today. Studying egalitarianism and naturalism in this period can therefore provide us with a deeper understanding of these ideas, of their tension-filled relationship, and of the fundamental rights conceptions they came to shape. Second, Salaville and Delamétherie are pertinent thinkers not just because of their innovative arguments about animals' and humans' fundamental rights. The very fact that their exchange is relatively obscure makes it attractive for the purposes of modelling ideal-types of fundamental rights, to which I turn next. With little secondary literature clouding our view, the debate between Salaville and Delamétherie gives us immediate access to the ideological currents that came to shape the Aristocratic and Meritocratic conceptions.

constitutional fundamental rights catalogue see eg arts 1–17 in Basic Law for the Federal Republic of Germany (1949, Grundgesetz, GG) <https://www.gesetze-im-internet.de/englisch_gg/> accessed 11 June 2023.

[48] See eg Liliane Bodson, 'Attitudes Toward Animals in Greco-Roman Antiquity' (1983) 4 International Journal for the Study of Animal Problems 312; Izhak Englard, 'Human Dignity: From Antiquity to Modern Israel's Constitutional Framework' (2000) 21 Cardozo Law Review 1903, 1905.

[49] We know of it only thanks to the French sociologist Valentin Pelosse, who discovered the debate in the 1980s, and Pierre Serna's in-depth study: see Pierre Serna, *L'animal en République, 1789–1802: genèse du droit des bêtes* (Anacharsis 2016).

As I have mentioned, I propose to understand the Aristocratic and the Meritocratic conceptions as *ideal-types* on opposing ends of a spectrum of fundamental rights conceptions. I borrow the concept of the ideal-type from Max Weber, according to whom it is a heuristic device that makes possible the formation of a 'unified analytical construct' out of 'more or less present and occasionally absent concrete individual phenomena'.[50] Ideal-types are attempts at distilling the core conceptual elements—or 'essential tendencies'[51]—that are buried within the history and practices of specific phenomena. This process of distillation is one of rational construction, the purpose of which is to provide the most intelligible and internally consistent version of those phenomena.[52]

To avoid confusion, it is worth emphasizing that ideal-types need not be morally desirable. They are 'ideal' not in a moral sense, but in a logical or conceptual sense.[53] That is why, according to Weber, one may well choose to construct an ideal-type that is at odds with one's own ethical views.[54] Ideal-types serve as standards against which concrete instances of phenomena can be measured. They are 'expository devices' which one can use as aids to analyse the extent to which the empirical reality approximates the utopian construct.[55] Because ideal-types can only serve their expository function if they are not confused with other ideal-types, Weber cautions against the temptation to merge elements from different ideal-types.[56] This is the reason why, as noted above, my proposal for a practical way forward avoids developing a theory that merges elements from the two antithetical fundamental rights conceptions. Nor does an ideal-type actually have to be instantiated anywhere in practice; it is, as Weber puts it, a conceptual 'utopia'[57] that may exist only in our minds. It would therefore be to misunderstand the method of the ideal-type to point out concrete human or animal rights accounts that do not evince all or any of the ideal-types' characteristic elements which I am highlighting. Do not get me wrong: there are such accounts. For example, there are animal rights accounts that deviate from the Meritocracy by adopting Aristocratic elements, such as *Equal Consideration*.[58] There are also human rights accounts

[50] Max Weber, *The Methodology of the Social Sciences* (Edward A Shils and Henry A Finch trs, Free Press 1949) 90. For more detail see Richard Swedberg, 'How to Use Max Weber's Ideal Type in Sociological Analysis' (2017) 18 Journal of Classical Sociology 181.
[51] Weber, *The Methodology of the Social Sciences* (n 50) 91.
[52] ibid 90.
[53] ibid 91–92.
[54] ibid 43.
[55] ibid 90, 92.
[56] Weber refers to the merging of elements from different ideal-types as 'syncretism': ibid 11, 57–58.
[57] ibid.
[58] See eg Tom Regan, *The Case for Animal Rights* (University of California Press 1983) 247. See also Chapter 5.

that deviate from the Aristocracy by endorsing Meritocratic elements, such as *Externalism*.[59] Considerable disagreement can exist among proponents of the same ideal-type.[60] For instance, as we will see, the Meritocracy can span from more deontological theories such as Delamétherie's to utilitarian ones such as Peter Singer's. The Aristocracy is a similarly broad church that includes accounts of different traditions, including religiously infused defences of human dignity and decisionist political theories. One and the same ideal-type can thus be made up of accounts from various traditions, and some accounts will come closer to the pure ideal than others. As always, reality is much messier than theorists would like it to be. But that does not change the fact that the ideal-typical elements which I will be fleshing out can be found in many accounts and practices.

Some may take issue with the particular selection I am making. Why say that Aristocrats focus on *Heredity*, for example? Or why argue that Meritocrats are *Externalists*? It is certainly possible to disagree with me on these and other points. I am not excluding the possibility of differently shaped ideal-types. In fact, I am not even excluding the possibility of different versions of the same ideal-types: for example, while the Meritocratic and the Aristocratic conceptions are on opposite ends of the fundamental rights spectrum, they may not be the most extreme representatives of these opposing ends. On the Meritocratic end, one could imagine, for instance, views that extend rights not only to animals, but to nature more generally.[61] And on the Aristocratic end, one can imagine views that restrict equal rights and dignity to a small subgroup of human beings, as was indeed the case with the real aristocracy. However, the two ideal-types which I will explore capture some of the most salient features of current human and animal rights debates and practices, and therefore tell a particularly interesting story. That story is not meant to replace other ways of carving up the debate space. Rather, its aim is to provide a novel—and I believe fruitful—way of understanding the relationship between human and animal rights. I cannot however demonstrate this here but have to trust that the ensuing chapters will do a good enough job of convincing the reader. The proof of the pudding, as it were, is in the eating.

[59] In fact, there is a major human rights school—sometimes referred to as the 'naturalistic' or 'orthodox' school of human rights—which is *Externalist* in its approach. See for a brief overview Cochrane, 'Evaluating "Bioethical Approaches" to Human Rights' (n 18) 319.

[60] eg Anne Phillips, despite adopting an *Internalist* approach, criticizes the hierarchical notion of human superiority which is linked to the idea of dignity: Anne Phillips, *The Politics of the Human* (Cambridge University Press 2015) 89. See Chapter 3, Section 4.1.

[61] See eg Aldo Leopold, *A Sand County Almanac* (Oxford University Press 1966).

Lastly, focus. Why does the book centre around fundamental rights? Today, discussion of fundamental rights is sometimes scoffed at as a sign of impoverished or even problematic thinking,[62] including in the context of animal rights.[63] Granted, law and morality have more on offer than rights-talk.[64] I focus on fundamental rights not because they are a magic bullet—they are not.[65] There are other approaches, such as those which take duties to be prior to rights,[66] or which put welfare regulations before rights claims,[67] that some find just as useful. However, the existence of these approaches does not change the fact that rights talk abounds. As John Tasioulas observes, human rights discourse in particular has acquired the status of a 'lingua franca'.[68] Given the widespread acceptance of rights discourse, we need to ask whether it is also applicable to nonhuman animals, and what implications this would have for human rights. What is more, the focus on fundamental rights ties in with the dominant role that rights discourse played in the Enlightenment, a period which I will explore in some detail. As the historian Vincenzo Ferrone has pointed out, 'the defining characteristic of the late Enlightenment—and the most positive aspect of its legacy to the Western world today—is the creation of a distinctive language of the rights of man, and the use of that language as an instrument in its struggles'.[69] The rights sceptic may be relieved to hear, however, that I will also discuss other concepts, such as equality and personhood. As will become evident, these concepts overlap with the concept of fundamental rights in numerous respects.

My focus throughout will be on human and nonhuman animals, and, within the latter category, sentient animals: animals who are able to have subjective experiences including but not limited to pain and pleasure.[70] For the most

[62] See eg Mary Ann Glendon, *Rights Talk: The Impoverishment of Political Discourse* (Free Press 1993). On the critical departure from rights found, say, in feminist scholarship see eg Isabelle Barker and Jasbir Kaur Puar, 'Feminist Problematization of Rights Language and Universal Conceptualizations of Human Rights' (2002) 5 Concilium 64.

[63] See eg Lee Nicholas H, 'In Defense of Humanity: Why Animals Cannot Possess Human Rights' (2013) 26 Regent University Law Review 457, 457–60.

[64] See James Griffin, *On Human Rights* (Oxford University Press 2008) 41.

[65] For an overview of rights critiques see Leif Wenar, 'Rights' in Edward N Zalta (ed), *The Stanford Encyclopedia of Philosophy* (Fall 2015) <https://plato.stanford.edu/entries/rights/> accessed 11 June 2023.

[66] See eg Philip Selznick, 'The Idea of a Communitarian Morality' (1987) 75 California Law Review 445, 454. See also Michael Sandel, *Liberalism and the Limits of Justice* (2nd edn, Cambridge University Press 1998) 184–218.

[67] See eg Jonathan R Lovvorn, 'Animal Law in Action: The Law, Public Perception, and the Limits of Animal Rights Theory as a Basis for Legal Reform' (2006) 12 Animal Law 133.

[68] John Tasioulas, 'The Moral Reality of Human Rights' in Thomas Pogge (ed), *Freedom From Poverty as a Human Right: Who Owes What to the Very Poor?* (Oxford University Press 2007) 75.

[69] Vincenzo Ferrone, *The Enlightenment: History of an Idea* (Elisabetta Tarantino tr, Princeton University Press 2015) xi.

[70] Nussbaum, *Justice for Animals: Our Collective Responsibility* (n 26) 119.

part, I will therefore not concentrate on animals that (to the best of our current knowledge) lack sentience. Nor will I focus on nonanimal beings that could potentially become sentient. With the fast-paced development of artificial intelligences (AIs) and robots, the question has arisen whether they, too, could be sentient and deserving of moral and legal rights.[71] There are numerous parallels between animal rights and the rights of AIs and robots, and the analysis and the SMA which this book develops may prove enlightening in the emerging debates around the moral and legal protection of nonanimal entities. However, I will not focus on that topic.[72]

4 How the book is organized

The book is structured into eight chapters. Chapter 2 turns the spotlight onto the two intellectual currents—naturalism and egalitarianism—which became prominent in the French Enlightenment and which came to form the basis of the Meritocratic and the Aristocratic fundamental rights conceptions. I begin by illuminating the egalitarian current, which influenced the Aristocracy, before showing how it conflicted with the naturalist current, which became the foundation of the Meritocracy. By drawing on the writings of the naturalist Jean-Claude Delamétherie and the egalitarian Jean-Baptiste Salaville, I illustrate how these two currents conflicted in a way that would come to inform the tension between the Meritocracy and the Aristocracy. It is to these conceptions that I will turn in the ensuing two chapters.

Chapter 3 will start by studying the Aristocratic conception. It first provides an account of the recent movement in human rights and dignity scholarship that proposes to understand concepts such as human dignity, human equality, and human rights as connected to ideas of nobility. I then spell out how exactly these concepts can be regarded as Aristocratic concepts by identifying two key characteristics of the Aristocracy: the principle of *Equal Consideration* and the *Internalist* approach. Finally, I show how *Internalists 'found'* concepts such as human rights, dignity, and equality, and I point to the virtues as well as the vices of this approach.

[71] See eg Blay Whitby, 'Sometimes It's Hard to Be a Robot: A Call for Action on the Ethics of Abusing Artificial Agents' (2008) 20 Interacting with Computers 326; David J Gunkel, 'The Other Question: Can and Should Robots Have Rights?' (2018) 20 Ethics and Information Technology 87; John Tasioulas, 'First Steps Towards an Ethics of Robots and Artificial Intelligence' (2019) 7 Journal of Practical Ethics 49, 69.

[72] But see some cursory thoughts in Chapter 7, Section 4.2 and Chapter 8.

In Chapter 4, I move to the other end of the fundamental rights spectrum and examine the Meritocratic conception. After excavating some of the fragmentary groundwork that has been laid in scholarship on the Meritocracy, I shed light on its two core characteristics: *Differential Consideration* and *Externalism*. Mirroring Chapter 3, I then discuss how exactly *Externalists* '*ground*' rights, what advantages this approach has, and what problems it creates.

Chapter 5 focuses on the increasingly popular sentientist rights approach, which combines arguments for extending rights to sentient animals with a commitment to equal status of rights-holders. The chapter asks whether this approach represents a third conception that stands outside the spectrum of fundamental rights conceptions and that is potentially more attractive than the Aristocratic and Meritocratic conceptions. Using Alasdair Cochrane's theory as a case study, I argue that, while his theory is a less pure instantiation of the Meritocracy than other theories, it nevertheless possesses sufficient features of the Meritocracy to warrant the label 'Meritocratic'. What is more, even if one does not categorize a sentientist rights theory like Cochrane's as Meritocratic, such a theory nevertheless does not escape the fundamental rights spectrum. Finally, I argue that Cochrane's theory faces problems even if we assume that it lies outside the spectrum and forms its own, third conception of rights: in particular, it threatens to undermine the equal status of vulnerable humans, which reduces its appeal.

In Chapter 6, I develop an argument for the adoption of a middle ground between the Aristocracy and the Meritocracy as the most attractive practical way forward. I propose that, given recent scientific advances that reveal striking similarities between humans and other animals, there is a good case for expanding the circle of rights-holders to at least some other animals. In the language of the spectrum, I argue that there is a need to 'Meritocratize' the Aristocracy. By focusing on possible Meritocratizations with respect to animals' property status and fundamental rights, I demonstrate concretely how this move to the middle could be achieved.

Chapter 7 qualifies these practical suggestions by making the case for the Species Membership Approach. I explain why, in law, the SMA is particularly attractive, and why we should abandon the orthodox view according to which species membership is off-limits as a criterion for extensions of rights and other legal protections. To illustrate the viability of the SMA, I discuss three cases—the cases of Sesha the human being, Minnie the elephant, and Knuckles the chimpanzee—and show that the SMA is better able to accommodate them than the Aristocracy, Meritocracy, and—to the extent that it is considered an alternative conception—the sentientist rights approach. The chapter ends by mapping out how the SMA could be operationalized and how it can respond to challenges that might arise from its implementation.

Finally, Chapter 8 concludes the book by summarizing its key contributions and by outlining some future directions of research.

2
Animal and Human Rights in the Enlightenment

1 Introduction

Leo Strauss once remarked that '"[o]ur ideas" are only partly our ideas. Most of our ideas are abbreviations or residues of the thought of other people . . . of the thought of the past. These thoughts were once explicit and in the centre of consideration and discussion.'[1] This chapter aims to show that Strauss's observation is particularly apt in the context of discussions about human and animal rights. Many of the ideas and arguments we encounter in contemporary debates on these topics are not new, but rather echo the ideas of the past; ideas which have often become tacit assumptions of our own conversations. To better understand our own ideas, we must therefore shed light on the underlying assumptions informing them. We must make explicit what is implicit. And, if Strauss is right, then the best—and indeed perhaps only—way of doing so is to investigate the history of these ideas.[2]

My focus in this chapter is on the French Enlightenment because it has been a singularly formative period for fundamental rights.[3] France may not be able to lay claim to having invented the idea of individual rights,[4] nor was it the first country in which unalienable rights were proclaimed.[5] However, it was in France and with the French Revolution more specifically that the idea of universal human rights became an international reference point with the adoption of the Declaration of the Rights of Man and Citizen in 1789. As Ernst Cassirer has noted, 'French philosophy of the eighteenth century by no

[1] Leo Strauss, *What is Political Philosophy? And Other Studies* (University of Chicago Press 1959) 73.
[2] I am using the terms 'history of ideas' and 'intellectual history' interchangeably.
[3] All translations in this chapter are mine, unless otherwise indicated.
[4] See Michel Villey, La formation de la pensée juridique moderne (Presses universitaires de France 2013) 240–68.
[5] See Johannes Morsink, *Inherent Human Rights: Philosophical Roots of the Universal Declaration* (University of Pennsylvania Press 2009) 20; Jack R Censer and Lynn Hunt, *Liberty, Equality, Fraternity: Exploring the French Revolution* (Pennsylvania State University 2001) 35.

More Equal Than Others. Raffael N Fasel, Oxford University Press. © Raffael N Fasel 2024.
DOI: 10.1093/oso/9780198907435.003.0002

means discovered the idea of inalienable rights; but it was the first to make a real moral gospel of this idea and to embrace it passionately and proclaim it enthusiastically'.[6]

Unbeknownst to many, the Enlightenment, and in particular the French Enlightenment, has not only played a key role in shaping how we understand human rights today.[7] Right around the time that the idea of human rights was formed, another—and, according to some, opposing—idea started to take shape: the idea of animal rights. In fact, the ideas of human rights and animal rights did not only emerge at the same time and from the same cradle. As I will show, they also emerged *together*, that is, in tandem with each other rather than in isolation from one another. As a result, we cannot expect to fully grasp either human rights or animal rights if we try to understand them as independent ideas.

This chapter provides an account of these shared origins by shedding light on the ideas that came to shape contemporary human rights approaches of the Aristocratic bent and animal rights approaches of the Meritocratic bent. To do so, I unearth two diverging intellectual currents that were prominent in the French Enlightenment. The first current is *egalitarianism*, which would come to form the basis of the Aristocratic conception of fundamental rights. The other current was *naturalism*, from which the Meritocratic conception sprang. As I will argue, naturalism's focus on the gradual differences between humans and animals challenged egalitarianism's emphasis on the equality of human beings and their separateness from other species.

To illustrate these two currents in action, I will focus on the exchange between two French Enlightenment thinkers: Jean-Claude Delamétherie, who developed a naturalist defence of fundamental rights for animals, and Jean-Baptiste Salaville, who objected to the idea of animal rights by defending an egalitarian account of human rights. To be sure, neither of these thinkers was consequential for our modern positions. They were relatively little known even at the time, and have faded into almost complete obscurity today. What makes their exchange deserving of our attention is therefore not so much who they were, but which views they defended. As I will show in this as well as the next two chapters, Delamétherie and Salaville developed some of the central arguments that we can find still today in debates between human and animal rights proponents.

The chapter is structured as follows. In Section 2, I discuss naturalism by shedding light on the background and on some of the central themes of

[6] Ernst Cassirer, *The Philosophy of the Enlightenment* (Fritz CA Koelln and James P Pettegrove trs, Princeton University Press 1979) 250. See also Lynn Hunt, *Inventing Human Rights: A History* (Norton 2007) 17.

[7] Hunt, *Inventing Human Rights: A History* (n 6) 22–26.

this intellectual current. I then turn, in Section 3, to egalitarianism and discuss what characterized this stream of thinking. Building on these accounts, Section 4 spells out more clearly in which respects the two approaches were in tension with each other. Finally, Section 5 illustrates this conflict by drawing on the writings of Delamétherie and Salaville.

2 Naturalism

The seventeenth and in particular eighteenth centuries saw the rise of a new way of looking at the world—one that would explain the lasting importance of the Age of Enlightenment.[8] That new paradigm was naturalism.[9] Naturalists rejected supernatural explanations of the world, believing instead that experience and empirical investigation provide us with the best account of nature.[10] Naturalism was not a novel paradigm, to be sure. Pre-Socratic philosophers had already made systematic attempts at understanding the world without reference to divine forces;[11] Aristotle, Epicurus, and Lucretius then took up the baton from their pre-Socratic precursors.[12] The existence of these precursors, however, does not detract from the momentous importance of Enlightenment naturalism.[13] Naturalism is the fruit of the Age of Enlightenment, even if its seeds were sown earlier.

The empirical method is often traced to Francis Bacon who, in *Novum Organum* (1620), argued against the then-predominant way of reasoning which operated in an abstract, *a priori* fashion. Bacon compared those who adopted this way of thinking with spiders weaving cobwebs 'out of their own substance'.[14] He proposed that we should instead be like bees who gather pollen

[8] For an account of the different senses of 'Enlightenment' see James M Byrne, *Religion and the Enlightenment: From Descartes to Kant* (Westminster John Knox Press 1996) 1–5.

[9] Alan Charles Kors, 'The Enlightenment, Naturalism, and the Secularization of Values' (2012) April/May Free Inquiry 24, 24.

[10] ibid 28.

[11] See James Warren, *Presocratics* (Routledge 2007) 23–37.

[12] Alan Charles Kors, 'The Age of Enlightenment' in Stephen Bullivant and Michael Ruse (eds), *The Oxford Handbook of Atheism* (Oxford University Press 2013) 204. See also Alan Charles Kors, *Naturalism and Unbelief in France, 1650–1729* (Cambridge University Press 2016) 6. On Aristotle see James Lennox, 'Aristotle's Biology' in Edward N Zalta (ed), *The Stanford Encyclopedia of Philosophy* (Fall 2021) <https://plato.stanford.edu/archives/win2019/entries/aristotle-biology/> accessed 11 June 2023. On Epicurus see Olivier Bloch, *Matière à histoires* (Librairie philosophique J Vrin 1997) 58–98.

[13] See Michael Shermer, 'Scientific Naturalism: A Manifesto for Enlightenment Humanism' (2017) 15 Theology and Science 220.

[14] Francis Bacon, *Selected Philosophical Works* (Rose-Mary Sargent ed, Hackett Publishing 1999) 128. See also RS Woolhouse, 'Empiricism' in Alan Charles Kors (ed), *Encyclopedia of the Enlightenment* (Oxford University Press 2002).

from the flowers and then turn this pollen into honey. Put differently, he advocated the collection of empirical data and the induction of principles from those data. This bottom-up process was at the heart of what Cassirer called the Enlightenment's new process of thinking: a process of 'doubting and seeking, tearing down and building up'.[15]

In their zeal to reveal nature's secrets, the naturalists not only scrutinized minerals, fungi, plants, and animals. Human beings were no longer immune from scientific examination either. Previously, humans had only been the ones who compiled taxonomies of other forms of life. Now, they themselves became an object of scientific study, to be assigned their proper place in the taxonomies. It was in the first edition of Carl von Linné's *Systema Naturæ* in 1735 that humans were, for the first time in modern history, classified as part of the natural order.[16] Two sets of views that many naturalists would adopt to make sense of the world were materialism and sensationalism.[17] Let us start with the former.

Materialists were influenced by a wide variety of thought, including Cartesian physics, Lockean sensationalism (about which I will say more below), mechanism, chemistry, mineralogy, biology, and libertinism.[18] However, as Olivier Bloch has identified, there are some positions that most of them had in common. These included atheism and antispiritualism; criticism of religiously and metaphysically infused moral and political values; the belief that everything in nature is necessary; and the view that humans are natural beings and form part of the same material unity as everything else in nature.[19] The last position is of particular interest to our study of the tension between naturalism and egalitarianism. Materialists arrived at the view that humans form part of nature by abandoning dualism, that is, the view made prominent by René Descartes that there are two separate substances: the material body and the immaterial soul.[20] Materialists adopted monism in its stead. According to monism, we only need one substance—matter—to explain everything there

[15] Cassirer, *The Philosophy of the Enlightenment* (n 6) xv. See also Peter Gay, *The Living Enlightenment* (1996) <https://tannerlectures.utah.edu/_resources/documents/a-to-z/g/Gay98.pdf> accessed 11 June 2023.

[16] B Ricardo Brown, *Until Darwin, Science, Human Variety and the Origins of Race* (Routledge 2015) 17; Carl von Linné, *Systema naturæ, sive regna tria naturæ systematice proposita per classes, ordines, genera, & species* (Theodorum Haak 1735) 10.

[17] On naturalists who were not materialists see Bloch, *Matière à histoires* (n 12) 332; Olivier Bloch and Charles Porset, 'Le matérialisme au siècle des Lumières' (1992) 24 Dix-huitième Siècle 5, 5.

[18] Bloch, *Matière à histoires* (n 12) 313–15; Olivier Bloch, 'L'héritage libertin dans le matérialisme des Lumières' (1992) 24 Dix-huitième Siècle 73, 73, 79.

[19] Bloch, *Matière à histoires* (n 12) 321.

[20] See Colas Duflo, *Diderot: Du matérialisme à la politique* (CNRS éditions 2013) 29–30.

is to explain in the world.[21] On the monistic view, nature is a whole—a 'mass of matter',[22] as the materialist Denis Diderot put it—which resists strict systematization and taxonomy. To monistic materialists, even the human being was nothing other than a complex aggregation of matter. This aggregation was seen as the product of mere accident and therefore lacking divine design.[23]

Importantly, even the soul was considered to be a mere product of matter, arising from humans' physical constitution.[24] To materialists, the belief in an immaterial soul amounted to 'a dead end, simply an admission of ignorance', as Alan Charles Kors observes.[25] Renouncing the belief in souls existing independently of matter entailed abandoning one of the central notions that had allowed humans to set themselves apart from animals, plants, and everything else in nature: the notion that only human beings have immaterial souls.[26] Once that notion was relinquished, it became more difficult to maintain that humans were fundamentally different from nonhumans. Instead, nature seemed characterized by gradual progression from the inanimate to the animate, from plants to animals to humans.[27] If the world is ultimately one, then every being in it—including human beings—is in one way or another related. In the words of Diderot: 'everything is connected in nature'.[28]

The second set of views that often intersected with naturalism and materialism was *sensationalism*.[29] Sensationalism is the view that sensations—which Diderot's famous *Encyclopédie* defined as 'impressions arising in us as a result of external objects'[30]—are a being's sole epistemic access to the world and constitute the very essence of knowing.[31] Put simply, according to sensationalism, I know what I know because I sense, and knowing means sensing. Sensationalists rejected 'innate ideas', that is, knowledge about the world that one has prior to any sensory experiences.[32] John Locke is generally credited

[21] See eg Pierre Lurbe, 'Matière, nature, mouvement chez d'Holbach et Toland' (1992) 24 Dix-huitième Siècle 53.

[22] Denis Diderot, *Pensées sur l'interprétation de la nature* (1754) 191. See also Denis Diderot, *Principes philosophiques sur la matière et le mouvement*, vol 9 (Le Club Français du Livre 1971) 613–14.

[23] Colas Duflo, *Diderot philosophe* (Honoré Champion 2003) 112.

[24] Kors, 'The Age of Enlightenment' (n 12) 203.

[25] Kors, 'The Enlightenment, Naturalism, and the Secularization of Values' (n 9) 31.

[26] Duflo, *Diderot: Du matérialisme à la politique* (n 20) 36.

[27] See ibid.

[28] Denis Diderot, *Entretien entre D'Alembert et Diderot* (Gilbert Maire ed, Éditions Bossard 1921) 94.

[29] See eg Bloch, *Matière à histoires* (n 12) 314–15.

[30] 'Sensations', *Encyclopédie, ou Dictionnaire raisonné des sciences, des arts et des métiers* (Sociétés Typographiques 1780) 731.

[31] See Sylvain Auroux, 'Sensationalism' in Michel Delton (ed), *Encyclopedia of the Enlightenment* (Fitzroy Dearborn 2001) 1208.

[32] See Jerry Samet, 'The Historical Controversies Surrounding Innateness' in Edward N Zalta (ed), *The Stanford Encyclopedia of Philosophy* (Fall 2008) <https://plato.stanford.edu/archives/fall2008/entries/innateness-history/> accessed 11 June 2023. See also Julien Offray de la Mettrie, 'Traité de l'âme', *Œuvres philosophiques de la Mettrie*, vol 1 (1796) 65–66.

with having laid the foundation for this rejection. On Locke's account, which influenced many French thinkers,[33] all our ideas and impressions stem from the senses and the sensations that external objects cause in them. The soul, according to Locke, does not possess any innate ideas: every idea it has comes from sensations or from reflection (which itself operates on already existing sensations).[34] Locke argued that depending on one's sense organs, one will have different ideas. He even suggested that there could be beings in other parts of the universe with entirely different senses. Because of their different senses, these beings would have entirely different ideas and thus entirely different ways of knowing the world.[35]

Materialism and sensationalism were not only scientific ways of viewing the world, but thinkers of the time also took them to have normative implications and used them to make concrete policy proposals. For example, Locke's argument that moral knowledge, like all other kinds of knowledge, is not innate but acquired by means of experience had radical consequences because experience could now serve as a critique of authorities that prescribed moral norms that conflicted with experience.[36] Although the materialists did not agree on which moral philosophy would flow from Lockeanism or materialism more generally, they were united in their rejection of Christianity as the basis of morality.[37] They agreed that the foundations of morality had to be secularized. According to Kors, this 'secularisation of the ethical debate' is one of the most important legacies of the Enlightenment.[38] Instead of basing their moral theories on theological arguments, the naturalists turned to nature.[39] Only by studying nature, they believed, can we discover what is moral. If we turn away from nature, we will fall prey to superstition and false prophets commanding us to act in ways that are incompatible with our natures.[40] Nature was thus seen as providing a more solid foundation for morality. Unlike Christian ethical principles, naturalized ethics could be validated by experiment and experience.[41] Specifically,

[33] Kors, 'The Enlightenment, Naturalism, and the Secularization of Values' (n 9) 31; Georges Lefebvre, *The French Revolution: From Its Origins to 1793* (Routledge 2001) 56.
[34] John Locke, *An Essay Concerning Human Understanding* (Penguin Books 1997) 1.II–III; 2.VII.
[35] ibid 4.III, §23.
[36] Kors, *Naturalism and Unbelief in France, 1650–1729* (n 12) 25.
[37] Jacques Domenech, *L'éthique des Lumières: Les fondements de la morale dans la philosophie française du XVIIIe siècle* (Librairie philosophique J Vrin 1989) 24. Note, however, that Locke himself adopted a theocentric and Christian position.
[38] Kors, 'The Enlightenment, Naturalism, and the Secularization of Values' (n 9) 24.
[39] ibid.
[40] ibid 33.
[41] RS Woolhouse, 'Empiricism' in Alan Charles Kors (ed), *Encyclopedia of the Enlightenment* (Oxford University Press 2002). See also Ann Thomson, 'French Eighteenth-Century Materialists and Natural Law, History of European Ideas' (2016) 42 History of European Ideas 243, 243, 252.

materialist naturalists believed that examining nature—in particular, human nature—revealed the centrality of the principle of utility, that is, the principle 'that the happiness of the species was the highest value and that all things might be judged by their contribution to happiness or suffering'.[42] As I will show in Chapter 4, the naturalists' view about the solid foundations that nature provides for normative principles plays a central role in the Meritocratic conception of fundamental rights.

Many naturalists extended their normative accounts beyond the moral sphere and developed economic and political proposals.[43] Materialism provided a powerful platform from which to launch such proposals.[44] As in ethics, materialists could make claims based on experiment or experience that often (but not always) served to attack existing ideologies.[45] It is 'the primary vocation of materialism', Bloch highlights, to 'fight and resolve, relying as much as possible on factual knowledge of the things of this world, the prejudices, illusions, and fantasies of the dominant opinion'.[46] Paul-Henri Thiry, Baron d'Holbach, another materialist, argued for example that governments and laws have to accord with the demands of human nature, which requires them to respect individuals' interests in liberty, safety, and property.[47]

3 Egalitarianism

The second important current of the Enlightenment was egalitarianism.[48] Like naturalism, egalitarianism was hardly an invention of this time,[49] but the Enlightenment turned out to be a formative period for it, too. This is in no small part due to the fact that the Enlightenment ushered in the abolition of the old, hierarchical system, which, according to Harvey Chisick,

[42] Kors, 'The Enlightenment, Naturalism, and the Secularization of Values' (n 9) 27. See also Jeremy Bentham, *An Introduction to the Principles of Morals and Legislation*, vol 2 (W Pickering 1823) 236.

[43] See JL Heilbron, 'Natural Philosophy and Science' in Alan Charles Kors (ed), *Encyclopedia of the Enlightenment* (Oxford University Press 2002).

[44] See Ann Thomson, *Bodies of Thought: Science, Religion, and the Soul in the Early Enlightenment* (Oxford University Press 2008) 231.

[45] See, with respect to Diderot, Duflo, *Diderot: Du matérialisme à la politique* (n 20) 104, 111.

[46] Bloch, *Matière à histoires* (n 12) 222.

[47] Thomson, *Bodies of Thought: Science, Religion, and the Soul in the Early Enlightenment* (n 44) 231.

[48] See William Bristow, 'Enlightenment' in Edward N Zalta (ed), *The Stanford Encyclopedia of Philosophy* (Summer 2011) <https://plato.stanford.edu/archives/sum2011/entries/enlightenment/> accessed 11 June 2023.

[49] Harvey Chisick, *Historical Dictionary of the Enlightenment* (Scarecrow Press 2005) 160.

> was in principle radically inegalitarian. It defined the individual in terms of the corporation, estate, occupation and religion to which he or she belonged, ascribing different dignities and statuses to each. The law was particularistic, recognising privilege and varying rights and customs throughout the country and across the social scale. It is worth bearing this in mind in considering the place of equality in Enlightenment thought.[50]

The Enlightenment started to replace this hierarchical order with an egalitarian one. For the first time, it 'extended a broad notion of equality to humanity as a whole'.[51] To be sure, as I will explain in the next section, egalitarianism was not universally accepted, and coincided with inegalitarian theories propounding different origins for different human races as well as other forms of scientific racism.[52] However, this should not detract from the fact that egalitarian thinking became prominent in the Enlightenment.

Although similar transformations occurred in other states, egalitarianism played an especially important role in France.[53] In the Ancien Régime, the social and political order that had shaped France since the late Middle Ages, equality existed neither in practice nor in theory. Significant wealth gaps between members of the Third Estate (ie the peasants and the bourgeoisie) and the upper classes were an important but by no means the only form of inequality that enraged the general population.[54] In almost every aspect of an ordinary person's life, social distinctions were pervasive, including in '[o]fficial parades, the order of seating in the parish church, the number of bells rung at a funeral, the clothes one wore and especially the material they were made of, [or] the size of one's house and its location'.[55] Eighteenth-century France still had between 140,000 and 1,500,000 serfs, and millions more peasants who owed their landlords seigneurial dues.[56] For the majority of the French population who did not belong to the nobility or the clergy, there were insurmountable barriers that made it impossible for them to own land or hold public office. Simply fighting for the abolition of serfdom was therefore not enough for the Third Estate.[57] It is for this reason that the struggle for liberty in France could

[50] ibid.
[51] ibid 161.
[52] See generally Devin J Vartija, *The Color of Equality: Race and Common Humanity in Enlightenment Thought* (University of Pennsylvania Press 2021).
[53] See eg on the US Philip A Hamburger, 'Equality and Diversity: The Eighteenth-Century Debate About Equal Protection and Equal Civil Rights' (1992) 8 The Supreme Court Review 295, 298.
[54] See Jack R Censer and Lynn Hunt, *Liberty, Equality, Fraternity: Exploring the French Revolution* (Pennsylvania State University 2001) 6.
[55] ibid 8.
[56] ibid 3.
[57] Lefebvre, *The French Revolution* (n 33) 104.

not be separated from the struggle for equality.[58] And it is for this reason that *égalité* became one of the central themes of the French Enlightenment and especially the French Revolution.[59]

Enlightenment egalitarianism was based on two key theses: the *Equality Thesis* and the *Separateness Thesis*. According to the *Equality Thesis*, all humans are fundamentally equal, notwithstanding any differences in their physical constitution or social conditions. According to the *Separateness Thesis*, all human beings are special and separate from all other species.

The *Equality Thesis* is best understood in light of the prevalence at the time of supernatural views of the world which informed many egalitarians' understanding of the basic equality of human beings. For despite naturalistic developments in the seventeenth and eighteenth centuries and their anti-Christian tendencies, Christian ideology was far from having lost its influence on society.[60] And with the prevalence of Christianity, one of its key dogmas—that all humans are fundamentally equal notwithstanding their differences—retained a prominent role. This idea was firmly rooted in the Christian belief that 'God created mankind in his own image', as the Old Testament states.[61] According to this *imago Dei* doctrine, the weakest human being is as much an image of God as is the strongest, the least intelligent as much as the brightest. It is in this equal creation in the image of God that Christians believe resides the dignity of humanity.[62] This notion was intimately connected to the dualist view that only human beings have souls that are immaterial, that is, that belong to a metaphysical plane that is separate from bodies.[63] In contrast to the material sphere of bodies, this plane is not subject to time and space. As a result, souls cannot deteriorate: they are immortal.[64] Despite the manifold differences between them, humans were thus viewed as having a basic equality in common simply in virtue of their immaterial souls.

Of course, one did not need to be a dualist to believe in the *Equality Thesis*. Some naturalists adopted egalitarian views, too. For example, despite his

[58] See also Louis chevalier de Jaucourt, 'Égalité naturelle' in Denis Diderot and Jean le Rond d'Alembert (eds), *Encyclopédie, ou dictionnaire raisonné des sciences, des arts et des métiers, etc.* (University of Chicago: ARTFL Encyclopédie Project, 2017) 5:415 <https://artflsrv04.uchicago.edu/philologic4.7/encyclopedie0922/navigate/5/1558?byte=4449109&byte=4449118> 11 June 2023.

[59] Lefebvre, *The French Revolution* (n 33) 88–89.

[60] See on this Byrne, *Religion and the Enlightenment: From Descartes to Kant* (n 8) 29–32, 34–36.

[61] Genesis 1:27 (NIV).

[62] See Janet Soskice, 'Human Dignity and the Image of God' in Christopher McCrudden (ed), *Understanding Human Dignity* (Oxford University Press 2014).

[63] Fernando Vidal, 'Soul' in Alan Charles Kors (ed), *Encyclopedia of the Enlightenment* (Oxford University Press 2002).

[64] See Bernard Baertschi, *Les rapports de l'âme et du corps: Descartes, Diderot et Maine de Biran* (Librairie philosophique J Vrin 1992) 64.

misgivings about immaterial souls, Locke believed that all men are fundamentally equal.[65] As Jeremy Waldron has argued, Locke based his theory of basic equality on humans' capacity for abstraction, that is, their ability to have general ideas. Although some other animals can reason, Locke claimed, only humans can reason *abstractly*.[66] In virtue of this capacity, humans—and only humans—can reason their way to the general idea of God, discover His commandments, and live their lives accordingly.[67] Others took a more secular tack to justifying basic human equality.[68]

Egalitarians often bolstered the *Equality Thesis* with another thesis: the *Separateness Thesis*. According to this thesis, humanity is not on a continuum with other natural entities, including animals. Rather, it is viewed as a special category that is separate and distinct from all other species. We have already encountered two of the frequently invoked justifications for the *Separateness Thesis* above: one of them is the idea that only human beings are created in the image of God, the other is that only human beings have immaterial souls. As we will see in our discussion of Salaville's work (Section 6), natural properties, such as intelligence, were also sometimes put forward as justifications for the separateness of humanity. Those who adopted the *Separateness Thesis* argued that, although we may find similarities between humans and members of other species, these similarities cannot undermine the strict dividing line that exists between humans and other animals. To put this point another way, there is a difference in kind, not merely degree, between humans and animals.

Not all egalitarians embraced the *Separateness Thesis*. Locke, for example, made his case for basic equality despite accepting the idea of a continuum between humans, animals, and other natural entities.[69] Yet, as we will see in the

[65] See Locke, *An Essay Concerning Human Understanding* (n 34) 4.III, §6; John Locke, *Two Treatises of Government* (Peter Laslett ed, 3rd edn, Cambridge University Press 1988) The Second Treatise, II, §4. See also William Uzgalis, 'John Locke: The Immateriality of the Soul and Personal Identity' (2012) <https://stanford.library.sydney.edu.au/archives/spr2014/entries/locke/supplement.html> accessed 11 June 2023.

[66] Jeremy Waldron, *God, Locke, and Equality: Christian Foundations of John Locke's Political Thought* (Cambridge University Press 2002) 75. However, in *An Essay Concerning Human Understanding*, Locke appears to have distinguished between 'person' and 'man', and he discussed the possibility that a parrot can count as a person: John Locke, *An Essay Concerning Human Understanding* (Penguin 1997) II, para 8. I am grateful to Joe Wills for this pointer.

[67] Waldron, *God, Locke, and Equality: Christian Foundations of John Locke's Political Thought* (n 66) 79–80.

[68] Milan Zafirovski, *The Enlightenment and Its Effects on Modern Society* (Springer 2011) 45. See eg Louis chevalier de Jaucourt, 'Égalité naturelle' in Denis Diderot and Jean le Rond d'Alembert (eds), *Encyclopédie, ou dictionnaire raisonné des sciences, des arts et des métiers, etc.* (University of Chicago: ARTFL Encyclopédie Project, 2017) 5:415 <https://artflsrv04.uchicago.edu/philologic4.7/encyclopedie0922/navigate/5/1558?byte=4449109&byte=4449118> accessed 29 October 2023.

[69] See Locke, *An Essay Concerning Human Understanding* (n 34) 3.VI, §12. See also Waldron, *God, Locke, and Equality: Christian Foundations of John Locke's Political Thought* (n 66) 53–55.

next section, the *Separateness Thesis* was closely connected to the *Equality Thesis*. Once the *Separateness Thesis* came under attack, basic human equality would become more difficult to uphold, too.

4 The tension between naturalism and egalitarianism

Having outlined both the naturalist and the egalitarian currents, we are now in a better position to understand the tension that arose between them. That tension, to be precise, did not arise between all forms of naturalism and egalitarianism. As we saw, some naturalists endorsed egalitarianism and vice versa. However, there was a tension between egalitarianism and a particular strand of naturalism: the strand that foregrounded the physical and social differences which distinguish individual human beings. Particularly prominent among materialists, this strand cast serious doubt on the idea that all human beings are equal. To parse the tension this created, it is helpful to focus on the *Equality Thesis* and *Separateness Thesis*.

As we saw above, the *Separateness Thesis*—which holds that the human species is special and separate from other animals—was invoked to support the *Equality Thesis*. A key challenge to the *Separateness Thesis* arose with the materialists' rejection of Cartesian dualism and their concurrent adoption of monism. According to monism, there can be no immaterial souls because everything that exists is present in the material world. For the materialists, everything in nature is on a continuum. And because humans are part of nature, they are on that continuum in the same way as animals are. As a result, humans were seen as differing from animals only in degree, but not in kind. Thinkers who adopted this position, Kors notes,

> insisted that human beings were not categorically distinct, and that the transition from other animals to man was gradual and founded upon observable physical differences of constitution, such as what was knowable from the evidence of comparative embryology and anatomy.[70]

The emphasis on the gradual rather than categorical differences in individuals' properties seemed to blur the lines that some egalitarians tried to draw between humans and nonhumans. This also had a normative upshot. For if there are no strict divisions between species and their members, then how can

[70] Kors, 'The Enlightenment, Naturalism, and the Secularization of Values' (n 9) 32.

one justify treating one species completely differently from another? The focus of this strand of naturalism on gradation, in other words, cast serious doubt on the *Separateness Thesis* and thereby on the common justification for treating animals in ways that one could not treat humans.

Once doubt was cast on the *Separateness Thesis*, the *Equality Thesis* would also become harder to defend. With the rejection of a sharp dividing line between humans and animals based on the insight that everything in nature is on a continuum, it became more difficult to maintain the position that all members of the human species are equals. If nature is rife with difference, then why should human nature be any different? Given that, as a matter of empirical fact, humans differ considerably from each other, why consider them one another's equals? As Ann Thomson notes, inegalitarian materialists 'emphasis[ed] individual differences arising from our innate organisation'.[71] According to them, '[i]f humans are determined by physical causes, then one might conclude that physical differences create fundamental divisions between humans'.[72] In other words, individual humans and groups of human beings can differ from each other physically to an extent that creates a deep—and, in the eyes of some, insurmountable—gulf between them.

Julien Offray de La Mettrie (not be confused with Jean-Claude Delamétherie whose work I discuss in Section 5) was one of the most prominent materialist foes of equality who rejected both the *Equality Thesis* and the *Separateness Thesis*. Like many others at the time, La Mettrie was a proponent of the idea of the great chain of being, or *scala naturae*.[73] According to this idea, there is a natural hierarchy in nature—a ladder whose steps are occupied by increasingly developed and therefore superior creatures.[74] La Mettrie took this to have two implications. First, he believed that there is an essential similarity between humans and other animals in that all are part of the same continuum. In both their behaviour and their physical organization, he argued, humans are comparable to animals.[75] There is no distinction in kind between them; no strict dividing line.[76] As he contended, if one could teach an ape how to speak, then that

[71] Thomson, *Bodies of Thought: Science, Religion, and the Soul in the Early Enlightenment* (n 44) 236. But see also ibid 245.

[72] ibid 237.

[73] ibid 239; Arthur M Wilson, *Diderot* (Oxford University Press 1972) 565.

[74] See Arthur O Lovejoy, *The Great Chain of Being: A Study of the History of an Idea* (Harvard University Press 1971).

[75] Julien Offray de La Mettrie, *Machine Man and Other Writings* (Ann Thomson ed, Cambridge University Press 1996) 'Preliminary Discourse', 147; 'Machine Man', 19. See also Ann Thomson, *Materialism and Society in the Mid-Eighteenth Century: La Mettrie's Discours Préliminaire* (Librairie Droz 1981) 41.

[76] La Mettrie, *Machine Man and Other Writings* (n 75) 'Machine Man', 18–19.

ape would be on a par with humans.[77] Second, he argued that there is a natural hierarchy also *within* the human species. According to him, some humans rank higher than others. Far from being equal by nature, they are unequal by nature.[78]

Another example of a naturalist who challenged egalitarianism is d'Holbach. He, too, argued that while humans have superior mental faculties to animals, there is no essential difference—no difference in kind—between them. Rejecting the *Separateness Thesis*, d'Holbach held that humans and animals are essentially similar because they are all sensitive beings.[79] Moreover, like La Mettrie, d'Holbach also rejected the *Equality Thesis*, arguing that 'although men have a general resemblance to each other, they differ essentially'.[80] Every individual human differs in their nature from other humans.[81] They differ with respect to the strength of their body and mind, their passions, their ideas about their own well-being, and the means they choose to achieve it.[82] These differences are so salient, according to d'Holbach, that they warrant categorizing humans into separate groups: 'divided into different classes according to the effects they produce, and according to the different qualities which we observe in them, which derive from the individual properties of their souls or particular modifications of their brain'.[83] Significantly, for d'Holbach, this diversity in human beings was no evil to be exorcised. Rather, he saw it as desirable that nature produces things that are complementary—creating weaker humans that can be ruled by stronger ones.[84] Because of the natural inequality among humans, he urged that we need to 'stop supposing an alleged equality which is believed to have existed originally between men. They have always been unequal. Let us not rail against this inequality which has always been necessary'.[85]

D'Holbach's argument nicely illustrates the tension between egalitarianism and naturalism. As Bloch observes, d'Holbach's rejection of egalitarianism 'is consistent with the naturalist character of his materialism':[86] whoever sees in human beings simply another product of the gradual processes of matter in

[77] ibid 'Machine Man', 12.
[78] See eg ibid 'Anti-Seneca', 139. See also Thomson, *Materialism and Society in the Mid-Eighteenth Century: La Mettrie's Discours Préliminaire* (n 75) 153–54.
[79] Paul-Henri Thiry d'Holbach, *La morale universelle, ou, les devoirs de l'homme fondés sur sa nature*, vol 1 (Marc Michel Rey 1776) 7–8.
[80] Paul-Henri Thiry d'Holbach, *Système de la nature, ou des lois du monde physique et du monde moral*, vol 1 (Étienne Ledoux 1821) 147.
[81] Bloch, *Matière à histoires* (n 12) 333–34.
[82] Paul-Henri Thiry d'Holbach, *La politique naturelle, ou, discours sur les vrais principes du gouvernement*, vol 1 (1773) 18.
[83] D'Holbach, *Système de la nature* (n 80) 146 (emphasis removed).
[84] D'Holbach, *La morale universelle* (n 79) 84. See also d'Holbach, *La politique naturelle* (n 82) 20, 44.
[85] D'Holbach, *La politique naturelle* (n 82) 19.
[86] Bloch, *Matière à histoires* (n 12) 333–34.

motion will be disinclined to postulate an equality between what is seen as 'very markedly'[87] different. For d'Holbach, it was therefore natural that the weak and the strong are not equals. Rather, '[t]he weak man, either of body or of mind, has always been forced to recognise the superiority of the strongest, the most industrious, the smartest'.[88]

La Mettrie, d'Holbach, and other critics of egalitarianism were writing at a time when the critique of the *Equality Thesis* was fuelled by theories of polygeny, according to which different human races originate from different human ancestors. As Thomson points out, these theories reinforced the inegalitarian view 'that certain peoples, in particular the Africans, were not totally human as their origin was different'.[89] Reports in the eighteenth century about the existence of great apes (summarily referred to then as 'orangutans') left many to wonder whether these apes belonged to the human species and whether the human tribes Westerners encountered in foreign lands belonged to the animal kingdom.[90] Against this backdrop, it is no surprise that the inegalitarian strand of naturalism 'can be linked to the emergence of racial classification in the late eighteenth and early nineteenth centuries', as Thomson points out.[91] Justin Smith has observed in a similar vein that

> a crucial feature of the emergence of the modern race concept was the collapse of a certain universalism about human nature, which had been sustained by a belief in the transcendent essence of the human soul, and this belief's gradual but steady replacement over the course of the early modern period by a conception of human beings as *natural* beings, and thus no less susceptible to classification in terms of a naturalistic taxonomy than any other natural being, plant or animal or mineral. The peculiar modern ontologisation of human difference, then, was made possible by the rejection of human nature, and the parallel insertion of humans into nature.[92]

[87] D'Holbach, *La politique naturelle* (n 82) 18.

[88] ibid 19. See however also d'Holbach, *Système de la nature* (n 80) 172.

[89] Thomson, *Bodies of Thought: Science, Religion, and the Soul in the Early Enlightenment* (n 44) 241.

[90] Justin EH Smith, *Nature, Human Nature, & Human Difference: Race in Early Modern Philosophy* (Princeton University Press 2015) 115–16, 133. See also Pierre Serna, *Comme des bêtes: Histoire politique de l'animal en Révolution (1750–1840)* (Fayard 2017) 333–41; Elisabeth de Fontenay, *La silence des bêtes: La philosophie à l'épreuve de l'animalité* (Fayard 1998) 331–32.

[91] Thomson, *Bodies of Thought: Science, Religion, and the Soul in the Early Enlightenment* (n 44) 237, 293; Vincenzo Ferrone, *The Enlightenment: History of an Idea* (Elisabetta Tarantino tr, Princeton University Press 2015) xii.

[92] Smith, *Nature, Human Nature, & Human Difference: Race in Early Modern Philosophy* (n 90) 7–8 (emphasis in original).

Before the 'naturalisation of the human being',[93] Smith argues, such subdivisions between members of the same species were 'unthinkable',[94] especially among human beings. With the rise of naturalism, however, humanity ceased to be an 'all-or-nothing affair'.[95] It now became possible to distinguish between humans who belong to higher races and humans who belong to lower races, or who, as individuals, have fewer or less weighty interests than other humans.[96]

Hence, although not only materialists rejected egalitarianism,[97] their dismissal of the idea that all humans are in equal possession of immaterial souls, and their view of nature as an interconnected mass of matter, was uniquely suited to undermining egalitarianism.[98] As Thomson observes, '[t]hose who paid attention to the ways in which we are affected by inherent differences in physical organisation were more willing to accept a certain innate inequality in individual capacities'.[99] Just as egalitarians were defending the equality of all humans and their separateness from other species, then, this strand of naturalist thinking led to the development of theories that undermined these very ideas.[100] Perhaps just as problematically, even the naturalists who tried to defend the idea of human equality could no longer do so on metaphysical grounds. Rather, their defences were based on contingent, empirical facts about humanity, such as that any differences between human beings are not as great as those between humans and other species. This is the case, for instance, with Locke's proposal that humans have basic equality because only they can reason abstractly—a claim that has come under attack in recent years.[101] In contrast to supernatural explanations of human equality, this naturalist justification of equality was always susceptible to empirical refutation.

[93] ibid 18.

[94] ibid 137. However, note the existence of pre-Adamite theories that antedated Enlightenment subdivisions of the human race: David N Livingstone, *Adam's Ancestors: Race, Religion, and the Politics of Human Origins* (Johns Hopkins University Press 2008). I owe this pointer to John Adenitire.

[95] Smith, *Nature, Human Nature, & Human Difference: Race in Early Modern Philosophy* (n 90) 137.

[96] ibid 8.

[97] See eg on Julien Joseph Virey, who believed in immaterial souls but not in natural equality: Thomson, *Bodies of Thought: Science, Religion, and the Soul in the Early Enlightenment* (n 44) 243–44.

[98] But see also ibid 244.

[99] ibid 237.

[100] See also Hunt, *Inventing Human Rights: A History* (n 6) 187.

[101] See eg on abstract thought in orangutans Jennifer Vonk, 'Matching Based on Biological Categories in Orangutans (Pongo Abelii) and a Gorilla (Gorilla Gorilla Gorilla)' (2013) 1 PeerJ e158.

5 Jean-Claude Delamétherie and the *droit d'animalité*

So far, the discussion of the tension between the naturalist and the egalitarian currents has remained relatively abstract. To illustrate the concrete ramifications of this tension, I now turn to an exchange between two eighteenth-century French philosophers: the naturalist Jean-Baptiste Salaville and the egalitarian Jean-Claude Delamétherie. As Chapters 3 and 4 will show, their positions anticipated many of the crucial claims that we can find in today's debates on human and animal rights. Let us begin with Delamétherie.

Jean-Claude Delamétherie (1743–1817) studied theology and medical sciences but never practised as a physician, instead preferring to focus on his scientific work. An expert on the Paris Basin, his publications made him a notable naturalist in Europe, writing on such topics as mineralogy, biology, and political philosophy. His work had a lasting impact on Jean-Baptiste Lamarck, whose theory of transformism was an important predecessor of the Darwinian theory of evolution.[102] Delamétherie himself believed in transformism and was a proponent of materialism.[103] Politically, he was a member of the Club de 89, which was founded in response to the radical and anti-aristocratic Jacobin Club.[104] The Club de 89 was sceptical of republicanism and favoured monarchy.[105]

In 1787, Delamétherie published the *Principes de la philosophie naturelle* (*Principes*), which would become one of the major foils to Salaville's essay of 1802 (discussed in Section 6).[106] In the *Principe*'s first volume, on which I will concentrate here, Delamétherie presents a theory of the fundamental rights of animals that anticipates many of the central arguments for animal rights that can be found in today's animal rights literature. Delamétherie's *Principes* should therefore be considered a pioneering work in that field. In contrast to Salaville's essay, which is strictly egalitarian, Delamétherie's *Principes* is in line with the naturalistic views of other Enlightenment thinkers discussed above. As Delamétherie makes clear in the preface, his work is one that is concerned

[102] See Ernst Mayr, 'Lamarck Revisited' (1972) 5 Journal of the History of Biology 55, 61.

[103] Raymond Corbey, *The Metaphysics of Apes: Negotiating the Animal-Human Boundary* (Cambridge University Press 2005) 62.

[104] William Doyle, *Aristocracy and Its Enemies in the Age of Revolution* (Oxford University Press 2009) 231–32.

[105] Timothy Tackett, *Becoming a Revolutionary: The Deputies of the French National Assembly and the Emergence of a Revolutionary Culture (1789–1790)* (Princeton University Press 1996) 284.

[106] Jean-Claude Delamétherie, *Principes de la philosophie naturelle, dans lesquels on cherche à déterminer les degrés de certitude ou de probabilité des connoissances humaines*, vols 1 and 2 (1787). See Jean-Baptiste Salaville, *De l'homme et des animaux* (Ch Crapelet 1805) ix, 12–13 (where Salaville implicitly references Delamétherie's 1787 treatise). See also Pierre Serna, *L'animal en République, 1789–1802: genèse du droit des bêtes* (Anacharsis 2016) 218 (footnote 24).

entirely with the study of 'nature'—a term he defines as comprising all existing beings and their qualities.[107] Like many other naturalists, Delamétherie was also an adherent of sensationalism.[108] Judgement, intelligence, reasoning, willpower, freedom, love, hatred—these and other qualities were nothing but variations of sensations for him.[109]

Considering the great weight that Delamétherie attached to sensations, it is not surprising that sensitive beings—or *êtres sensibles*, as he called them—played the lead in his theory. A sensitive being, according to him, can be defined as a union between body and consciousness.[110] Intelligence (the faculty of knowing things) is the first quality of sensitive beings, which serves as a foundation for all their other qualities. According to Delamétherie, the core unit of sensation is the same in all sensitive beings. However, due to differences in their nature, different beings have different sensations, and they have these sensations to different degrees. As beings who are able to experience both pain and pleasure, he argued, all sensitive individuals have a tendency to maximize pleasant sensations and to minimize harmful ones.[111] In fact, he claimed that there is a universal, natural law requiring the good and prohibiting the bad.[112] This view had important normative implications. To Delamétherie, sensitive beings not only have a negative duty to not impose harm on others, but they also have a positive duty to promote others' happiness.[113] A consequence of this is that it would be irrational to treat conspecifics better than other sensitive beings. In his view, the only thing that matters is that a being has the same degree of sensitivity, regardless of its species.[114]

These were far-sighted views that have found many adherents today. As I will point out in Chapter 4, modern scholars call the focus on individual capacities 'moral individualism', and 'speciesism' the irrationality of holding a view that gives preference to members of one's own species. Delamétherie did not shrink from following these prescient arguments to their logical conclusions either. He argued for example that we need to reason in the same way with respect to sensitive beings on other planets and any other sensitive being that

[107] Delamétherie, *Principes*, vol 1 (n 106) viii, xx.
[108] See ibid 23.
[109] ibid xvi.
[110] I use the term 'sensitive', not 'sentient', to translate Delamétherie's term 'sensible'. In contrast to contemporary usage of the term 'sentient', Delamétherie also included plants under the definition of 'sensible beings' (*êtres sensibles*): see ibid 199.
[111] ibid 27–33, 41.
[112] ibid 140–41. See on the idea of universal law also Jacques Proust, *Diderot et l'Encyclopédie* (Slatkine 1982) 405–08.
[113] Delamétherie, *Principes, vol 1* (n 106) 148, 197.
[114] ibid 206–07.

may exist.[115] Delamétherie called this moral relationship which all sentient beings have among each other *droit naturel* (natural law). Due to epistemic and practical constraints on helping the sensitive beings that live on other planets, he considered it to be sufficient to wish these beings the kind of happiness which their nature permits. 'But we can act directly', he emphasized, 'on those who coexist with us'.[116] Because other humans and animals share this planet with us, we have direct responsibilities towards them; responsibilities which depend on the sensations they are capable of experiencing. These less universal moral relations are called *droit de nature* (law of nature) and form part of the abovementioned *droit naturel*.[117] Unfortunately, Delamétherie complained, most humans neglect these obligations because they have suppressed their natural empathy for animals and, sometimes, other humans.[118]

On Delamétherie's account, humans' duties towards other sensitive beings necessarily correlate with the rights that these beings possess in having their well-being protected and promoted.[119] Both humans and animals possess such rights to well-being. Delamétherie further unpacked the duties and rights of sensitive beings by introducing a distinction within the *droit de nature* between *droit d'animalité* (law of animality) and *droit d'humanité* (law of humanity).

The *droit d'animalité* describes what all animals, including human beings, owe each other. Because of what he saw as their limited knowledge and their relatively strong urges to pursue momentary passions, Delamétherie argued that animals have much fewer obligations.[120] Humans, on the other hand, are more perfect than the other animals. They are able to observe the laws of equity, which is why they have to respect and cater for other sensitive beings' needs. But just how far do these duties towards other sensitive beings, and in particular animals, go? Answering this question reveals how ground-breaking Delamétherie's argument for the *droit d'animalité* is. He proposed that animals have a triad of fundamental rights. First, they have a *right to life*. Because life is the basis of all their sensations, he argued, taking away a sensitive being's life is the greatest injustice one can commit against them.[121] Indeed, it would be equally wrong as the killing of a human being, he contended, because the same reasons that command respect for a human being's life (namely, that she is a sensitive being whose well-being is connected with her life) also apply

[115] ibid 196–97.
[116] ibid 198.
[117] ibid.
[118] ibid 141–42, 205–06, 212.
[119] ibid 148.
[120] ibid 202–04.
[121] ibid 199–200, 237.

to animals. Because life alone does not get an animal far, Delamétherie proposed a second fundamental right: the *right to health*. Every animal, he argued, should be able to have a life free from illness.[122] Finally, he put forward a third fundamental right, which builds on the former two as its preconditions. This third right is the *right to enjoyments* (*plaisirs*). Delamétherie failed to specify what this right entails exactly but he suggested that *plaisirs* are connected to a sensitive being's senses, spirit, and heart.[123] The right to enjoyments could thus encompass experiences such as play, friendship, and even sex, considering that he recognized reproduction as one of every animal's two basic needs (the other being food).[124]

As this shows, the *droit d'animalité* does not stop at prohibiting unnecessarily cruel acts towards animals. Instead, it entails that animals should possess similar rights to human beings because animals are sensitive beings like humans. This is particularly remarkable considering that France only enacted its first laws against the cruel treatment of animals in 1850, more than half a century after the publication of Delamétherie's *Principes*.[125] Delamétherie not only advocated the protection of animals from cruelty, as did these first welfare laws concerning the protection of animals. Rather, his arguments went beyond such animal *welfare* proposals and instead presented a genuine theory of fundamental animal *rights*.[126] As will become clearer in Chapter 4, Delamétherie's theory is hardly inferior to today's theories of animal rights which only emerged in the third quarter of the twentieth century. These more recent theories brought the idea of fundamental animal rights back into the public sphere. But they by no means invented it.

In contrast to the *droit d'animalité*, which concerns the rights and duties of all animals towards each other, the *droit d'humanité* describes rights and obligations that apply only to human beings. The reason why there is such a law, Delamétherie explained, is that the members of every species have more sensibility for conspecifics than for members of other species. What a fellow human being experiences will touch another human more than what an animal experiences. As a result, humans will be more ready to help secure other humans' well-being and can expect others to do the same for them.[127] To the extent

[122] ibid 200.
[123] ibid 201.
[124] ibid 217.
[125] See Éric Pierre, 'Réformer les relations entre les hommes et les animaux: fonction et usages de la loi Grammont en France (1850–1914)' (2007) 31 Déviance et Société 65.
[126] See on this distinction Nicola Taylor, 'Whither Rights? Animal Rights and the Rise of New Welfarism' (1999) 3 Animal Issues 27.
[127] Delamétherie, *Principes*, vol 1 (n 106) 209–10.

that no one else's rights are infringed by this, he argued, every human has a right to everything conducive to his well-being.[128] This is because, as he suggested, humans have special needs arising from their social condition, such as the need to clothe themselves, to have adequate accommodation, and so on.[129] These special needs give rise to rights in human beings that do not exist in animals lacking these needs. However, as Delamétherie made clear, the *droit d'humanité* is just one particular set of 'laws', regulating the special rights and obligations that govern the relationship between human beings. Because intensified intra-species concern also exists in other species, there are specific laws that apply exclusively to the members of these species.[130] For example, there is a *droit de chevalité*—regulating the special rights and duties that exist among horses.

Delamétherie's reliance on naturalism and his emphasis on individual animals' sensations led him to conclude that each animal should assist others in attaining their triad of rights as much as possible. However, he argued that this duty only applies to animals who have no interest in harming others. It therefore does not apply to carnivores who live off the flesh of other animals. Carnivores must have the *right to kill and eat other animals*, Delamétherie reasoned, 'because they have no other way to survive, and because, as sensitive beings, they have to procure their own well-being'.[131] Despite realizing that carnivores may be necessary to prevent an overpopulation of animals,[132] he struggled to comprehend nature's motives in creating sensitive beings that have no other way to survive than by causing great suffering and death to others. Questioning the universal law of the good which he stipulated at the beginning of his treatise, Delamétherie wondered: 'Can we say that nature wanted the happiness of all these beings?'[133] I will return to this problem in Chapter 4. Although Delamétherie himself did not have an answer to the problem, he knew how to respond to human beings who kill other animals for food. In contrast to carnivores, he pointed out, humans have no right to kill other animals because they do not need to eat them. Barring exceptional circumstances, humans can live off plants and are therefore only permitted to eat animals who die of a natural cause.[134]

[128] ibid 215–17.
[129] ibid 217–18.
[130] ibid 215.
[131] ibid 201–02, 231.
[132] ibid 232–33.
[133] ibid 231.
[134] ibid 238–46.

In 1802, Delamétherie published *De l'homme considéré moralement, de ses mœurs, et de celles des animaux*,[135] a two-volume treatise applying his naturalistic insights to political philosophy. This treatise explicitly renounced egalitarianism by proposing a full-blown hierarchical account of nature.[136] Delamétherie laid the groundwork for this account by rejecting the *Separateness Thesis*, arguing that the bodies of both humans and animals have a similar constitution because they are both machines controlled by a central nervous system. Although humans have certain special traits, he argued, they share most things with animals, including their desire for pleasure.[137] 'Man', Delamétherie claimed, is simply 'the foremost species of ape'[138] who evolved to become the most powerful being on the planet.[139] In the process of this evolution, humans abandoned vegetarianism and became hunters, which had a negative impact on their mores: they started to stand out from all other animals with their violence and oppressive tendencies—making humans, paradoxically, more shrewd and intelligent than other animals.[140] According to Delamétherie, humans have to be placed at the top of the natural hierarchy, where the most perfect beings with the most excellent qualities belong.

However, he also held that hierarchies are justified *within* one and the same species, if the members of that species possess dissimilar qualities. According to Delamétherie, this holds for the human species, whose members are marked by important differences. The central difference, for him, was that between 'civilised' human beings and those who, like animals, have not left the state of nature.[141] Hence, in his view, 'civilised' people rank higher in his hierarchy than 'barbaric' ones.[142] Within the higher-ranked category of 'civilised' humans, Delamétherie placed those on top who are rich and well-educated. Those who are poor or who perform manual labour, by contrast, rank lower.[143] The difference between educated and non-educated people, he contended, can be so great as to raise the question whether the latter are human at all:

> It is knowledge and education that elevates this class [the educated class] above the one we have just discussed [the non-educated class]. They establish

[135] Jean-Claude Delamétherie, *De l'homme considéré moralement; de ses moeurs, et de celles des animaux*, vol 1 (Guilleminet 1802). See also Serna, *L'animal en République* (n 106) 218.
[136] See also Serna, *L'animal en République* (n 106) 213, 219.
[137] See Delamétherie, *De l'homme considéré moralement* (n 135) vi–xi.
[138] ibid xxxvi.
[139] See for a similar view already Delamétherie, *Principes*, vol 1 (n 106) 196, 205, 349.
[140] Serna, *L'animal en République* (n 106) 214–15.
[141] Delamétherie, *De l'homme considéré moralement* (n 135) vii.
[142] ibid 38.
[143] ibid 256–61. See also Serna, *L'animal en République* (n 106) 218–20.

> such a great distance between the two that one would be tempted to believe that they belong to two different species. There is no apparent relation between Caesar or Newton, and a Papuan or a Hottentot.[144]

According to Delamétherie, justice requires 'conferring to everyone what he is owed'.[145] What we owe to one another, in turn, is determined by our place in society and our merit.[146] Unless we give more rights to those who are more perfect and therefore superior to those who are less perfect, we act unjustly.[147] Delamétherie thus also rejected the *Equality Thesis*. And as was the case with other inegalitarian naturalists, his rejection of the *Separateness Thesis* cleared the way for this move.

Let us recapitulate. Delamétherie's *Principes* have illustrated the central marks of the inegalitarian strand of naturalism: drawing on sensationalism and materialism, Delamétherie developed a difference-based theory of fundamental rights that grounds these rights in the relevant physical properties of individual beings (most importantly their sensitivity). This approach allowed him to defend a conception of animal rights that anticipated more recent theories. By grounding rights in empirical properties that may differ from being to being, however, Delamétherie also opened the door for inegalitarianism. Applying his differentialist account to the human species, he argued for a hierarchy of higher and lower humans who have to be treated differently in accordance with their respective place in society.

6 Jean-Baptiste Salaville and the sentiment of humanity

Delamétherie's views came into serious conflict with those of another French thinker at the time, the egalitarian Jean-Baptiste Salaville (1755–1832). Salaville was a Parisian journalist and political theorist who wrote on topics as diverse as mesmerism, the organization of society, morality, the abolition of

144 Delamétherie, *De l'homme considéré moralement* (n 135) 260.

145 ibid 123.

146 ibid 124.

147 See ibid. Perhaps taken aback by these conclusions, Delamétherie included in *De l'Homme considéré moralement* a short subsection on 'political equality': ibid 274–75. There, he argued that at least those differences (or 'inequalities') between human beings which have a physical cause—that one is stronger, has a larger brain, or has more exquisite sensations than another—should not infringe on the political equality and the right to equal protection under the law that all citizens have in civil society. However, Delamétherie believed that there are also differences or 'inequalities' that are not caused by one's physical nature, but by one's upbringing. The rich who can afford healthy nutrition and a good education for their children, he held, acquire 'a decisive superiority over the people who work for them, and the equality between citizens ceases to exist': see ibid 255, 258.

the duel, and the death penalty. In 1789, he made a name for himself with the publication of *De l'organisation d'un État monarchique*, in which he criticized the French monarchy and discussed the need for a new constitution. A staunch republican with democratic sympathies, Salaville served as the secretary of the Comte de Mirabeau, then deputy for the Third Estate, until 1791.

Salaville's essay *De l'homme et des animaux*, which is of primary interest to our analysis, was written in 1802 and published in 1805. Salaville submitted it to an essay competition run by the *Institut national de France*.[148] The competition question was: 'To what extent is the barbaric treatment of animals of interest to public morality? And would it be appropriate to adopt laws in this regard?'[149] A total of twenty-eight essays were sent to Paris by authors from a wide variety of backgrounds.[150] However, due to a change in the political regime that left little room for radical ideas like animal rights, the competition was ended abruptly. Furious, Salaville decided to publish his essay independently to ensure it would receive the attention he thought it deserved.[151] In the foreword of his essay, Salaville explained why he deemed it crucial that his piece be made accessible to a broad audience. In recent times, he pointed out, numerous theories had been put forward which challenged the natural excellence of human beings and therefore violated their inherent dignity. A particularly grave degradation, he deplored, was perpetrated by modern scientists who argued that human beings differ from other animals only in degree.[152] 'If we are to believe a physicist of our day', Salaville pointed out tauntingly, ' "man, belonging to the family of apes, was originally covered with hair like them, [and] inhabited the warm countries", etc.'[153] Salaville's 'physicist of our day' was none other than Delamétherie.

The declared aim of Salaville's essay was to salvage the special status of humanity by putting a stop to the kind of moral degradation that he believed to result from naturalistic accounts such as Delamétherie's.[154] There are too many doctrines, Salaville argued, which try to cast human beings in a terrible light, demonizing them for their desires and practices, especially those that affect animals. According to him, these doctrines are pernicious because they

[148] See for an account of the competition and its context Serna, *L'animal en République* (n 106). The competition essays themselves are available at Editions Anacharsis Blog, 'L'Animal en République' <http://blogs.editions-anacharsis.com/animal/> accessed 11 June 2023.
[149] Serna, *L'animal en République* (n 106) 35.
[150] See for the complete list ibid 41–51.
[151] ibid 206–07.
[152] Salaville, *De l'homme et des animaux* (n 106) vi–viii.
[153] Salaville quotes Delamétherie, *De l'homme considéré moralement* (n 135) xxii.
[154] See Jean-Baptiste Salaville, 'À M. Foullière, sur sa Lettre contre l'ouvrage intitulé: de l'Homme et des Animaux' (30 Thermidor Year XIII) T46 La Décade philosophique, littéraire et politique 339, 343.

undermine human excellence and violate human dignity by representing man, 'if it be allowed to say so, as a vulgar being'.[155] We ought therefore to reject all theories about the supposed fatalism of human barbarism towards animals.[156] Salaville's answer to the *Institut*'s competition question as to whether the brutal treatment of animals is a matter of public morality and should be regulated legally was thus a resounding 'No!'.

Salaville developed his answer in three steps. First, he analysed whether the cruel treatment of animals is of concern to *private morality*, that is, morality as it relates to individuals in the private sphere. According to him, private morality is part of public morality, that is, morality in the public sphere. Hence, he reasoned, if the barbaric treatment of animals were to violate private morality, then it would also violate public morality.[157] For Salaville, private morality can only be violated if animals possessed rights against cruel treatment: 'for where there is no violation of a right, there is no injustice'.[158] So the question for him becomes: do animals have such rights? Pointing to two potential sources of rights—positive law rights and natural rights—Salaville denies that they do. First, rights deriving from positive law, he argued, can only result from contracts and conventions.[159] Because only humans have the capacity to submit themselves to contractual relationships and to reciprocate the duties arising from such contracts, animals cannot have positive law rights.[160] Second, animals also lack natural rights because they lack the ability to translate these rights into positive law. Salaville's reasoning here is that if a being is unable to conduct such a legal translation, then surely it has no natural rights in the first place. Because only humans have that ability, they deserve a special kind of respect, and possess what he called—in ways that are reminiscent of Hannah Arendt's later term—'[un] droit à avoir des droits';[161] a right to have rights.

His second step was to argue that the barbaric treatment of animals is not a matter of public morality either. For as he pointed out, public morality could theoretically also be violated in circumstances which are of no concern to private morality. This is because public morality is more 'delicate'[162] than private morality. For example, he notes that private morality is not generally affected by

[155] Salaville, *De l'homme et des animaux* (n 106) vi.
[156] ibid xi–xiii.
[157] ibid 2.
[158] ibid 7.
[159] There is an interesting parallel here to social contract arguments put forward by modern courts dealing with animal rights cases, see eg *Nonhuman Rights Project, Inc v Patrick C Lavery et al* [2014] State of New York Supreme Court, Appellate Division, Third Judicial Department No 518336, 4.
[160] Salaville, *De l'homme et des animaux* (n 106) 2–3, 6.
[161] ibid 6. See Hannah Arendt, *The Origins of Totalitarianism* (Harvest 1973) 296.
[162] Salaville, *De l'homme et des animaux* (n 106) 8.

the 'relationships' that two spouses can have at home; but public morality can be affected if these relationships are carried out in public.[163] This is when they can offend sentiments of decency and shame, as well as the sentiment which Salaville believes society accords most weight to: the *sentiment of humanity*, that is, the sentiment that makes people willing to help others in need. If this sentiment is lost, we are left with nothing but the 'cold calculation of egoism'.[164] The question thus is: does the way we treat animals, or the sight of such treatment, distort or destroy our sentiments, specifically the precious sentiment of humanity?[165] To answer that question, Salaville explores whether animals are capable of suffering. His (somewhat puzzling) assumption here seems to be that the sentiment of humanity cannot be weakened if animals are unable to suffer. According to him, there are three positions on this matter: the Cartesian position that animals are automata that are completely lacking in the ability to suffer; the Comte de Buffon's position that animals can suffer but lack intelligence; and Étienne Bonnot de Condillac's position that animals suffer just like humans.

Condillac's position is the most problematic, according to Salaville. To Condillac, a noted adherent of sensationalism, humans and animals are cut from the same cloth and possess intelligence and sensibility that differ only in degree. This, Salaville believed, would mean that treating animals cruelly would have a similarly corrosive effect on the sentiment of humanity as treating humans cruelly. Rather than refuting Condillac's position on empirical grounds, Salaville points out the two equally unattractive choices to which it gives rise. On the one hand, the similarity of humans' and animals' capacities to suffer could be taken to mean that humans must become the guardians of animals and protect them from pain. As this would amount to giving up our superiority over other species, Salaville believed this would undermine the sentiment of humanity. On the other hand, if humans instead chose to exploit at least those animals that are inferior to them in their capacity to feel pain, then humans would open themselves to potential exploitation by beings that are superior to humans. Even more problematically, such oppression could take place not only between different species, but also within one and the same species. As Salaville asked: '[i]s there not also a greater and lesser among human beings? Are not some superior to others in intelligence, corporeal strength, natural faculties and acquired faculties?'[166] If we were to adopt this line of reasoning, he suggested, it would follow that superior human beings could exploit those who are less perfect. However,

[163] ibid.
[164] ibid 9.
[165] ibid 9–10.
[166] ibid 16.

he maintained, it would be wrong to say that more developed faculties in one human being would give her the right to oppress and treat cruelly those with lesser faculties. For these reasons, we should reject Condillac's theory.[167]

Buffon's more moderate position fares no better. According to Buffon, animals can suffer but are not intelligent. Salaville rejects this position on the ground that one cannot separate suffering from intelligence. One mistaken reason why many people believe that animals can suffer, he notes, is that animals squeal. However, such cries are not necessarily indicative of pain. After all, human babies cry more often than adults but, he claims, we would not think that they suffer, or at least not as much as adults do. What is more, sometimes we forget even great pain if we are distracted by something else. Mere bodily or behavioural signs of pain are thus no evidence for suffering. All this, he believes, suggests that consciousness of pain is necessary, too. If suffering had no such intellectual component, then the solidarity and empathy linking humans like an 'invisible chain' would be lost, and everyone would only be concerned with their own suffering. This is the case in the animal kingdom, he argued, because animals lack intelligence and, therefore, the ability to suffer.[168] Rejecting Delamétherie's view that sensitivity grounds rights, Salaville contended that intelligence is the sole reason for rights. Only intelligence can explain why humans suffer from degrading treatment. Hence, it alone gives rise to the moral dignity that commands respect for humans by the sentiment he calls humanity.[169] In Salaville's view, animals completely lack any such dignity, which is why we ought not apply it to them. Not mincing his words, he insists that 'extending the sentiment of humanity to animals is . . . to give it a wrong direction; it is to profane the feeling; to prostitute it to beings whom nature has not formed to be able to participate in this noble assignment of its finest work'.[170] Even Buffon's more moderate position must therefore be rejected because it fails to distinguish strictly between humans and animals, and thus 'confound[s] what must be carefully differentiated'.[171]

Having rejected Condillac's and Buffon's positions, Salaville effectively sided with the third camp: the Cartesians arguing that animals lack the ability to suffer. Because Salaville assumed that being able to suffer would be the only possibility for animals' barbaric treatment to have a negative impact on the sentiment of humanity, he therefore concluded that the way we treat animals has no

[167] ibid 15–18.
[168] ibid 27.
[169] ibid 35.
[170] ibid 37.
[171] ibid 35.

effect on public morality and that no laws are therefore required to protect animals. Interestingly, however, he added a third step to his argument: he adduced practical reasons 'based on facts and experience'[172] to drive his point home. Among other things, he speculated that if cruel treatment of animals were indeed deadening to human beings, then it would follow that butchers, hunters, vivisectionists, and the like would have lost all sense of compassion. But this is not the case, he claimed, because there are many such individuals who are perfectly caring. In fact, he continued, if we followed this hypothesis then everyone who enjoyed a meaty meal would be an accomplice of the butcher and be more inclined to become cruel. 'As for me', Salaville observed, 'I know very well that never, having risen from a table where, for my part, I had become the accomplice of the murder of several animals, have I felt a disposition to barbarity toward my fellow human beings.'[173] If those who eat meat do not lose their sense of morality, then neither do those who torture and kill animals in a professional capacity.

As Salaville underlined in the final pages of his essay, it is not only unnecessary to enact laws protecting animals from cruel treatment. It would also be actively harmful to human rights. This is because it would require extending the sentiment of humanity to those for whom it is not intended. Only humans possess the excellence and dignity that elicit the sentiment of humanity, which is why extending it beyond the human species would be to corrupt and debase it: '[i]n trying to lift animals to the status of humans, humans are brought down to the status of animals. This doctrine, ostensibly human, is in fact full of injustice and inhumanity.'[174] Extending the sentiment of humanity to animals would thus be to destroy it. Putting each being on the same level would annihilate the harmony and beauty of the whole. 'By giving everything the same colour, you disenchant the nature you think to embellish.'[175] In order to protect this invaluable sentiment once and for all, Salaville proposed that

> [i]t is, therefore, not by calling for sympathy towards animals that we can hope to increase and consolidate sympathy towards man; if there is a means of assuring the inviolability of the latter, it is, we dare to say, to render it exclusive; it is to admit that man and animals differ by their respective nature and that this difference authorises and makes legitimate with respect to them what it prohibits with respect to us.[176]

[172] ibid 40.
[173] ibid 43.
[174] ibid 53.
[175] ibid 56.
[176] ibid 51.

In other words, Salaville argued that only if we insist on the separation between humans and other animals (*Separateness Thesis*) can we protect the fundamental equality between all human beings (*Equality Thesis*). Salaville's *De l'homme et des animaux* thus nicely illustrates the two central theses of egalitarianism, and his attack on inegalitarian naturalists like Delamétherie reveals the ways in which their ideas challenged these theses.

7 Conclusion

In Leo Strauss's spirit, this chapter has shed light on 'the thought of the past'[177] in order to render explicit some of the views that have come to influence our thinking today. Focusing on the French Enlightenment, the chapter has provided an account of two important currents of thinking: naturalism and egalitarianism. As I have argued, the strand of naturalism which emphasized difference over equality conflicted with egalitarianism's thesis that all humans are fundamentally equal (*Equality Thesis*) and the neighbouring *Separateness Thesis*, according to which all humans are special and separate from all nonhumans. I then illustrated this conflict with the aid of the exchange between Delamétherie and Salaville.

As I have indicated, Delamétherie's naturalist account contains some of the core arguments that we can find in contemporary animal rights approaches. Salaville's egalitarian response to Delamétherie, on the other hand, foreshadowed some of the central claims in contemporary human rights literature. In order to be able to understand how exactly they have anticipated contemporary positions, we now need to move beyond the intellectual history of this chapter and approach the respective positions analytically. In Chapter 3, I will shed light on the conceptual structure of the Aristocratic conception of fundamental rights. As I will point out there, Salaville took the same egalitarian position on its central features—*Equal Consideration* and *Internalism*—as many modern Aristocrats do today. In Chapter 4, I will then elucidate the key features of the Meritocratic rights conception—*Differential Consideration* and *Externalism*—and will show that Delamétherie's views are cut from the same naturalistic cloth as those of contemporary Meritocrats.

[177] Strauss, *What Is Political Philosophy? And Other Studies* (n 1) 73.

3

The Aristocratic Conception

1 Introduction

Human rights reject special privileges for the few and promote equal protection for all—this is generally believed to be a founding idea of human rights.[1] Human rights, and cognate concepts such as human dignity and equality, are thus often seen as being premised on a rejection of aristocratic thinking, which prioritizes the interests of the few. In this chapter, I argue that this belief is incomplete, if not misguided. Still to this day, human rights bear the marks of aristocracy. It is true that these marks are less obvious than they were in, say, Ancien Régime defences of the nobility. However, many human rights approaches still endorse an aristocratic logic insofar as they only accord fundamental rights to a privileged group of beings and withhold them from other beings. The privileged group is the human species itself; and those excluded from it are all nonhumans.

There are, of course, numerous ways one can conceive of human rights, equality, and dignity without relying on aristocratic thinking. The Aristocratic conception of human rights that I portray in this chapter is therefore not the only game in town.[2] However, this conception captures many of the key elements that make up a lot of human rights thinking and practice today.[3] I say 'many' and 'a lot' because the Aristocratic conception, like any other one conception, is unable to cover 'all' of the central ideas of the sundry ways human rights are thought of and practised today. The point of this chapter is not to provide an exhaustive description of the manifold human rights accounts and practices that exist, but rather to focus on one particularly pertinent

[1] See eg UNESCO, 'Human Rights Day' (2021) <https://en.unesco.org/events/human-rights-day-0> accessed 18 December 2023.

[2] See Will Kymlicka, 'Human Rights Without Human Supremacism' (2018) 48 Canadian Journal of Philosophy 763, 765.

[3] See also ibid 770.

More Equal Than Others. Raffael N Fasel, Oxford University Press. © Raffael N Fasel 2024.
DOI: 10.1093/oso/9780198907435.003.0003

ideal-type—the Aristocratic conception—whose elements we can find in a good number of such accounts and practices.

The Aristocratic ideal-type is characterized by two elements: *Equal Consideration* and *Internalism*. *Equal Consideration* (which should not be conflated with Peter Singer's notion of 'equal consideration of interests', as I will explain in the next chapter) concerns the nature of the status that rights-holders possess in the Aristocratic conception. In other words, it answers the question of *what* the Aristocratic status is. I will show that the Aristocratic conception considers human rights to be entitlements that all members of a high rank—the rank of human dignity—possess equally and to the exclusion of all other beings. *Internalism*, by contrast, deals with the question of *how* the special status of *Equal Consideration* for human beings is explained. I will show that this is done in an *Internalist* manner: *Internalism* explains human rights, equality, and dignity by drawing on normative ideas about how human beings should be treated. As such, *Internalism* contrasts with the *Externalist* approach that is characteristic of the Meritocracy, as we will see in the next chapter. *Externalism* justifies rights and other concepts by drawing on empirical facts about human nature. To put this another way, we can say that *Externalists* '*ground*' rights, equality, and dignity in empirical facts, whereas *Internalists* '*found*' these concepts without relying on any such facts.

Drawing on both contemporary Aristocratic accounts as well as Jean-Baptiste Salaville's egalitarian theory, which I discussed in the previous chapter, I will show what the advantages of the Aristocratic approach are and where its shortcomings lie. It will be worth keeping in mind that the Aristocratic conception of fundamental rights is representative of one end of a spectrum of fundamental rights approaches. On the other, opposing end of that spectrum we find the Meritocratic conception of fundamental rights. Because the two conceptions stand in an antithetical relationship, we will be better able to appreciate the Aristocracy's characteristics once we can compare them with the opposing characteristics of the Meritocracy in Chapter 4.

The chapter is structured as follows. In Section 2, I will lay the groundwork for the Aristocratic conception by shedding light on a recent movement in scholarship which describes human rights, equality, and dignity as Aristocratic concepts. I will then turn to an analysis of the two characteristic elements of the Aristocratic ideal-type. I will start by examining the element of *Equal Consideration* (Section 3), before turning to *Internalism* (Section 4). I will critically evaluate these features, before summarizing the chapter's main findings in the conclusion.

2 Human rights Aristocracy

In recent times, a scholarly movement has emerged which understands human rights and related concepts such as basic equality and human dignity as essentially Aristocratic concepts. This movement may come as a surprise. After all, as indicated above, the notion of 'Aristocratic human rights' can appear oxymoronic considering that the central impetus behind human rights is one that is opposed to the notion that the few should have special privileges, and that the many be left with nothing. For that seems to be exactly what the aristocracy was all about. Hence, those who adopt this view may baulk at the idea of using the term 'human rights Aristocracy' to refer to a lot or even just some of contemporary human rights thinking and practice. Yet, as I hope to show in the following, human rights today do in fact share many of the core traits of the former nobility. As counterintuitive as it may seem at first, it is no stretch to talk of 'Aristocratic' human rights. Far from being misleading, I propose that the lens of the Aristocracy allows us to make better sense of current human rights thinking and practices.

One of the first recent thinkers to draw an explicit analogy between aristocracy and human rights and dignity was Gregory Vlastos.[4] In a 1984 essay, Vlastos described the special status and privileges of human beings as 'a "rank of dignity" in some ways comparable to that enjoyed by hereditary nobilities of the past' and as 'first-class citizenship [that has] been made common'.[5] Human society, Vlastos argued, is 'like a caste society (with a *unique* caste)'.[6] Membership in this caste is independent of individual merit and available to all human beings as an equal birthright.[7] In the same way as aristocrats acquire their special status and privileges simply in virtue of being born noble, human beings acquire their dignity and rights simply in virtue of being born human. Because all humans are equally born human, none of them can be considered superior or inferior to others.[8]

In a similar vein, James Whitman has argued that in continental Europe, human dignity has taken on the same meaning aristocratic dignity once had in the Ancien Régime: '"Human dignity", as we find it on the Continent today,

[4] For precursors of this view see HLA Hart, 'Are There Any Natural Rights?' (1955) 64 The Philosophical Review 175, 180–81; Joel Feinberg, 'The Nature and Value of Rights' (1970) 4 The Journal of Value Inquiry 243, 252; Thomas E Hill, 'Servility and Self-Respect' (1973) 57 The Monist 87, 93–94, 97. I am grateful to an anonymous reviewer for these pointers.

[5] Gregory Vlastos, 'Justice and Equality' in Jeremy Waldron (ed), *Theories of Rights* (Oxford University Press 1984) 54.

[6] ibid (emphasis in original).

[7] ibid.

[8] ibid 74.

has been formed by a pattern of *levelling up*, by an extension of formerly high-status treatment to all sectors of the population.'[9] Whitman points to examples in the law of criminal punishment, hate speech, and privacy to show that in all these areas, treatments that were previously reserved for high-status persons have been made available to everyone. Formerly low-status treatments, on the other hand, have been abolished.[10]

Arguably the most important contribution to the dissemination of the rank idea of human rights, equality, and dignity is Jeremy Waldron's *Dignity, Rank, and Rights*, which he delivered as his Tanner Lectures in 2009.[11] Building on an earlier article,[12] Waldron argues that human dignity, as it is used in legal practice, is best understood as a rank (or status) concept akin to that previously held by aristocrats. Dignity, he explains, 'expresses the idea of the high and equal rank of every human person'.[13] According to him, this understanding of dignity is in line with the ancient connotation of dignity as a term denoting the honour, esteem, and deference that were owed to a high rank or office.[14] He also anticipates the concern, mentioned above, that it is somewhat counterintuitive to associate human rights thinking with notions such as rank and aristocracy, which by definition imply a hierarchy between higher and lower beings. Waldron dispels this worry by arguing that the noble rank of human dignity is now accorded to *all* members of the human species: it has been universalized and is thus no longer restricted to a specific class of humans. As he points out, this egalitarian understanding of dignity is in line with Judeo-Christian beliefs about the equality and uniqueness of all human beings. Created in the image of God, all and only humans possess a rank which they hold not over other humans, but over all other creatures in the great chain of being.[15]

[9] James Q Whitman, '"Human Dignity" in Europe and the United States: The Social Foundations' in Georg Nolte (ed), *European and US Constitutionalism* (Cambridge University Press 2005) 110 (emphasis in original). See also Michael Rosen, *Dignity: Its History and Meaning* (Harvard University Press 2012) 8; Stéphanie Hennette-Vauchez, 'A Human Dignitas? Remnants of the Ancient Legal Concept in Contemporary Dignity Jurisprudence' (2011) 9 International Journal of Constitutional Law 32, 55; Aharon Barak, 'Human Dignity: The Constitutional Value and the Constitutional Right' in Christopher McCrudden (ed), *Understanding Human Dignity* (Oxford University Press 2014) 363.

[10] Whitman, '"Human Dignity" in Europe and the United States: The Social Foundations' (n 9) 116.

[11] Jeremy Waldron, *Dignity, Rank, and Rights* (Jeremy Waldron and Meir Dan-Cohen eds, Oxford University Press 2012) 13. For criticism of this idea see eg Don Herzog, 'Aristocratic Dignity?' in Jeremy Waldron and Meir Dan-Cohen (eds), *Dignity, Rank, and Rights* (Oxford University Press 2012) 99; Michael Rosen, 'Dignity Past and Present' in Jeremy Waldron and Meir Dan-Cohen (eds), *Dignity, Rank, and Rights* (Oxford University Press 2012) 79; A John Simmons, 'Human Rights, Natural Rights, and Human Dignity' in Rowan Cruft, S Matthew Liao, and Massimo Renzo (eds), *Philosophical Foundations of Human Rights* (Oxford University Press 2015) 143.

[12] See Jeremy Waldron, 'Dignity and Rank: In Memory of Gregory Vlastos (1907–1991)' (2007) 48 European Journal of Sociology 201.

[13] Waldron, *Dignity, Rank, and Rights* (n 11) 14.

[14] ibid 30.

[15] ibid 32. See on this also Chapter 2, Section 3.

That this is a plausible account of human rights and dignity is supported by the fact that aristocratic interpretations of these concepts are not a new phenomenon.[16] At least some contemporaries of the French Revolution adopted a similar understanding. The Marquis de Ferrières, a writer and deputy to the Second Estate, for example, wrote in a letter of 1789 that '[t]here is nothing better the Nobility can do than to join with the Third Estate in good faith, and to *lift up to itself* the wealthy and decent citizen of the bourgeoisie'.[17] In the same year, an observer from Great Britain pointed out that '[t]he greater part of the Noblesse could not bear the idea that persons of no rank or consideration in the Country should be *raised* to a dignity so important as this, and should be *put upon a level with themselves*'.[18] And in 1790, Armand-Gaston Camus, a revolutionary and representative to the National Assembly, declared that '[a]ll the French were now noble'.[19] These examples illustrate that understanding the abolition of the nobility's privileges and the recognition of commoners' fundamental rights as an 'upwards equalisation of rank'[20] is not a recent invention. As the French historian Jules Michelet put it succinctly: 'It is said that the Revolution destroyed the nobility. But quite the contrary, it has made thirty-four million nobles.'[21]

It is likely no coincidence that the idea of upwards equalization can be found both in the discourse of contemporaries of the French Revolution and in post-World War II human rights discourse. In each of these cases, experiences of outright denial of human rights had preceded the (re)assertion of these rights.[22] As David Bilchitz points out,

> The assertion of the dignity of all human beings in post-World War II human rights documents represented a reaction against the Holocaust and the War itself, both of which undeniably saw the massive devaluation in human

[16] Anne Phillips, *The Politics of the Human* (Cambridge University Press 2015) 23.

[17] Letter from Ferrières to his sister, 10 August 1789, Henri Carré (ed), *Marquis de Ferrières, Correspondance inédite: 1789, 1790, 1791* (Armand Colin 1932) 120 (emphasis added).

[18] Copy of a letter from Mr Jenkinson, 17 September 1789, Oscar Browning (ed), *Despatches from Paris: 1784–1790*, vol ii (Offices of the Society 1910) 261 (emphases added).

[19] William Doyle, *Aristocracy and Its Enemies in the Age of Revolution* (Oxford University Press 2009) 257.

[20] Waldron, *Dignity, Rank, and Rights* (n 11) 33.

[21] Jules Michelet, *Le peuple* (Comptoir des Imprimeurs-unis 1846) 18. See also James Q Whitman, 'Enforcing Civility and Respect: Three Societies' (2000) 109 Yale Law Journal 1279, 1279.

[22] See also Phillips, *The Politics of the Human* (n 16) 37; David Hollenbach, 'Human Dignity: Experience and History, Practical Reason and Faith' in Christopher McCrudden (ed), *Understanding Human Dignity* (Oxford University Press 2014) 123; Johannes Morsink, *The Universal Declaration of Human Rights: Origins, Drafting, and Intent* (University of Pennsylvania Press 2010) 36–38.

> life. Dignity was designed as a corrective to assert the universal value of all human-kind.[23]

As Richard Cupp has pointed out, in its reassertion of the equal value of all human beings, the post-war emphasis on human rights and human dignity has 'rejected individual intelligence or autonomy as a necessary foundation of legal personhood for humans'.[24] In order to extend the same protection to all members of the human species, differences between human beings, such as pertaining to cognitive disabilities, had to be de-emphasized.[25]

Remedying past injustices by elevating all human beings equally to a high rank would not be without its problems, however. As Bilchitz warns, the exaltation of one group of beings at the expense of others has echoes of the darkest moments of twentieth-century history.[26] What inevitably happens if one group is lifted to a high status with special rights is that the gap is automatically increased between this group and groups which are not included in the status. In fact, the levelling up of one group often occurs with the specific intention to level down another group. In the case of human rights, the group that is being levelled up is all members of the human species; the group that is levelled down is the members of all other species. As Will Kymlicka explains, this exaltation of the human species at the expense of other species which has become common in the current human rights discourse is often conducted for the strategic purpose of protecting vulnerable human beings, that is,

> to help battle forms of prejudice and discrimination against subaltern or marginalised groups, including racialised groups, women, the poor, immigrants, indigenous peoples, and people with disabilities. The hope and expectation is that asserting a sharp hierarchy between humans and animals will make it more difficult to disparage these groups.[27]

Jacques Maritain, who was a driving force behind the Universal Declaration of Human Rights (1948, UDHR), made it plain that a central part of the human

[23] David Bilchitz, 'Moving Beyond Arbitrariness: The Legal Personhood and Dignity of Non-Human Animals' (2009) 23 South African Journal on Human Rights 38, 51.

[24] Richard L Cupp, 'Cognitively Impaired Humans, Intelligent Animals, and Legal Personhood', *Pepperdine University Legal Studies Research Paper No 12* (2016) 28 <http://papers.ssrn.com/abstract=2775288> accessed 11 June 2023.

[25] See ibid.

[26] Bilchitz, 'Moving Beyond Arbitrariness: The Legal Personhood and Dignity of Non-Human Animals' (n 23) 51.

[27] Kymlicka, 'Human Rights Without Human Supremacism' (n 2) 772.

rights project was to 'tame[] the irrational'[28] that is a part of all human beings. For Maritain, we only become fully human once we learn how to overcome the 'immense burden of animality'[29] by distinguishing ourselves from all beings who are 'mere' animals.

In contrast to what sceptics of the idea of a 'human rights Aristocracy' may believe, then, Aristocratic thinking did not disappear with the upwards equalization of all human beings. The Aristocratic approach conceptually requires the existence of an 'other' who is not an equal member of the high rank.[30] As Angus Taylor puts this thought: 'human exceptionalism is at least as much about whom we are determined to exclude from the moral community as about whom we wish to include within it'.[31] This explains why Salaville, in his 1805 essay, was so intent on rejecting all talk about animal rights. As we saw in Chapter 2, he argued that extending the sentiment of humanity to animals would be 'to prostitute it to beings whom nature has not formed to be able to participate in this *noble* assignment of its finest work'.[32] In Salaville's as well as contemporary Aristocratic theories, nonhuman animals assume the quintessential role of the unequal other.

3 *Equal Consideration*

Having discussed the scholarly trend of conceiving of human rights, equality, and dignity as Aristocratic concepts, the stage is now set for an analysis of the features that are distinctive of the Aristocratic conception of fundamental rights. In this section, I focus on the first of the two characteristic elements of this conception: its commitment to *Equal Consideration* of rights-holders. As suggested above, an analysis of this element answers the question of *what* exactly the Aristocratic status is. I will demonstrate that it is three things: a high status that all human beings possess from the moment they are born[33]

[28] Jacques Maritain, *Christianity and Democracy and The Rights of Man and Natural Law* (Doris C Anson tr, Ignatius Press 2011) 100.

[29] ibid 37.

[30] See eg Tina Beattie, 'The Vanishing Absolute and the Deconsecrated God: A Theological Reflection on Revelation, Law, and Human Dignity' in Christopher McCrudden (ed), *Understanding Human Dignity* (Oxford University Press 2014) 270.

[31] Angus Taylor, 'Review of Wesley J Smith's A Rat Is a Pig Is a Dog Is a Boy: The Human Cost of the Animal Rights Movement' (2010) 13 Between the Species 10, 223, 228. I borrow this quote from: Kymlicka, 'Human Rights Without Human Supremacism' (n 2) 5.

[32] Jean-Baptiste Salaville, *De l'homme et des animaux* (Ch Crapelet 1805) 37 (emphasis added).

[33] If not earlier: see eg Nigel S Rodley, 'Integrity of the Person' in Daniel Moeckli, Sangeeta Shah, and Sandesh Sivakumaran (eds), *International Human Rights Law* (3rd edn, Oxford University Press 2018) 176. See also, for differing views on when a foetus has the status of a newborn, Margaret Olivia Little, 'Abortion and the Margins of Personhood' (2008) 39 Rutgers Law Journal 331, 347; Kate Greasley,

(*Heredity*); a status which all humans hold equally, and which gives them equal rights (*Equality*); and a status which excludes all nonhuman beings (*Exclusivity*). In brief, *Equal Consideration* considers humans to be separate *and* equal.

The three features of *Equal Consideration* are heavily influenced by the egalitarian current which I discussed in Chapter 2, and they can all be found in Salaville's essay *De l'homme et des animaux*. Although not explicitly mentioned, the first feature, *Heredity*, emerges from Salaville's argument that the status of humans as rights-holders is inherent in their humanity.[34] As we saw, he does not distinguish between human beings when he invokes their intelligence as an explanation for why only they have dignity.[35] This also corroborates the finding that Salaville embraced *Equality*. Salaville considered it to be neither here nor there that some humans surpass others in their intelligence or strength.[36] According to him, using these differences as a reason for allowing superior human beings to exploit inferior ones would be 'revolting'.[37] He tried to uphold the idea of basic human equality by arguing that our best course of action is to 'admit'[38] that humans differ from animals to such an extent that we may treat animals in ways we could not treat humans. Finally, Salaville also defended the *Exclusivity* of humans' high rank and equal rights. This feature follows conceptually from his acceptance of *Heredity* and *Equality*, for if humans have their status and equality by birth, then all those not born human are automatically excluded. In addition, Salaville of course explicitly argued that animals ought to be excluded from our scope of moral and legal consideration. Animals, according to him, lack intelligence, and therefore dignity.[39] The only way of securing the status and rights of humanity, he claimed, is by refusing to grant them to those who are not human. To guarantee human inviolability, human dignity and rights need therefore be rendered 'exclusive'.[40]

Let us now focus on *Heredity*, the first feature of *Equal Consideration*. *Heredity* is the idea that the Aristocratic status of human beings, their dignity, and the rights that it entails are considered to belong to humans by birth.[41]

Arguments about Abortion: Personhood, Morality, and Law (Oxford University Press 2017) 199. See also the discussion in Chapter 7, Section 4.2.

34 Salaville, *De l'homme et des animaux* (n 32) 6.
35 ibid 33–35. See also Aristotle, *On the Soul* (WS Hett tr, Harvard University Press 1957) II.2–3, 414a30–414b20.
36 cf Salaville, *De l'homme et des animaux* (n 32) 15–17.
37 ibid 16.
38 ibid 51.
39 ibid 36–37.
40 ibid 51.
41 See n 33.

This idea emerges clearly from the central founding documents of the human rights canon. The French Declaration of the Rights of Man and the Citizen (1789), for example, states in its Article 1 that '[m]en are *born* and remain free and equal in rights.' Inspired by the French Declaration, the UDHR stipulates that '[a]ll human beings are *born* free and equal in dignity and rights', and the International Covenant on Civil and Political Rights (1966, ICCPR) recognizes in its preamble the '*inherent* dignity and . . . equal and inalienable rights of all members of the human family'.[42]

According to these foundational documents, being born human is the only condition one needs to satisfy to enjoy human dignity and equal rights. John Tasioulas stresses this point when he argues that '[w]e possess [human] rights not in virtue of any personal achievement or social status, nor because they are conferred upon us by a positive legal order or social conventions, but simply in virtue of our standing as human beings'.[43] To say that we hold human dignity and rights *simply in virtue of being human* is, indeed, a common way of putting the point that this status and these rights are hereditary.[44] A prominent advocate of this view is James Griffin, who claims that a human right is 'a right that we have simply in virtue of being human'.[45] The *Heredity* of human dignity and rights is also recognized by many courts.[46]

The status that human beings are born into is, of course, not just any kind of status. It is one of *high elevation* and inherent worth: a status of dignity. Many contemporary human rights scholars draw on Immanuel Kant to explain this special worthiness of humans. According to Kant, human beings exist as ends-in-themselves because they are rational beings who are their own moral law-givers. Ends-in-themselves are priceless beings, who ought never to be treated as mere means to an end.[47] They have inner worth, or 'dignity'.[48] No rational

[42] Declaration of the Rights of Man and of the Citizen (1789) <http://avalon.law.yale.edu/18th_century/rightsof.asp> accessed 11 June 2023; International Covenant on Civil and Political Rights (1966, ICCPR) <http://www.ohchr.org/en/professionalinterest/pages/ccpr.aspx> accessed 11 June 2023 (emphasis added).

[43] John Tasioulas, 'Human Dignity and the Foundations of Human Rights' in Christopher McCrudden (ed), *Understanding Human Dignity* (Oxford University Press 2014) 292.

[44] See Raffael N Fasel, '"Simply in Virtue of Being Human"? A Critical Appraisal of a Human Rights Commonplace' (2018) 9 Jurisprudence 1.

[45] James Griffin, *On Human Rights* (Oxford University Press 2008) 2. But see also ibid 95, 276. See further Alan Gewirth, *Human Rights: Essays on Justification and Applications* (Chicago University Press 1982) 41.

[46] See eg Constitutional Council of France, decision no 94/343/344 DC, 27 July 1994, para 18; Constitutional Court of Germany, 1 BvR 357/05, para 124. See for further references Catherine Dupré, *The Age of Dignity: Human Rights and Constitutionalism in Europe* (Hart Publishing 2015) 82–112.

[47] See Immanuel Kant, *Groundwork of the Metaphysics of Morals* (Mary Gregor and Jens Timmermann trs, Cambridge University Press 2012) 4:434–35, 446.

[48] ibid.

being can demand respect from his fellow man if he is not in turn willing to accord the same respect to that man. Hence Kant's imperative to 'act that you use humanity, in your own person as well as in the person of any other, always at the same time as an end, never merely as a means'.[49] Following this imperative, dignity requires that special respect be accorded to its holders (and only to them).[50]

The second feature of *Equal Consideration* is *Equality*. This feature is based on egalitarianism's *Equality Thesis*, and holds that every human being has equal status and value (or worth) as a member of the high rank of dignity-holders. As members of that high status, humans also have equal rights.[51] Having 'equal rights' means two things. First, all humans can in principle possess the same fundamental rights. In other words, their rights come wholesale, not retail. They are, as this idea is sometimes put, 'indivisible': everyone can in principle have the same rights.[52] Of course, Aristocrats will readily acknowledge that not all human beings always meet the conditions for exercising all human rights. For example, a minor does not yet meet the conditions of maturity to exercise political rights. However, all humans are said, at least in principle, to possess all human rights simply in virtue of being human. Second, 'equal rights' means that everyone's rights are of the same strength. That is, a particular right generates reasons of equal stringency regardless of who its right-holder is. Hence, an elderly person's right to life has the same strength as a young person's, even if the former has fewer days to live. A particular right generally also binds the same number of entities to respect it, meaning that the elderly person's right does not bind fewer (or more) entities than the young person's.

The *Equality* feature plays a key conceptual role, for if there were some who possessed a higher status than others within the high status of dignity, then dignity would not signify the highest rank.[53] There would, instead, be two

[49] ibid 4:429, 41 (emphasis removed).

[50] Tasioulas, 'Human Dignity and the Foundations of Human Rights' (n 43) 305–06.

[51] Which is not to say that everyone who endorses human equality does so based on an Aristocratic theory, see eg Diego H Rossello, 'All in the (Human) Family? Species Aristocratism in the Return of Human Dignity' (2016) 45 Political Theory 6, 13. For the view that human rights are not egalitarian but sufficientarian, see eg Samuel Moyn, *Not Enough: Human Rights in an Unequal World* (Harvard University Press 2018).

[52] See eg UN Human Rights Office of the High Commissioner, 'What Are Human Rights?' <https://www.ohchr.org/en/what-are-human-rights> accessed 11 June 2023; Georg Lohmann, 'Die Menschenrechte: unteilbar und gleichgewichtig?' in Georg Lohmann and others (eds), *Die Menschenrechte: unteilbar und gleichgewichtig?* (Universität Potsdam 2005) 30; George Kateb, *Human Dignity* (Harvard University Press 2011) 89. On the history of the indivisibility principle, see Daniel J Whelan, *Indivisible Human Rights: A History* (University of Pennsylvania Press 2010). See, on the extent to which practice does not live up to this principle, Chapter 5, Section 2.

[53] But see also Michael Meyer, 'The Simple Dignity of Sentient Life: Speciesism and Human Dignity' (2001) 32 Journal of Social Philosophy 115.

ranks: that of superior beings who hold dignity, and that of inferior beings who do not. But such distinctions are precisely what the egalitarianism of human rights aims to combat. As George Kateb puts it,

> [e]qual status means that the question of which individuals in the human species are 'best of breed', let alone 'best in show', is out of order. Of course people vary in their talents and innate abilities, and in the manner of their acculturation, but that undefinable fact is irrelevant to human status.[54]

In Kateb's conception of dignity, the equal status of every human being constitutes the necessary correlate to the high rank of the human species as a whole (which he calls humanity's 'stature').[55]

Equality is also connected to *Heredity*. Every human being, regardless of their capacities, possesses equal human rights and dignity simply in virtue of being born human. As Vincenzo Ferrone highlights, it was one of the Enlightenment egalitarians' main claims that the rights of man are 'equal for all individuals, with *no distinction of birth*, census, nationality, religion, gender, or skin color'.[56] This is also reflected in the Catholic *imago Dei* doctrine. As discussed in Chapter 2, this doctrine has long formed a cornerstone of egalitarian thinking. According to this doctrine, God's creation of man in His own image established a special bond between the human species and God. Because of this bond, an assault on a human being constitutes an assault on God, who is mirrored in the human.[57]

The third and final feature of *Equal Consideration* is *Exclusivity*. The high hereditary status and equal rights of humans entail the exclusion of all those who are not members of the status. *Exclusivity* thus echoes the *Separateness Thesis* discussed in Chapter 2, according to which all human beings are special and separate from all other species. As Kateb has rightly emphasized with respect to human dignity, the equal status and rights of individual human beings is but one side of the coin. The other side is the exceptional stature of the human species as a whole and, consequently, the unexceptional stature of all other species: 'The core idea of human dignity is that on earth, humanity is the

[54] Kateb, *Human Dignity* (n 52) 9.
[55] ibid 130–31.
[56] Vincenzo Ferrone, *The Enlightenment: History of an Idea* (Elisabetta Tarantino tr, Princeton University Press 2015) xi (emphasis changed). This is not to say, of course, that all Enlightenment thinkers consistently defended this view. See eg on Kant, Pauline Kleingeld, 'Kant's Second Thoughts on Race' (2007) 57 The Philosophical Quarterly 573.
[57] James Hanvey, 'Dignity, Person, and Imago Trinitas' in Christopher McCrudden (ed), *Understanding Human Dignity* (Oxford University Press 2014) 216–17.

greatest type of beings [sic]'.[58] Ascertaining the special status of human beings therefore necessarily implies distinguishing members of this status from non-members. The relationship tends to be an inversely proportional one: the more one lifts humanity's status and praises its dignity, the more one lowers the status of others.

Interestingly, this exclusionary function of human dignity and rights is often neglected in current human rights discourse.[59] A possible reason for this neglect may be that many regard it as difficult enough to secure for all human beings the protection of their dignity and human rights. The fact that there are other beings who are excluded from this status and the concomitant privileges is, at best, of secondary concern.[60] Yet, the issue remains that, necessarily, some will not share in humans' high status and equal rights. Inequality is as much a part of human dignity as equality.[61]

4 *Internalism*

Having analysed what the nature of the status of rights-holders is under the Aristocracy, we can now address the question of *how* proponents of the Aristocracy explain humans' equal status and rights. I argue that they follow an *Internalist* approach. On this approach, which has become widespread since the second half of the twentieth century,[62] concepts such as human rights, equality, and dignity are explained by drawing on normative ideas about human beings. In contrast to *Externalists* (which I discuss in Chapter 4), *Internalists* do not *ground* concepts in empirical facts about the nature of individual human beings, such as their sentience or capacity for abstract thought.[63] As Marion Albers, Thomas Hoffmann, and Jörn Reinhardt define it, internalism is the

[58] Kateb, *Human Dignity* (n 52) 3, 6.

[59] See Alasdair Cochrane, 'From Human Rights to Sentient Rights' (2013) 16 Critical Review of International Social and Political Philosophy 655, 655.

[60] For criticism of this antagonistic understanding see Kymlicka, 'Human Rights Without Human Supremacism' (n 2); Joe Wills, 'Animal Rights, Legal Personhood and Cognitive Capacity: Addressing "Levelling-down" Concerns' (2020) 11 Journal of Human Rights and the Environment 199, 218–22; Saskia Stucki, *One Rights: Human and Animal Rights in the Anthropocene* (Springer 2023) 68–75.

[61] I adapt this phrase from Doyle, *Aristocracy and Its Enemies in the Age of Revolution* (n 19) 20.

[62] See Christopher McCrudden, 'In Pursuit of Human Dignity: An Introduction to Current Debates' in Christopher McCrudden (ed), *Understanding Human Dignity* (Oxford University Press 2014) 18–19.

[63] As a reminder, my use of the terms 'internalism' and 'externalism' is different from their meaning in other contexts, such as in epistemic justification. See eg George Pappas and Clayton Littlejohn, 'Internalist vs. Externalist Conceptions of Epistemic Justification' in Edward N Zalta and Uri Nodelman (eds), *The Stanford Encyclopedia of Philosophy* (Spring 2023, Metaphysics Research Lab, Stanford University 2023) <https://plato.stanford.edu/archives/spr2023/entries/justep-intext/> accessed 11 June 2023.

attempt 'to justify the universal validity of human rights by referring to a concept of human nature that is *normative from the beginning*'.[64] To use Francis Bacon's image from Chapter 2, we can say that *Internalists* are like spiders who are trying to weave cobwebs out of their own substance.

In this section, I will first address how exactly *Internalism* works. To do so, I will focus on two of its main strategies: decisionism on the one hand, and story-telling and interpretation on the other (Section 4.1). In Section 4.2, I will discuss the main advantage of the *Internalist* approach—namely its capacity to *found* human rights and human dignity—before arguing that this is not only a strength but also a weakness because it runs the risk of forming concepts that are arbitrary.

4.1 How-to

How exactly do *Internalists* explain and defend human rights, equality, and dignity? There are, as I have suggested, roughly two ways in which this can be done: by *deciding* that human beings ought to be the only ones with a high status and with equal human rights; and by *telling stories or constructing interpretations* according to which only human beings possess this status and these rights.

Let us start with *decisionism*, which is the more straightforward approach. One particularly lucid defence of decisionism can be found in Anne Phillips's work on 'the politics of the human'[65]—although Phillips herself has recently expressed dislike of the term 'decisionism'.[66] According to her, human rights, equality, and dignity should not be understood as 'the outcome of an argument, . . . something to be established by reference to certain facts about human beings'.[67] Rather, humans hold rights, equality, and dignity as the result of a decision or claim we make: 'People assert, rather than prove, their claims to be regarded as human.'[68] In her view, this claim is not one that merely describes already existing realities. Rather, it is constitutive of such realities in that it wills into existence a certain normative state of affairs. It is 'something we make happen':[69]

[64] Marion Albers, Thomas Hoffmann, and Jörn Reinhardt, 'Human Rights and Human Nature: Introduction' in Marion Albers, Thomas Hoffmann, and Jörn Reinhardt (eds), *Human Rights and Human Nature* (Springer 2014) 2 (emphasis added).
[65] Phillips, *The Politics of the Human* (n 16).
[66] Anne Phillips, *Unconditional Equals* (Princeton University Press 2021) 51, 60. See also n 83.
[67] Phillips, *The Politics of the Human* (n 16) 8.
[68] ibid 9.
[69] Phillips, *Unconditional Equals* (n 66) 41 (emphasis removed).

> Equality is not something we need to justify by reference to a shared humanity… it is something we bring into existence at the moment we claim it. It is not that we 'recognise' a pre-existing equality or pre-existing humanity: identify something that was always there but had escaped our attention while we were still at the mercy of false ideas about some being born to rule and others having a slavish nature. We are not equal *because* of certain facts about ourselves, *because* we have a soul, *because* we are rational agents, *because* we are vulnerable to pain. Though we may, and often do, articulate our claims in one or other of these languages, equality is something we assert and to which we commit ourselves rather than something we find out. There is no argumentative structure here, of the form, 'I am X therefore Y'.[70]

Why does Phillips refuse to draw on facts about human nature to justify human dignity, rights, and equality? She gives two main reasons.[71] First, she argues that doing so is necessary to underscore the fact that equality is a commitment that societies and individuals make.[72] Second, and more importantly for our purposes, she stresses that grounding equality in empirical facts risks justifying hierarchies between human beings on the basis of differences that (are claimed to) exist between them. 'When we invoke the language of the human', she points out, 'we are refusing the distinctions and hierarchies that otherwise divide us. We are asserting our equality, insisting that we are human too.'[73] On her account, then, equality is not dependent on the possession of any properties; it is 'unconditional'.[74] To put this thought another way, we should consider ourselves equals normatively, irrespective of whether we are equals descriptively.[75]

This is also the reason why she calls her account one about the 'politics' of the human: that humans have dignity and equal rights is not something 'cognitive',[76] a truth that can be determined empirically. Rather, it is a political decision or claim.[77] According to her, this also explains why, as we have seen above, claims about human dignity and equal rights are particularly prevalent after experiences of humans being denied their equal status and rights.[78]

[70] Phillips, *The Politics of the Human* (n 16) 69 (emphasis in original).
[71] This is brought out most clearly in her more recent book Phillips, *Unconditional Equals* (n 66) 15–16.
[72] ibid 16.
[73] Phillips, *The Politics of the Human* (n 16) 4.
[74] Phillips, *Unconditional Equals* (n 66) 41.
[75] I am grateful to Saskia Stucki for this point.
[76] Phillips, *The Politics of the Human* (n 16) 9.
[77] ibid 26.
[78] ibid 37.

As Diego Rossello has observed, the decision to confer human rights on humans is often made in an effort to distinguish the human from the animal.[79] Phillips herself expresses some unease with this consequence, and has signalled openness to the view that their shared sentience may explain why harming and killing both humans and animals is wrong. Nevertheless, she has insisted that equality requires a clear distinction between humans and animals.[80] As she argues in her most recent book, explaining human equality requires a 'line drawn around the human that marks us out from other beings'.[81] That is, it requires 'choosing a side' between human and animal.[82] This exclusionary approach is also manifested in her discussion of Hannah Arendt's theory, on which her own account builds: 'she represents us as only really human to the extent that we are *not* natural beings. If the only thing we ever did, for example, was labour, . . . we would not be distinguishing ourselves from animals in any significant way.'[83]

As should be obvious by now, decisionism is an *Internalist* approach because it starts not with a reference to facts about what human nature *is*, but with a decision as to how things *should be*. Thus, if we ask why humans have the high rank of dignity and equal rights, the decisionist's answer is: because we have decided they should have these entitlements. And that will be the end of the matter. This answer has struck some as unsatisfactory. For why should one accept this decision? Why not take another decision? And how can we find out which decision is better? It may not be enough simply to stipulate that humans and only humans have dignity and equal rights. We may also need to explain and defend this decision.[84]

Dissatisfied with the *fiat*-based nature of decisionism, which makes rights, dignity, and equality contingent on decisions,[85] some have proposed an

[79] Diego H Rossello, '"To Be Human, Nonetheless, Remains a Decision": Humanism as Decisionism in Contemporary Critical Political Theory' (2016) 16 Contemporary Political Theory 439, 453–54.

[80] Phillips, *Unconditional Equals* (n 66) 59, 61.

[81] ibid 61.

[82] ibid 53.

[83] Phillips, *The Politics of the Human* (n 16) 61 (emphasis in original). As Kymlicka has astutely noted, there is a certain irony in this revival of decisionism among human rights theorists because 'the original decisionist defender of human supremacism is Carl Schmitt, the Nazi theoretician. Defenders of the UN Declaration such as Maritain understood themselves to be making a decisive break with decisionism.' Kymlicka, 'Human Rights Without Human Supremacism' (n 2) 780.

[84] See also Jeremy Waldron, *God, Locke, and Equality: Christian Foundations of John Locke's Political Thought* (Cambridge University Press 2002) 76.

[85] See on this also Arnd Pollmann, 'Menschenwürde nach der Barbarei: Zu den Folgen eines gewaltsamen Umbruchs in der Geschichte der Menschenrechte' (2010) 1 Zeitschrift für Menschenrechte 26, 44 (endnote 33). Note that this is an aspect of decisionism that Philipps herself takes issue with: Phillips, *Unconditional Equals* (n 66) 51. Phillips is not opposed to the idea of explaining principles such as the equality principle by using narratives, as long as they are not invoked as justifications: Phillips, *The Politics of the Human* (n 16) 78.

Internalist approach that emphasizes the need to *tell stories or construct interpretations* that explain the special status of humanity.[86] A prominent proponent of the stories-based approach is Richard Rorty. In his famous essay *Human Rights, Rationality, and Sentimentality*, Rorty agrees with decisionists when he rejects the idea that human rights are best defended by grounding them in specifically human attributes that distinguish them from other animals:[87] 'nothing relevant to moral choice separates human beings from animals except historically contingent facts of the world, cultural facts'.[88] According to Rorty, grounding human rights in nature seems to do nothing for them in practice, which is why he proposes a 'pragmatist'[89] approach instead. On this approach, which contrasts with decisionism, we should 'concentrate our energies' not on finding metaphysical grounds for human rights, but 'on manipulating sentiments, on sentimental education'.[90] According to him, the most efficient defence for human rights is the telling of 'sad and sentimental stories'.[91] Such stories are uniquely suited to help us see that human beings whose rights are being violated, though different from us in some respects, are just 'like us'[92] in the respects that matter. Hence, on his account, what explains humans' special rank and rights is not their natural capacities, nor simple decisions, but the stories we tell as part of our culture.[93]

Rorty's call for sentimental stories is not the only *Internalist* approach that rejects decisionism. Another such approach is defended by Ronald Dworkin, according to whom the question as to which concept (or principle) we adopt is the result of a refined process of *interpretation*.[94] If we want to explain a moral principle such as human dignity, he argues, we cannot simply postulate it, as decisionists would. Nor can we simply resort to external, empirical facts, as *Externalists* would. This is because, according to Dworkin, the realm of morality has an independent existence on which non-normative facts have no

[86] See Rossello, 'All in the (Human) Family? Species Aristocratism in the Return of Human Dignity' (n 51) 4–6. On the 'looping effects' that are at play in both types of *Internalism*: Ian Hacking, 'The Looping Effects of Human Kinds' in Dan Sperber, David Premack, and Ann James Premack (eds), *Causal Cognition: A Multi-Disciplinary Debate* (Oxford University Press 1995) 366–70.

[87] Richard Rorty, *Human Rights, Rationality, and Sentimentality*, vol 3 (Cambridge University Press 1998) 169–72.

[88] ibid 170.

[89] ibid 172.

[90] ibid 176.

[91] ibid 172. See on the role of emotions in human rights also Lynn Hunt, *Inventing Human Rights: A History* (Norton 2007).

[92] Rorty, *Human Rights, Rationality, and Sentimentality* (n 87) 181.

[93] Though decisions may provide the basis for the stories we tell.

[94] Ronald Dworkin, *Justice for Hedgehogs* (Belknap Press of Harvard University Press 2011) 67, 102. See on interpretivism also Bernd Ladwig, 'Human Rights and Human Animals' in Marion Albers, Thomas Hoffmann, and Jörn Reinhardt (eds), *Human Rights and Human Nature* (Springer 2014) 29.

bearing.[95] For this reason, both the justification of a moral principle as well as challenges to it cannot proceed except by invoking other principles and assumptions that are already within the normative domain. Interpretation takes existing principles—some of which we have come to endorse deliberately, others unreflectively—and weaves them together in order to 'achieve an overall integrity so that each [interpretation] supports the others in a network of value that we embrace authentically'.[96] Dworkin's approach also illustrates the collective character of *Internalist* interpretations: they are not developed by an individual theorist, but discovered by her implicit within our thinking and our practices. The best interpretation of a principle, according to Dworkin, is one that fits best with shared social practices and other principles, rendering them more appealing than alternative interpretations.[97] In the best interpretation, the whole body of moral principles of a society stands together in a self-supporting manner. Hence, following his approach, when interpreting for example the concept of human dignity, one would draw on other principles internal to one's society, such as perhaps the assumption that humanity's creation in the image of God gives humans a special status, or the assumption that only humans have free will. One could however not explain dignity by referring to any external properties, such as the fact that most humans have highly developed mental capacities.

Phillips, Rorty, and Dworkin are not the only ones who have endorsed some version of *Internalism*. As Rossello has pointed out, 'the predominant theoretical approaches to human rights, despite their obvious and multiple differences, share an investment in stabilising the human being as a ground of the political'.[98] According to Michael Rosen, for example, '[s]tatuses are . . . agreed social conventions'. For Rosen, concepts such as human rights or dignity do not, in themselves, bear any content, in the same way as 'there is no fact beyond social acceptance that underlies the chess piece with a horse's head entitled to move in an "L"-shape'.[99] Kateb argues in a similar vein that 'the uniqueness of humanity and its superiority over the rest of creation . . . was for the most part just *assumed*'.[100] This 'assumedness' of human dignity and rights is also emphasized by Paolo Carozza, who reminds us that the drafters of the UDHR could not agree on a specific justification for human rights, and simply settled for

[95] Dworkin, *Justice for Hedgehogs* (n 94) 11.
[96] ibid 101.
[97] See ibid 6–7 and chapter 2.
[98] Rossello, '"To Be Human, Nonetheless, Remains a Decision": Humanism as Decisionism in Contemporary Critical Political Theory' (n 79) 440.
[99] Rosen, *Dignity: Its History and Meaning* (n 9) 145.
[100] Kateb, *Human Dignity* (n 52) 120 (emphasis added).

pragmatic consensus. 'The human rights enterprise', he infers, 'is built on practical agreement, *tout court*.'[101]

4.2 *Founding*

Let us now consider what speaks in favour of, and against, the *Internalist* approach. To do so, we can use the two opposing notions of '*founding*' and '*grounding*' to help us understand the contrasting ways in which *Internalism* and *Externalism* give an account of rights, equality, dignity, and similar concepts. *Internalism*'s central strength is that it makes it possible to explain that humans hold a high status and equal rights without having to *ground* these concepts in empirical facts about human nature. That is, the main advantage of *Internalism* is that it enables us to *found* human dignity and human rights. By '*founding*' I mean that *Internalism* engages in an act of establishing or creating something new without drawing on external resources. Like the abovementioned spiders, *Internalists* create their own foundations by drawing on existing (internal) normative assumptions and concepts.[102] '*Founding*' stands in contrast with '*grounding*', which is characteristic of the Meritocracy's externalist approach (which I discuss in Chapter 4). To *ground* a concept is to justify it with facts about nature; to *found* it is to refuse to draw on such facts.[103]

Why is *founding* attractive? Because of the problems that arise if we try to *ground* a concept in an empirical account of human nature. Say we *ground* human rights, as *Externalists* would, directly in individual humans' ability to think abstractly, or their linguistic abilities, or their ability to plan for the future, and the respective interests which arise from these abilities. The human beings who possess these abilities and interests will receive human rights. But those who do not possess them, or who possess them to a lesser extent, do not qualify for rights or would only get some weaker form of rights. As we will see in Chapter 4, this is one of the reasons why many critical disability scholars reject *Externalist* theories of rights. To make things even thornier, there can be nonhuman animals who possess these abilities, perhaps to a greater extent

[101] Paolo G Carozza, 'Human Rights, Human Dignity, and Human Experience' in Christopher McCrudden (ed), *Understanding Human Dignity* (Oxford University Press 2014) 621 (emphasis in original).

[102] See Raffael N Fasel, 'The Old "New" Dignitarianism' (2019) 25 Res Publica 4, 15.

[103] Perhaps counterintuitively, my use of the term '*founding*' therefore corresponds to what is generally called 'antifoundationalism'. See, for a useful definition of foundationalism and antifoundationalism, Amy Gutmann, 'Democracy, Philosophy, and Justification' in Seyla Benhabib (ed), *Democracy and Difference: Contesting the Boundaries of the Political* (Princeton University Press 1996) 340.

than some humans do. Would we have to grant these animals human rights in virtue of their abilities? Phillips puts the issue succinctly:

> If we link the entitlement to human rights to characteristics like vulnerability to pain or capacity for conscious planning, the empirical evidence may well lead to the conclusion that some of the great apes qualify for at least some of the so-called human rights. But it may also lead . . . to the conclusion that some humans who currently qualify—day-old infants who have not yet developed consciousness; those in a coma who have lost it—are not entitled.[104]

Thus, the danger of *grounding* rights, equality, and dignity in facts about human nature is that it opens them up to empirical challenge. If it can be shown that there are significant differences in the capacities of different human beings then we would have to treat these human beings differently in equally significant ways. In Phillips's words, we would have to 'attach hierarchical significance to difference'.[105] However, this could create different categories of human beings, some with more or stronger rights and a higher status than others. And this, in turn, would undermine the idea of equal status and equal rights. In fact, as Phillips argues, even if no significant empirical differences could be found, the mere act of opening up rights, equality, and dignity to empirical justification or proof risks eroding these concepts because it accepts the possibility of hierarchy. 'Proving equality', as she puts it, 'is a game it is almost impossible to win'.[106] This problem is exacerbated by the fact that, frequently, pseudo-science is invoked to claim that certain groups of human beings are inferior to other groups. Historically, such arguments have been all too common and have served to exclude women, people of colour, and other disadvantaged groups from rights under the pretence that they lacked the capacities deemed necessary.[107]

The appeal of *Internalism* lies in its refusal to play this game. It takes human rights, equality, and dignity to be based on decisions, stories, or interpretations that are normative through and through. Because *Internalism* does not view these concepts as empirical claims,[108] new empirical discoveries cannot serve to overturn them.[109] To use Arnd Pollmann's term, *Internalism*

[104] Phillips, *The Politics of the Human* (n 16) 40.
[105] ibid 46.
[106] ibid 45.
[107] See eg Hunt, *Inventing Human Rights: A History* (n 91) 186–88.
[108] See also Markus Rothhaar, 'Species, Potentiality and Their Manipulation' in Marion Albers, Thomas Hoffmann, and Jörn Reinhardt (eds), *Human Rights and Human Nature* (Springer 2014) 177.
[109] Phillips, *The Politics of the Human* (n 16) 44.

'impregnates'[110] rights, equality, and dignity against all external criticism. That is, it immunizes them against such criticism. This is particularly important for those human beings who lack some of the capacities that would otherwise be considered relevant for the possession of rights: humans who would not be considered equals, for instance because they factually differ from 'normal' rational human agents in important respects. Humans with severe mental disabilities, for example, may lack some of the capacities that, under a Meritocratic approach, would be considered necessary for the holding of certain rights, say the right to vote, or the right to marriage. Failing to possess the same rights as humans without mental disabilities, these beings might then not be considered equals, and could be deemed undeserving of the status of dignity.

This is what Salaville had in mind with his provocative question to the naturalists who emphasized difference over equality: 'Is there not also a greater and lesser among human beings? Are not some superior to others in intelligence, corporeal strength, natural faculties, and acquired faculties?'[111] Like modern Aristocrats, Salaville understood that there are important differences between human beings. His point was that these differences should not matter when it comes to granting equal status and equal rights. To avoid forming groups of human beings with lesser rights and lesser status, Aristocrats hold that it is imperative that we refuse to *ground* humans' rights and status in an account of their nature. Only if we *found* rights, equality, and dignity—or, as Salaville put it, only if we 'admit'[112] that there is a fundamental chasm between humans and animals—is the fact that not all human beings possess the same capacities irrelevant for their status and rights.[113]

This explains why the Aristocracy is a particularly appealing conception after crises that have witnessed the denial of the rights of marginalized humans.[114] As Kateb notes, '[it] is often true that what came first, in time and importance, were the denial of equal human dignity, of equal individual status, and the consequent reduction of human beings into the not-fully-human'.[115] In cases such as the post-World War II period, the emphasis on the special dignity

[110] See Arnd Pollmann, 'Human Rights Beyond Naturalism' in Marion Albers, Thomas Hoffmann, and Jörn Reinhardt (eds), *Human Rights and Human Nature* (Springer 2014) 123.

[111] Salaville, *De l'homme et des animaux* (n 32) 16. See Chapter 3, Section 6.

[112] Salaville, *De l'homme et des animaux* (n 32) 51. To be sure, Salaville also argued that only human beings are intelligent and that rights and dignity are based on intelligence rather than sentience (ibid 35). However, in my view, this is best interpreted not as an *Externalist grounding* of rights in intelligence. Rather, it is a founding myth: an *Internalist* story that invokes the alleged uniqueness of humans to explain their dignity and equal rights. See on this also Chapter 4, Section 2.

[113] See Kateb, *Human Dignity* (n 52) 9.

[114] See Section 2.

[115] Kateb, *Human Dignity* (n 52) 39.

and rights of all human beings is what Catherine Dupré has called a 'never again'[116] reaction: a repudiation of the systematic debasement and destruction of supposedly lesser humans, and a clarion call for unification.

Uniquely suited to respond to such crises, *Internalism* has served as a popular tool for the thwarting of empirical challenges to humans' dignity and their equal rights, as it has for the thwarting of animal rights claims—which are often seen as posing a similar threat.[117] And the *Internalist* approach has lost none of its relevance today. As Thomas Williams has observed, 'the experimental and human sciences, often weighed down by materialist philosophical presuppositions and the constraints of their objectivist methodology, tend ever more to emphasise the continuity between man and other creatures'.[118] This calls for a firm *Internalist founding* of human dignity. As Roger Brownsword has put it pithily, 'we appeal to human dignity in order to stop science'.[119]

To recapitulate, then, the *Internalist* approach is attractive because it allows the *founding* of concepts such as equal status and rights independently of facts about human nature. It therefore avoids the problem of having to assign normative importance to empirical differences that could lead to hierarchization between humans.

However, the *Internalist* approach also has a *downside*. Paradoxically, this downside is the flipside of its strength: by *founding* concepts without regard to empirical facts, *Internalism* risks creating concepts that bear no reasonable connection to reality and that can therefore have an all the more consequential impact on it. '[D]istinctions that are not about something real', as Justin Smith has cautioned, 'are not for that reason not real distinctions'.[120] To illustrate this problem, consider the example Waldron gives of a principle—*founded* in an *Internalist* fashion—which states that we ought to 'treat trees, tigers, teapots, and teenagers as one another's equals'.[121] As he points out, it would be 'slightly mad'[122] to treat things as equals which bear so little similarity as teapots and teenagers. Because teapots and teenagers are so different from each other, it would make little sense to adopt this principle.

[116] Catherine Dupré, 'Constructing the Meaning of Human Dignity: Four Questions' in Christopher McCrudden (ed), *Understanding Human Dignity* (Oxford University Press 2014) 117–18.
[117] See also Kymlicka, 'Human Rights Without Human Supremacism' (n 2) 779–80.
[118] Thomas D Williams, *Who Is My Neighbor? Thomistic Personalism and the Foundations of Human Rights* (Catholic University of America Press 2005) 207.
[119] Roger Brownsword, 'Human Dignity, Human Rights, and Simply Trying to Do the Right Thing' in Christopher McCrudden (ed), *Understanding Human Dignity* (Oxford University Press 2014) 347.
[120] Justin EH Smith, *Nature, Human Nature, & Human Difference: Race in Early Modern Philosophy* (Princeton University Press 2015) 52.
[121] Jeremy Waldron, *One Another's Equals: The Basis of Human Equality* (Belknap Press of Harvard University Press 2017) 59.
[122] ibid.

To put this thought in more general terms: once and to the extent that a *founded* principle loses a meaningful connection to reality, it becomes *arbitrary*. And once it becomes arbitrary, it becomes unreasonable to choose this principle over another principle which is more in line with facts about reality.[123] Of course, arbitrariness cannot directly affect the internal normative validity of a principle. The principle remains immunized against empirical evidence. However, arbitrariness can at least *indirectly* serve to challenge a principle by raising the question as to whether one should not adopt another principle which is more in line with empirical facts.

As I will discuss in Chapters 4 and 6, the concrete question that arises for the Aristocracy is whether the complete exclusion of all nonhuman animals from the fundamental rights of humans makes sense from a factual point of view or whether this exclusion should be considered arbitrary and abandoned in favour of a principle that is less arbitrary. Jean-Claude Delamétherie's argument that we should not exclude animals from rights-holdership, which I discussed in Chapter 2, was based on exactly the view that it would be arbitrary to exclude them. He must have been alive to the problematic consequences that arbitrary distinctions can have. The contemporary Meritocrat Jeff McMahan draws attention to this ugly side of our Aristocratic bias towards all human beings:

> [T]he other side of species partiality is a tendency to treat the interests of animals as morally insignificant. If we compare the number of radically cognitively impaired human beings who benefit from our partiality with the number of animals who suffer from our tendency to regard them primarily as means to our ends, it is hard to believe that the effects of species partiality are desirable overall from an impartial point of view.[124]

Bilchitz draws a parallel between the arbitrary exclusion of animals and other arbitrary distinctions, such as that between people of colour and white people in apartheid South Africa. According to Bilchitz, arbitrariness is not only problematic in itself (though it is also that), but also because it 'leads to the disregarding of the interests of individuals, often those who are most vulnerable'.[125] To him, it is paramount that we recognize and overcome 'the arbitrariness and unjustifiability of the current legal framework relating to animals'.[126]

[123] Some *Internalists* are not put off by this fact: see eg Pollmann, 'Human Rights Beyond Naturalism' (n 110) 123.
[124] Jeff McMahan, 'Our Fellow Creatures' (2005) 9 The Journal of Ethics 353, 361.
[125] Bilchitz, 'Moving Beyond Arbitrariness: The Legal Personhood and Dignity of Non-Human Animals' (n 23) 66.
[126] ibid 71.

As Bernard Williams, himself an Aristocrat,[127] acknowledges, followers of this approach ought to be 'sceptical about the coercive rhetoric, the lies about differences, and the sheer violence that are often associated with such ideas [of species loyalty] and with the movements that express them'.[128]

5 Conclusion

This chapter has presented the Aristocratic conception of fundamental rights. My analysis is part of a broader movement in scholarship to understand concepts such as human rights, basic equality, and human dignity as Aristocratic concepts. To elucidate the Aristocratic conception, I identified two of its key characteristics, *Equal Consideration* and *Internalism.*

Equal Consideration addressed our question of what the Aristocratic status of human beings exactly is. I have shown that it is three things: a high status that humans possess simply in virtue of being born human (*Heredity*); a status which they hold equally, and which gives them equal rights (*Equality*); and a status from which all nonhumans are excluded (*Exclusivity*). *Equal Consideration* was thus shown to be based on central egalitarian ideas, which I introduced in Chapter 2. For both past and modern adherents of *Equal Consideration*, I argued, humans are separate *and* equal.

Internalism answered our question as to how the special rank and rights of humans can be explained. I argued that the ideal-typical approach is to explain them from an *Internalist* perspective, that is, by invoking decisions, by telling stories, or by constructing interpretations that are already within the normative domain. *Internalism*'s capacity to *found* rights, equality, and dignity in this way was shown to be its strength. By refusing to *ground* these concepts in facts about human nature, *Internalism* avoids making them vulnerable to empirical challenge. As Phillips has put it, '[w]hen the human is invoked today, it is most commonly in order to deny the significance of difference'.[129] However, as I demonstrated, *Internalism*'s refusal to accord normative significance to physical differences is at the same time also its weakness. By *founding* a status and rights in a way that is resistant to facts, one runs the risk of giving them an interpretation that it would make little sense to adopt. I will take up this point again in Chapter 6, when I will argue that the problem with the current human

[127] cf Bernard Williams, *Philosophy as a Humanistic Discipline* (Princeton University Press 2009) 138.
[128] ibid 151.
[129] Phillips, *The Politics of the Human* (n 16) 10.

rights Aristocracy is that it arbitrarily excludes all nonhuman beings from the possession of fundamental rights and legal personhood, despite the fact that some of these beings have similar capacities to human beings.

In the next chapter, I will turn the spotlight on the nonhumans who have been excluded from humans' high rank and equal rights. I will do so by unveiling another conception of fundamental rights—the Meritocratic conception—which is considerably more receptive to their interests.

4
The Meritocratic Conception

1 Introduction

The predominant fundamental rights conception today is the Aristocratic conception.[1] Among human rights lawyers in particular, the idea that human beings have a high and equal status as well as equal rights is a fixture. Because of the dominance of the Aristocratic conception, there is a tendency to forget that it is not the only fundamental rights conception. In this chapter, I will show that there is another conception that is crucial to our understanding of contemporary and past arguments about rights: the Meritocratic fundamental rights conception. I am not the first to discover this conception. Gregory Vlastos has laid some important groundwork with his theory of the 'M-system',[2] about which I will say more in the next section. However, no one has spelled out what the different features of this conception are.

As with the Aristocracy, I take the Meritocracy to be an ideal-type that I will be constructing by drawing on existing fundamental rights accounts and by taking their inherent implications to (what I believe to be) their conceptual conclusion. As I have indicated, the Meritocratic and Aristocratic conceptions are on opposite ends of a spectrum of fundamental rights (see Figure 1.1 in the Introduction). This chapter analyses the exact respects in which the Meritocracy is antithetical to the Aristocracy. It will do so by focusing on two central features which mirror the Aristocracy's two features that I have analysed in the previous chapter. First, the Meritocratic conception is based on *Differential Consideration* rather than *Equal Consideration*, which is characteristic of the Aristocracy and which should not be conflated with Peter Singer's notion of 'equal consideration of interests', as I explain in Section 3. Second, in contrast to Aristocrats who follow *Internalism* to explain their views, Meritocrats are *Externalists*.

[1] I will substantiate this claim in Chapter 6.

[2] Gregory Vlastos, 'Justice and Equality' in Jeremy Waldron (ed), *Theories of Rights* (Oxford University Press 1984) 41.

More Equal Than Others. Raffael N Fasel, Oxford University Press. © Raffael N Fasel 2024.
DOI: 10.1093/oso/9780198907435.003.0004

Whereas the Aristocratic conception has proven popular among human rights thinkers, the Meritocratic conception resonates particularly with proponents of animal rights. That is not to say that human rights advocates cannot endorse Meritocratic views or that animal rights proponents do not also argue for human rights. Yet, as I will show in this chapter and take up again in the next, the Meritocratic conception is particularly well-suited for arguing for the rights of nonhuman beings. This should not surprise us given that the Meritocratic conception is based on the naturalist current of the Enlightenment which challenged egalitarianism by emphasizing the normative importance of gradual differences in nature. In the same way as Jean-Baptiste Salaville's egalitarian essay proved illustrative for the Aristocracy, Jean-Claude Delamétherie's naturalist writings will be used to exemplify core Meritocratic ideas. As I will show, Delamétherie's account anticipated both *Differential Consideration* and *Externalism*.

The chapter is structured as follows. In Section 2, I will outline Vlastos's theory of the 'M-system', which anticipated important elements of the Meritocracy. Section 3 analyses the element of *Differential Consideration*, which will serve to answer the question what it means to hold fundamental rights based on merit. Section 4, finally, considers how proponents of the Meritocracy explain *Differential Consideration* and how animals should have certain rights. It argues that Meritocrats adopt an *Externalist* approach that *grounds* rights in natural facts. I will discuss the strengths and weaknesses of this approach before retracing the main steps of the chapter in its conclusion.

A terminological note is in order before we begin. When Meritocrats say that animals 'merit' (a term I use synonymously with desert[3]) fundamental rights or legal personhood,[4] they do not mean that animals deserve these rights because of any acts they perform. Rather, they take desert to be based on animals' characteristics, in particular their interests. I will use the term 'merit' in this sense, and will say more in Section 4 about how characteristics-based merit of rights works.[5]

[3] For a non-synonymous use see George Sher, *Desert* (Princeton University Press 1987) 109.

[4] See eg Paola Cavalieri, *The Animal Question: Why Nonhuman Animals Deserve Human Rights* (Catherine Woollard tr, Oxford University Press 2004). For critical voices see Anne Peters, 'Liberté, Égalité, Animalité: Human–Animal Comparisons in Law' (2016) 5 Transnational Environmental Law 25, 46–47; Christine M Korsgaard, *Fellow Creatures: Our Obligations to the Other Animals* (Oxford University Press 2018) 109–11.

[5] See on this type of desert Sher, *Desert* (n 3) 8; Fred Feldman, *Utilitarianism, Hedonism, and Desert: Essays in Moral Philosophy* (Cambridge University Press 1997) 183. On a challenge to characteristics-based desert, see John Rawls, *A Theory of Justice* (Harvard University Press 1971) 74, 104.

2 The 'M-system'

The first to describe the contrast between what I call the Aristocratic conception and the Meritocratic conception was Vlastos. Vlastos, to be sure, was critical of what I call the Meritocracy and did not emphasize, as I do in Section 4.2, its strong suits. However, we can nonetheless use his analysis as our starting point because it captures some of the key ideas underpinning the Meritocracy. In his much-praised article 'Justice and Equality', Vlastos introduced the term 'M-system'[6] to express an idea that is similar to what I call the Meritocracy. He argued that in contrast to the Aristocratic 'caste society', which we encountered in the previous chapter, the M-system 'has no place for a rank of dignity which descends on an individual by the purely existential circumstance (the "accident") of birth and remains his unalterably for life'.[7] Instead, the M-system grades individuals based on their merit: 'If *A* is valued for some meritorious quality, *m*, his individuality does not enter into the valuation. As an individual he is then dispensable; his place could be taken without loss of value by any other individual with as good an *m*-rating.'[8] As a result, Vlastos believed, the M-system reduces individuals to mere 'place-holder[s] of qualities'.[9] They possess no inherent value, no equality, and no 'rank of dignity'[10] that, in the Aristocracy, they would possess simply in virtue of belonging to the human species. The sole factor that determines how one ought to treat beings in the M-system is their individual merit.

If the M-system resembles utilitarianism, that is no coincidence. As we will see in Section 3, some utilitarian theories come close to being pure instantiations of the Meritocracy. However, that is not to say that only utilitarian or other forms of consequentialist theories can form part of the Meritocracy. Rights-based approaches can in principle also come under the Meritocracy if they are sufficiently based on *Differential Consideration* and *Externalism*. Some recent sentientist rights approaches incorporate an egalitarian element that make them less obviously 'Meritocratic'. I will consider these theories separately in the next chapter.

What is important for our current purposes is that, in the account Vlastos outlines, rights depend on merit in two ways.[11] First, they are what we can call

6 Vlastos, 'Justice and Equality' (n 2) 54.
7 ibid.
8 ibid 52 (emphasis in original).
9 ibid.
10 ibid 54.
11 ibid 55. In contrast to how I use the term 'merit' in this book, Vlastos assumes that a characteristic can serve as basis for desert only if it is '"acquired", that is, if it represents what its possessor has himself made of his natural endowments and environmental opportunities': ibid 51. However, the contrast he

justified by merit in that someone who lacks merit will not receive a particular right. Second, they are *proportioned to merit* in that someone with less merit will receive rights of lesser strength. As Vlastos rightly highlights, these implications are antithetical to the Aristocratic understanding of rights because they permit applying terms to rights-holders such as 'superior' and 'inferior' which we believed to have eradicated.[12]

A sceptic of Vlastos's theory of the M-system and my account of the Meritocracy might want to object at this stage that by distinguishing between these conceptions and the Aristocratic 'caste society', we are drawing a distinction without a difference. For could one not argue that the Aristocratic conception also accords membership in the community of equals on the basis of merit? After all, it could be said that what makes a being deserve equal status and equal rights is the fact that it is born into the human species, or that it possesses intelligence or other features believed to be uniquely human.

It is true that the Aristocracy is not necessarily incompatible with some notions of merit. In Ancient Greece, for example, 'aristocracy' and 'meritocracy' were not thought to be conflicting concepts. Aristocracy was defined as the rule by the best, and the best were chosen—in a more or less meritocratic way—based on virtue and wealth.[13] Even in the eighteenth century, aristocrats saw no conflict with merit. Their status was one they believed they deserved because they were born as aristocrats, or because they behaved as was expected of aristocrats.[14] The Aristocratic conception of fundamental rights, too, need not reject the notion that human beings are said to 'deserve' equal status and equal rights in virtue of their birth or certain features believed to be uniquely human. This would seem to support the view that the Aristocracy and the Meritocracy are not at odds. However, things are more complex than they appear.

In contrast to Meritocrats' invocation of features such as an individual's capacity to feel pain, Aristocratic pointers to birth as a human or the possession of intelligence are not meant to serve as grounds for rights that can be tested—and challenged—empirically. Rather, they are stories—founding myths if you like—that humans tell to explain why humans should have fundamental rights, equality, and dignity. They are irrevocable criteria that, though not necessarily

draws between the 'M-system' and the caste system is one that, *mutatis mutandis*, also applies to the Meritocratic and the Aristocratic fundamental rights conceptions.

[12] cf Vlastos, 'Justice and Equality' (n 2) 74.
[13] See William Doyle, *Aristocracy and Its Enemies in the Age of Revolution* (Oxford University Press 2009) 40. See also Aristotle, *Politics* (Harris Rackham tr, Harvard University Press 2014) IV.4, 1294a2–4.
[14] Doyle, *Aristocracy and Its Enemies in the Age of Revolution* (n 13) 56–57.

pure fictions, are not grounded in empirical facts in the way that Meritocratic rights are. Hence, if Aristocrats talk of humans 'deserving' rights because they are, say, intelligent, they do not mean to say that these rights could be taken away from unintelligent humans. Rather, intelligence—or membership in the human species—is simply an *Internalist* story that we draw on to explain why humans should have these entitlements. As pointed out in Chapter 3, this is the strong suit of the Aristocratic conception: by *founding* dignity and equal rights, individuals' status and their rights cannot be revoked by pointing to empirical facts about these beings.

The Meritocratic conception of fundamental rights, by contrast, rejects basing rights on group-membership, and instead focuses entirely on individuals' characteristics. It tests, in each and every case, whether the individual at hand actually has the characteristics required for the possession of the relevant rights. Only if these characteristics are present in the individual do Meritocrats say that that individual 'deserves' the rights. That is why, contrary to Aristocrats, Meritocrats allow for a revocation of an individual's rights if it cannot be shown to possess the required characteristics. Bernard Williams realized that this testing of each and every individual on their merit follows necessarily once one rejects the Aristocratic conception (which he called the 'human prejudice'): 'the criteria which determine what you can properly do to a creature, are applied to examples one at a time: it is always a question whether this particular individual satisfies the criteria'.[15] Hence, even if the Aristocrats can be said to use 'desert' in some sense, they do not use it in the more specific sense that Meritocrats employ.

3 *Differential Consideration*

Let us now turn to the first characteristic feature of the Meritocratic conception: *Differential Consideration.* This feature addresses the question of *what* it means to hold fundamental rights in the Meritocratic conception. As I will show, *Differential Consideration* has three central components: it makes rights-holding dependent on an individual's characteristics and interests (*Merit*); it rejects equal rights in favour of a gradual approach to distributing rights (*Gradualism*); and it allows for the inclusion of any type of being in the category of rights-holders as long as that being possesses the relevant characteristics (*Inclusivity*). *Differential Consideration* has inherited its emphasis on natural

[15] Bernard Williams, *Philosophy as a Humanistic Discipline* (Princeton University Press 2009) 142.

differences from the naturalist stream which, as I have shown in Chapter 2, also rejected the idea of equality in favour of a more differentiated approach.

The first and most central component of *Differential Consideration* is *Merit*. According to *Merit*, rights-holding is dependent not on an individual's membership in a particular species or group, but rather on whether that individual possesses the characteristics and interests that are deemed relevant for fundamental rights. In other words, *Merit* makes rights-holding contingent on whether an individual being deserves these rights. The philosophical idea that underpins *Merit* is also known as moral individualism.[16] James Rachels, one of its main proponents, defines moral individualism as 'a thesis about the justification of judgements concerning how individuals may be treated'.[17] According to moral individualism,

> how an individual may be treated is to be determined, not by considering his group memberships, but by considering his own particular characteristics. If *A* is to be treated differently from *B*, the justification must be in terms of *A*'s individual characteristics and *B*'s individual characteristics. Treating them differently cannot be justified by pointing out that one or the other is a member of some preferred group, not even the 'group' of human beings.[18]

Moral individualism is not oblivious to the fact that members of a group generally share some characteristics.[19] For example, many human beings share the characteristic of being agents, that is, beings who can make reflective choices about their actions.[20] This makes it wrong to treat these humans as if they were unable to make such choices. However, according to moral individualism, what matters is not whether an individual belongs to a group whose members characteristically possess agency, but only whether that individual being itself possesses agency. The fact that an individual also belongs to a group whose members characteristically possess agency is 'morally epiphenomenal', as Jeff McMahan puts it.[21] As a result, Meritocrats like him reject the view, defended by the Aristocrats, that being born into the human species is a morally

[16] *Differential Consideration* is also similar to proportional equality in Aristotle's sense, see Stefan Gosepath, 'Equality' in Edward N Zalta (ed), *The Stanford Encyclopedia of Philosophy* (Spring 2011 edn) <https://plato.stanford.edu/archives/spr2011/entries/equality/> accessed 11 June 2023.

[17] James Rachels, *Created From Animals: The Moral Implications of Darwinism* (Oxford University Press 1999) 173.

[18] ibid 173–74.

[19] ie apart from the characteristic of being a member of the group.

[20] Lori Gruen, *Ethics and Animals: An Introduction* (2nd edn, Cambridge University Press 2021) 64.

[21] Jeff McMahan, 'Our Fellow Creatures' (2005) 9 The Journal of Ethics 353, 354 (footnote 2).

relevant criterion for the possession of fundamental rights. To Meritocrats, membership in the human species is no different from other extended social relationships, like belonging to a particular race or sex. None of these extended relationships, Meritocrats believe, have inherent moral value.[22]

Aristocrats object to this by arguing that there are some uniquely human values that make belonging to the human species morally relevant. For example, according to John Finnis, concern for life, truth, co-operation, procreation, play, and a conception of what is mine and what is yours are values that all and only humans have.[23] Meritocrats, however, can respond to such arguments by pointing out that the relevant values are not uniquely human. The values that Finnis highlights can to some extent also be observed in nonhuman animals, such as the great apes.[24] Those who, in the face of such similarities, maintain that human beings nonetheless deserve special treatment are guilty of 'speciesism' in the Meritocrats' eyes.[25] According to Singer, who popularized the term, speciesism is understood as 'a prejudice or attitude of bias toward the interests of one's own species and against those of members of another species'.[26] As pointed out in Chapter 2, speciesism is by no means a new idea. Long before Richard Ryder coined the term in 1970,[27] Delamétherie rejected speciesist thinking, arguing that '[a]s soon as in reality there is the same degree of sensitivity in two individuals, *their species is irrelevant*. For any animal that thinks and reasons, our interest should be the same.'[28] As will be recalled, Delamétherie even went as far as to argue that it does not matter whether sensitive beings are earthlings or not.[29]

Because Meritocrats place no importance on group memberships, such as membership in the human species, they are open to extending moral and legal concern to nonhumans. As Rachels argues, '[i]f we think it is wrong to treat a human in a certain way, because the human has certain characteristics, *and a particular non-human animal also has those characteristics*, then consistency requires that we also object to treating the non-human in that way'.[30] In other words, if someone deserves a certain treatment, then they deserve it no matter

[22] See ibid 361.
[23] John Finnis, *Natural Law and Natural Rights* (2nd edn, Oxford University Press 2011) 81–85.
[24] See eg Sarah F Brosnan, 'Property in Nonhuman Primates' (2011) 132 New Directions for Child and Adolescent Development 9, 13.
[25] See Richard D Ryder, 'Speciesism Again: The Original Leaflet' (2010) 2 Critical Society 1.
[26] Peter Singer, *Animal Liberation: A New Ethics for Our Treatment of Animals* (HarperCollins 1975) 6.
[27] Ryder, 'Speciesism Again: The Original Leaflet' (n 25) 1.
[28] Jean-Claude Delamétherie, *Principes de la philosophie naturelle, dans lesquels on cherche à déterminer les degrés de certitude ou de probabilité des connoissances humaines*, vol 1 (1787) 207 (emphasis added; my translation).
[29] ibid 196–97.
[30] Rachels, *Created From Animals: The Moral Implications of Darwinism* (n 17) 175 (emphasis in original).

who or what they are. It is in this sense that we have to understand Vlastos's claim that, in the M-system, individuals are simple 'place-holder[s] of qualities'.[31] What matters for *Differential Consideration* are one's qualities and not one's identity as, say, a human being or a Caucasian.

Consider the following example. In 2013, the Nonhuman Rights Project (NhRP) started filing writs of *habeas corpus* in US state courts to have chimpanzees recognized as legal persons with fundamental rights. In its court filings, the NhRP consistently argued that the individual animals on whose behalf it was suing have the capacities required for them to possess the common law rights to bodily integrity and liberty. In its petition on behalf of the chimpanzee Tommy, for example, the NhRP maintained that in addition to being able to suffer pain,[32] Tommy

> possess[es] the capacities for autonomy and self-determination[,] . . . self-consciousness, self-knowingness, self-agency, referential and intentional communication, empathy, a working memory, language, metacognition, numerosity, and material, social, and symbolic culture . . . the ability to understand cause-and-effect and the experiences of others, to imagine, imitate, engage in deferred imitation, emulate, to innovate and to use and make tools.[33]

In a later *habeas corpus* suit, which the NhRP filed on behalf of the elephants Beulah, Minnie, and Karen, it devoted more than half of its thirty-six-page petition to providing an account of these elephants' characteristics, which it backed up with several affidavits from pachyderm experts. 'Elephants are autonomous beings who can choose how to live their rich and fulfilling lives', the NhRP argues its Memorandum of Law, concluding that 'Beulah, Minnie, and Karen should be recognised as "persons" with the common law right to bodily liberty'.[34]

The *Merit*-based reasoning on which the NhRP's cases rely was subsequently defended in an *amici curiae* brief that seventeen philosophers submitted. The philosophers argue that '[i]f chimpanzees possess the same relevant capacities

[31] Vlastos, 'Justice and Equality' (n 2) 52.

[32] *Nonhuman Rights Project, Inc v Patrick C Lavery et al, Memorandum of Law in Support of Petition for Habeas Corpus* (2 December 2015) Supreme Court of the State of New York, County of New York, 1 <https://www.nonhumanrights.org/content/uploads/Tommy-Memo-of-Law-Dec-2-2015.pdf> accessed 11 June 2023.

[33] ibid 7–8.

[34] *Nonhuman Rights Project, Inc v Commerford & Sons, Inc et al*, Memorandum of Law in Support of Verified Petition for Common Law Writ of Habeas Corpus (13 November 2017) Superior Court, Judicial District of Litchfield, <https://www.nonhumanrights.org/content/uploads/CT-Memo-11.13.17.pdf> accessed 11 June 2023.

that qualify humans as persons, then the reasonable conclusion should be that chimpanzees are also persons'.[35] As a judge who ruled on one of the chimpanzee cases has put it, the NhRP's key argument in all its cases is that these animals 'should be accorded rights consonant with their abilities, and that their autonomy and self-determination *merit* the right to be free from illegal detention'.[36]

The second element of *Differential Consideration* is *Gradualism*. This component is closely related to the first one—*Merit*—because *Merit is* a grading concept. *Gradualism* starts from the fact that individuals differ in their characteristics. Some are bright, others are dim; some are sociable, others are hermits; some are virtuous, while others are wicked. That is not a new insight, of course. As the Enlightenment *philosophe* Denis Diderot observed, the materialist universe is one 'in which everything is connected, & where the beings rise above or below each other, in imperceptible degrees, so that there is no gap in the chain [of beings]'.[37] 'The more we examine nature', he continued, 'the more we become convinced that in order to express ourselves precisely, there would have to be as many different denominations as there are individuals'.[38] According to Meritocrats, if an individual's characteristics differ in degree from the characteristics of another individual, then so do their respective merits. In Vlastos's terminology, the 'M-system' requires 'grading individuals . . . with respect to their qualities'.[39] As we saw, this works on two levels: first, the level of who deserves a particular fundamental right and, second, the level of strength of that particular right.

On the first level, only those who actually possess the relevant characteristics that ground a particular fundamental right deserve that right. This is what it means for a right to be *justified by merit*. Because there are important differences in characteristics even among conspecifics, not all members of the same species will possess the same fundamental rights. What is more, beings from other species who possess the same characteristics may deserve some of the

[35] *Nonhuman Rights Project, Inc* v *Patrick C Lavery et al and Nonhuman Rights Project, Inc v Carmen Presti et al* (23 February 2018) Proposed Brief by Amici Curiae Philosophers, 28 <https://www.nonhumanrights.org/content/uploads/In-re-Nonhuman-Rights-v.-Lavery-Proposed-Brief-by-PHILOSOPHERS-74435.pdf> accessed 11 June 2023. See also Kristin Andrews et al, *Chimpanzee Rights: The Philosophers' Brief* (Routledge 2019).

[36] *Nonhuman Rights Project, Inc v Samuel L Stanley et al* [2015] Supreme Court of the State of New York, New York County No 152736/15, 26 (emphasis added).

[37] Denis Diderot and Louis-Jean-Marie Daubenton, 'Animal' in Denis Diderot and Jean le Rond d'Alembert (eds), *Encyclopédie, ou dictionnaire raisonné des sciences, des arts et des métiers, etc.* (University of Chicago: ARTFL Encyclopédie Project, 2017) 1:468 <https://artflsrv04.uchicago.edu/philologic4.7/encyclopedie0922/navigate/1/2753> accessed 11 June 2023 (my translation).

[38] ibid (my translation).

[39] Vlastos, 'Justice and Equality' (n 2) 51.

same rights. This has important implications for two common human rights notions: that human rights are *indivisible*, meaning that human beings in principle possess *all* human rights; and that human rights are *universal*, that is, that *all* human beings possess human rights. Together, indivisibility and universality entail that *all* humans possess *all* human rights.

The commonplace that human rights are *indivisible* (ie that they come on a wholesale basis) holds that if *A* has fundamental rights, then *A* has all fundamental rights.[40] As we saw in the previous chapter, this is encompassed in the Aristocracy's feature of *Equality*, and of equal rights more specifically. As we will see in the next chapter, some have pointed to human rights practice to question whether human rights are actually indivisible in their operation. Even if these scholars are right, the Meritocracy still differs markedly from the Aristocracy because its distribution of rights is both in theory and practice *retail*-based. That is, in the Meritocracy, individual merit determines which fundamental rights the individual gets. In contrast to the Aristocracy, there is no package deal on offer here.[41] The retail approach can already be found in Delamétherie's theory. As will be recalled from Chapter 2, Delamétherie argued that while humans and animals share some rights-grounding characteristics—such as their sensitivity—there are some fundamental rights that not all possess because they are based on characteristics that not all have. For example, according to Delamétherie, there is a *droit d'humanité* which describes the rights and obligations that apply only to human beings.[42] As part of this *droit d'humanité*, he argued, humans possess rights that protect the special needs that they have because they have left the state of nature, giving them, for instance, a right to clothing or to adequate housing.[43]

The second notion—that of human rights *universality*—holds that if *A* is a human being, then *A* holds fundamental rights. Note that, in contrast to the indivisibility thesis, on the universality thesis, it is not necessary for A to hold *all* fundamental rights.[44] It is sufficient for universality that A hold at least one human right.[45] This difference often goes unnoticed. Some assume that

[40] See on the indivisibility principle Chapter 3, Section 3.

[41] This is not to say that, if deserved, fundamental rights cannot come in sets.

[42] Delamétherie, *Principes*, vol 1 (n 28) 209–10.

[43] See ibid 217–18.

[44] In the Aristocracy, the indivisibility and universality principles overlap insofar as all humans are seen to possess (at least conditionally) all human rights. However, because the whole of human rights thinking and practice does not follow this view, I focus in Chapter 3 on the indivisibility principle rather than the universality principle to characterize the Aristocracy.

[45] See Raffael N Fasel, '"Simply in Virtue of Being Human"? A Critical Appraisal of a Human Rights Commonplace' (2018) 9 Jurisprudence 1, 17.

humans have to possess all fundamental rights for those rights to be universal, and thereby confound the universality principle and the indivisibility principle.[46] Unlike the latter, the universality principle is not discarded outright by Meritocrats. However, the Meritocracy takes away the unconditional validity universality has in the Aristocracy by making it contingent upon empirical corroboration: whether or not it is true that all human beings possess at least one fundamental right depends on whether all human beings possess the characteristics that ground at least one fundamental right. This may or may not be the case. Even if, as I believe, we have good reasons for assuming that this is the case,[47] the Meritocratic conception has no in-principle commitment to universality.

The second level on which *Gradualism* works is that of the *strength* of a right, that is, that rights are *proportioned to merit*. Under the Meritocratic conception, different beings do not only deserve different rights, but they deserve these rights to different extents. If being *A* possesses characteristic *c* to a higher degree than being *B*, and if *c* grounds fundamental right *r*, then *A*'s right *r* is *prima facie* stronger than *B*'s. Consider what Delamétherie says, for example, about the rights of predators to kill other animals for food.[48] According to him, the right to life of predators encompasses what is necessary for their self-preservation and can outweigh the conflicting right to life of their prey if it is sufficiently weighty, that is, if there is no other way for the predator to survive. Humans, on the other hand, have alternative ways of procuring their survival without having to eat another animal's flesh. As a result, their right to life will generally not be strong enough to outweigh that of other animals in such circumstances.[49]

Or consider a situation in which both a human being and a rabbit are in need of a life-saving cancer treatment, but the state-run health care system only has enough resources to give the treatment to one of them. Would the human being and the rabbit have an equally strong right to that treatment? Not necessarily. According to *Differential Consideration*, the being with the stronger interest in remaining alive would have a stronger right to life, or health, allowing the right of the other to be outweighed. Many would say that humans have an interest in continued existence that is stronger than a rabbit's, if they consider the rabbit

[46] See eg James W Nickel, 'Personal Desert and Human Rights' in Rowan Cruft, Matthew S Liao, and Massimo Renzo (eds), *Philosophical Foundations of Human Rights* (Oxford University Press 2015) 153.

[47] Fasel, '"Simply in Virtue of Being Human"? A Critical Appraisal of a Human Rights Commonplace' (n 45) 25.

[48] Delamétherie, *Principes*, vol 1 (n 28) xviii, 50, 68. See also Chapter 2, Section 5.

[49] See Delamétherie, *Principes*, vol 1 (n 28) 235–37.

to have any such interest at all. As a result, the human's right to life would be stronger and would outweigh the rabbit's.

In this situation, the Meritocratic conception vindicates common practice: it provides a justification for how human interests outweigh the interests of animals. This outcome would not be different from that entailed by an Aristocratic theory. However, the Meritocracy is a double-edged sword. If the rights-grounding characteristics of an animal are more developed than those of a human being, then the right of the animal will outweigh that of the human being. Imagine the rabbit in our example mutates because of a radioactive spill. Transformed, our rabbit has acquired extraordinary mental capacities and the ability to plan far ahead into the future, farther still than any human can. Assume also that the human being in our example lacks these characteristics because of a severe mental disability. In this alternative scenario, the rabbit's right to life would be stronger, outweighing the human's. Hence, the rabbit, not the human, should be given the life-saving treatment. This is a conclusion no Aristocrat would ever reach.

Gradualism would also have far-reaching implications among human beings.[50] Similar to the rabbit case, human beings with more advanced mental capacities and with a more developed ability to plan their future could be considered to have a stronger interest in continued existence. As a result, their right to life would outweigh that of human beings with severe mental disabilities who are considered to lack this ability. It is here that the connection between the Meritocracy and utilitarian conceptions becomes evident. As Allen Buchanan has argued, for utilitarians, too,

> there is only a gradation, a continuum of beings with lesser and greater capacities for well-being and harm, and sacrificing some beings for the sake of others further along the continuum is always in principle not only permissible, but even required.[51]

Like utilitarian gradualism,[52] Meritocratic *Gradualism* leaves little or no room for a status of equality.[53] This is because such a status would have to 'supervene upon facts about our nature', as McMahan explains, 'yet there are

[50] See also Jeff McMahan, *Killing in War* (Oxford University Press 2009) 161.

[51] Allen Buchanan, *Beyond Humanity? The Ethics of Biomedical Enhancement* (Oxford University Press 2011) 224.

[52] Tim Mulgan, 'The Ethics of Killing: Problems at the Margins of Life by Jeff McMahan' (2004) 34 Canadian Journal of Philosophy 443, 459.

[53] Nickel, 'Personal Desert and Human Rights' (n 46) 153.

really no relevant respects in which we are by nature equal'.[54] *Gradualism* thus inherits naturalism's rejection of the *Equality Thesis*. And for the same reason, the Meritocracy, in its pure form, is also unsuited to accommodate other threshold-concepts, such as personhood or dignity.[55] Thresholds (or range properties[56]) constitute discontinuous strategies, which, as Nigel Simmonds has noted, 'cannot be mapped onto a continuous distinction'.[57] Thresholds presuppose that the beings on one side of the threshold are categorically distinct from those on the other. They are an all-or-nothing matter. And, as such, they are incompatible with *Gradualism*.[58] Take the example of personhood. Those who meet the threshold of being persons are all equally persons. Those who do not meet it, are not persons at all. No one who passes the threshold is more or less of a person.[59] I will return to this issue in the next chapter.

As Delamétherie's 1802 treatise *De l'homme considéré moralement, de ses mœurs, et de celles des animaux* anticipated, *Gradualism* paves the way for hierarchies between human beings, with some possessing more rights and a higher status than others. While the divide need not be between 'civilised' peoples and 'barbaric' peoples, or rich and poor, as Delamétherie suggested,[60] *Gradualism* makes it likely that some kind of rights hierarchy will emerge. Even if we have good reasons for rejecting the view that some human groups deserve more or stronger rights than others because no group can be said to be superior to others, the fact that the Meritocratic conception is not in principle opposed to such categorizations shows how radical it is.[61] In the eyes of the Aristocrats, it is precisely this fact that makes the Meritocracy so odious. I will analyse this issue in more detail in Section 4 when considering the Meritocracy's strong suit and weakness.

Before we turn to the Meritocracy's second central feature—*Externalism*—we need to address an objection that threatens to undermine the distinction between the Meritocracy's *Differential Consideration* and the Aristocracy's *Equal Consideration*. As I have suggested in this section, Meritocrats embrace difference, whereas Aristocrats embrace equality. But what if this dichotomy is

[54] Jeff McMahan, 'Challenges to Human Equality' (2008) 12 The Journal of Ethics 81, 95.
[55] See ibid 101–02.
[56] Rawls, *A Theory of Justice* (n 5) 506.
[57] Nigel E Simmonds, *Law as a Moral Idea* (Oxford University Press 2007) 196.
[58] See McMahan, 'Challenges to Human Equality' (n 54) 93.
[59] See Buchanan, *Beyond Humanity?* (n 51) 218.
[60] Jean-Claude Delamétherie, *De l'homme considéré moralement; de ses moeurs, et de celles des animaux*, vol 1 (Guilleminet 1802) vii, 38, 256–61.
[61] See also Anne Phillips, *The Politics of the Human* (Cambridge University Press 2015) 45; Allen Buchanan, 'The Egalitarianism of Human Rights' in Roger Crisp (ed), *Griffin on Human Rights* (Oxford University Press 2014) 691.

false? What if difference and equality are not mutually exclusive? That is precisely what the objection tries to establish. *Equal Consideration*, the objection goes, can accommodate individuals' different characteristics. In fact, *Equal Consideration requires* that we treat beings with different interests differently.[62] This is because *Equal Consideration* neither implies that all humans are the same, nor that all humans should be treated the same. Under the Aristocratic conception, the objection holds, human beings need not be treated *equally*, but *as equals*.[63] Ronald Dworkin elucidates this distinction between equal treatment and treatment as equals (also called 'equal concern') by submitting that the former entails the 'right to an equal distribution of some opportunity or resource or burden', whereas the latter describes the right 'to be treated with the same respect and concern as anyone else'.[64] For example, if a teacher gives the same mark for student *A*'s excellent paper as for student *B*'s mediocre paper, both *A* and *B* are treated equally. However, they are not treated as equals, because in order to respect student *A*'s achievement she should be given a higher mark. Aristocrats can thus point out that their position is no stranger to differential concern. Quite the opposite: *Equal Consideration* requires taking into account the differences between human beings and treating them differently based on these differences.

In response to this objection, Meritocrats can insist that there is a real and important difference between *Equal Consideration* and *Differential Consideration*. The difference is that, in contrast to *Equal Consideration*, *Differential Consideration* is not committed to the view that all humans have equal value (or worth). This difference is easily overlooked because even some Meritocrats put forth principles that seem to render the distinction between *Equal Consideration* and *Differential Consideration* moot. Singer, for example, has made the 'equal consideration of interests' principle a cornerstone of his theory.[65] According to Singer, this principle requires 'that we give equal weight in our moral deliberations to the like interests of all those affected by our actions', regardless of who the interest-holders are.[66] At first glance, Singer's principle seems to be the spitting image of the Aristocratic principle of *Equal Consideration*. The similarity is in name only, however. For while Singer's

[62] See eg Elizabeth Fenton, 'Genetic Enhancement—A Threat to Human Rights?' (2008) 22 Bioethics 1, 6.

[63] See Ronald Dworkin, *Sovereign Virtue: The Theory and Practice of Equality* (Harvard University Press 2000) 11.

[64] Ronald Dworkin, *Taking Rights Seriously* (Bloomsbury 2013) 273.

[65] Singer, *Animal Liberation: A New Ethics for Our Treatment of Animals* (n 26) 6.

[66] Peter Singer, *Practical Ethics* (3rd edn, Cambridge University Press 2011) 20.

principle requires that like *interests* be treated alike, the Aristocratic principle requires that like *interest-holders* be treated alike.

This is an inconspicuous but important difference. Under Singer's principle, as under the Meritocracy, individuals are placeholders of interests. As we saw above, their identity as members of a particular group is considered to carry no moral significance in itself. As a result, an individual's moral worth depends entirely on the number and the strength of the interests they have. The greater these interests, the greater the moral worth of the individual. Recall our example of the rabbit and the human in need of a life-saving medical treatment. As we saw, in the standard situation, the human being's interest in life is taken to be stronger than the rabbit's, which is why the right of the human being outweighs that of the rabbit. However, in the alternative situation, in which we imagined the rabbit to have been altered due to a radioactive spill and the human being to have a severe mental disability, the rabbit's interest in life would have been stronger, meaning his right to life would have outweighed the human being's. It is in this sense that Singer's equal consideration of interests principle treats interests equally, but not interest-holders. The human's and the rabbit's moral value are not necessarily equal because their value depends on their interests.

As we will see in the next chapter, some animal rights proponents have rejected Singer's principle precisely for this reason, and have adopted a more egalitarian approach. According to Tom Regan, for instance, Singer's principle 'has no room for the equal moral rights of different individuals because it has no room for their equal inherent value or worth. What has value for [Singer] is the satisfaction of an individual's interests, *not the individual whose interests they are*.'[67] Indeed, in a discussion of the moral status of humans with mental disabilities, Singer explicitly suggested that we should 'abandon the idea of the equal value of all humans, replacing that with a more graduated view in which moral status depends on some aspects of cognitive ability, and that graduated view is applied both to humans and nonhumans'.[68]

By contrast, the Aristocracy's *Equal Consideration* is based on the assumption that all fundamental rights-holders (ie all human beings)—and not just their similar interests—have equal status. This thought is often expressed in the idea that humans are *persons* with equal value or worth. As John Rawls

[67] Tom Regan, 'The Case for Animal Rights' in Peter Singer (ed), *In Defence of Animals* (Basil Blackwell 1985) 19 (emphasis added).
[68] Peter Singer, 'Speciesism and Moral Status' (2009) 40 Metaphilosophy 567, 575.

puts it, for example, the term 'equality . . . applies to the respect which is owed to persons'.[69] Personhood is taken to be a moral baseline that determines which treatments we owe to persons in order to respect them as equals. *Equal Consideration* thus has an underlying commitment to equal status which governs its sensitivity to individual differences.[70] This type of commitment to equality is completely absent in the Meritocracy. While *Equal Consideration* is sensitive to certain differences between human beings (differences in interests), its commitment to an underlying moral baseline inhibits it from accommodating other differences (differences in moral value between rights-holders). *Differential Consideration*, on the other hand, is restricted by no such commitment, and can therefore accommodate all kinds of differences between beings, including differences in moral value between human beings.

Let us now turn to the third and last feature that is characteristic of *Differential Consideration*: *Inclusivity*. This feature mirrors the third feature of the Aristocracy's *Equal Consideration*, *Exclusivity*. As I explained above, *Differential Consideration* does not limit fundamental rights to the human species, nor to any other group. We saw that its *Merit*-based *Gradualism* is open to recognizing fundamental rights in any kind of individual. The only condition for this is that the individual possesses the capacities that are considered relevant for the possession of the right. In other words, *Differential Consideration* admits to the category of rights-holders any individual who deserves it, including nonhuman animals and, as Delamétherie argued, any other sensitive being that may exist.

Once one extends rights to nonhuman animals, as Meritocrats do, one loses the exclusively human character of 'human' rights.[71] As some have pointed out, it would therefore be apposite to replace the label 'human rights' with a more suitable term that does justice to the fact that there is a broader category of beings than just humans who are possible rights-holders.[72] For example, Saskia Stucki has advanced a holistic understanding of human and animals rights as 'One Rights', in analogy to the more well-known One Health framework.[73]

[69] Rawls, *A Theory of Justice* (n 5) 511.
[70] See also Peter Westen, *Speaking of Equality: An Analysis of the Rhetorical Force of 'Equality' in Moral and Legal Discourse* (Princeton University Press 2014) 7.
[71] Alasdair Cochrane, 'Evaluating "Bioethical Approaches" to Human Rights' (2012) 15 Ethical Theory and Moral Practice 309, 319.
[72] ibid 320; Alasdair Cochrane, 'From Human Rights to Sentient Rights' (2013) 16 Critical Review of International Social and Political Philosophy 655.
[73] Saskia Stucki, *One Rights: Human and Animal Rights in the Anthropocene* (Springer 2023) 9.

4 *Externalism*

Let us now consider the second element of the Meritocracy: *Externalism*. This element addresses the question of *how* exactly Meritocrats explain fundamental rights. As I will show in this section, Meritocrats *ground* these rights in an individual's characteristics and interests. Drawing on Francis Bacon's metaphor which we encountered in Chapter 2, we can say that *Externalists* are like bees who gather pollen from flowers and then turn the pollen into honey.[74] I will first shed light on how exactly *Externalists* gather their empirical 'pollen' and turn it into rights 'honey' by considering two objections that can be raised against the *Externalist* approach. I will then discuss *Externalism*'s strong suit, namely its capacity to *ground* rights in natural features, before drawing attention to its main weakness, namely its tendency to give fewer and weaker rights to human beings with fewer and weaker interests.

4.1 How-to

What exactly is *Externalism*? Marion Albers, Thomas Hoffmann, and Jörn Reinhardt define it as an attempt 'to justify elementary moral and legal principles from "outside" our normative or evaluative vocabularies. The reductive ambition is to trace a normative concept back to certain non-normative descriptions of human beings as formulated in the vocabularies of the natural sciences.'[75] This definition is useful as it foregrounds *Externalists*' ambition to ground normative concepts in empirical facts about humans or other beings. However, it misleadingly suggests that the ambition has to be a 'reductive' and purely non-evaluative one. As I will show below, *Externalism* is neither reductive nor purely non-evaluative. For the moment, however, we can use this definition to construe a working account of *Externalism* which understands it as an attempt to trace fundamental rights back to facts about the natural characteristics and interests of human and nonhuman beings. This account contrasts with the Aristocracy's *Internalism*, which refuses to leave the normative domain. *Externalism*'s willingness to draw on natural facts makes evident its indebtedness to the naturalist current which I described in Chapter 2.

[74] As a reminder, my use of the terms 'internalism' and 'externalism' is different from their meaning in other contexts, such as in epistemic justification.

[75] Marion Albers, Thomas Hoffmann, and Jörn Reinhardt, 'Human Rights and Human Nature: Introduction' in Marion Albers, Thomas Hoffmann, and Jörn Reinhardt (eds), *Human Rights and Human Nature* (Springer 2014) 2.

To illustrate *Externalism*, consider Delamétherie's theory. As will be recalled, Delamétherie applied the *droit d'animalité* to all sensitive beings in virtue of the empirical fact that they are capable of sensation. He took this fact, and the interests it gives rise to in sensitive beings, to ground his triad of rights. The rights to health and to enjoyments, for example, are grounded in the fact that sensitive beings have an interest in leading lives free from illness, and in having pleasurable experiences. The right to life, in turn, is grounded in sensitive beings' interest in being alive, which serves as a precondition for all their other sensations and rights.

The philosophically trained reader will be itching at this stage to point out that Meritocrats' *Externalism* commits a logical fallacy. It derives rights from natural facts about beings. But that is to derive an 'ought' from an 'is', which is to violate what is often called 'Hume's Law' (I will refer to this as the *Objection from Hume's Law*).[76] Although it is a matter of some dispute as to what David Hume argued exactly in the relevant passage of his *Treatise on Human Nature* (*Treatise*),[77] it is commonly thought that his point was that propositions about what ought or ought not to be the case cannot logically be derived from propositions about what is or is not—or, as it is sometimes put, that 'values' cannot be derived from 'facts'.[78] Morality, as Dworkin summarizes the position, is considered to be completely independent from 'facts about the basic structure of the universe'.[79] Have the reader's philosophy seminars paid off? Have they caught Meritocrats red-handed? Or is there a way the Meritocrats can save their necks?

Before we answer these questions, let us consider another challenge, which builds on the *Objection from Hume's Law*. In addition to the logical problem that may arise for attempts to derive fundamental rights from interests and characteristics, one could object that *Externalism* suffers from a fatal practical problem. There may be numerous benign characteristics and interests that we will undeniably find deserving of normative promotion. For example, the interest many have in maintaining their family life and extra-familial social ties seems to be deserving of some form of protection. However, there are also other, more pernicious interests that we think not only undeserving of such protection, but even deserving of repudiation. The interest that some people

[76] See eg Arnd Pollmann, 'Human Rights Beyond Naturalism' in Marion Albers, Thomas Hoffmann, and Jörn Reinhardt (eds), *Human Rights and Human Nature* (Springer 2014) 121–22.

[77] David Hume, *A Treatise of Human Nature* (LA Selby-Bigge ed, Clarendon Press 1960) Book 3, Part 1, Section 1, 469–70.

[78] See PD Magnus and Jon Mandle, 'What Kind of Is-Ought Gap Is There and What Kind Ought There Be?' (2017) 14 Journal of Moral Philosophy 373, 374.

[79] Ronald Dworkin, *Justice for Hedgehogs* (Belknap Press of Harvard University Press 2011) 17, 44–46.

have in oppressing others, for example, deserves only condemnation. Yet, under an unqualified *Externalist* approach, any kind of natural property and interest that would arise from that property would have to be promoted, with potentially disastrous consequences. Drawing on Martha Nussbaum, I will call this the *Objection from Nature Worship*.[80]

Delamétherie seemed to accept this implication of the Meritocratic approach when he claimed that carnivores have a right to kill other animals 'because they have no other way to survive, and because, as sensitive beings, they have to procure their own well-being'.[81] He believed that predators have an interest in killing others that, under his *Externalist* approach, seemed to require the granting of corresponding rights to these predators. He also believed that, in yielding such conclusions, *Externalism* raised serious issues regarding nature's purposes. As we saw, these issues had him questioning, for a moment at least, the plausibility of his own theory about the universal law of the good.[82]

Meritocrats can respond to these two objections by arguing that they are targeted at a strawman version of *Externalism* that does not represent the ideal-type of the Meritocracy, even though some of its advocates (including Delamétherie) may have embraced it.[83] The Meritocracy, properly understood, adopts a more sophisticated *Externalism* that avoids the issues raised by the *Objection from Hume's Law* and the *Objection from Nature Worship*.

To see this, we require a better understanding of what Hume said and, more importantly, what he did *not* say. On closer inspection, Meritocrats can argue, it becomes evident that Hume did not claim that normative propositions cannot be linked to factual ones. Hume in fact had no objection in principle to deriving an 'ought' from an 'is', as long as one *explains* how one establishes the relation between these two distinct realms.[84] This becomes plain from the wording of the relevant passage in the *Treatise*: 'For as this ought, or ought not, expresses some new relation or affirmation, 'tis necessary that it shou'd be observ'd and *explain'd*; and at the same time that *a reason should be given* . . . how this new relation can be a deduction from others, which are entirely different from it.'[85]

[80] See Martha C Nussbaum, *Frontiers of Justice: Disability, Nationality, Species Membership* (Harvard University Press 2006) 366.
[81] Delamétherie, *Principes*, vol 1 (n 28) 201–02, 231.
[82] ibid 231. See on the predation problem also Korsgaard, *Fellow Creatures: Our Obligations to the Other Animals* (n 4) 173–90.
[83] See also John Tasioulas, 'On the Foundations of Human Rights' in Rowan Cruft, S Matthew Liao, and Massimo Renzo (eds), *Philosophical Foundations of Human Rights* (Oxford University Press 2015) 45–46.
[84] See James Rachels, 'Naturalism' in Hugh LaFollette (ed), *The Blackwell Guide to Ethical Theory* (Blackwell 2000) 76–78.
[85] Hume, *A Treatise of Human Nature* (n 77) Book 3, Part 1, Section 1, 469 (emphasis changed).

As this shows, Hume accepted that 'ought'-propositions can be connected to 'is'-propositions in the sense that the latter can serve as reasons that justify the former.[86]

Meritocrats can argue that facts about individuals' characteristics serve as reasons that justify the derivation of normative principles, such as fundamental rights. *Externalism*, in other words, is not an attempt to logically derive an 'ought' from an 'is'. Rather, it is an attempt to use the 'is' as a *reason for* the 'ought'. That is why, for instance, Meritocrats state that it would be 'unreasonable'[87] not to grant animals fundamental rights given their capacities. They thus take characteristics of animals to be reasons that render fundamental rights intelligible. In Jeremy Waldron's words, '[t]he point of looking for an underlying property [is] to find a way of *making sense* of the relevant principle or principles and providing a well-organised basis for their application'.[88]

On what grounds can Meritocrats argue that it 'makes sense' to ground rights in facts about a being's characteristics? Why see a connection at all between what a being is like and how we ought to treat it? The answer to these questions reveals that Meritocrats accept a simple normative assumption, namely that the good should be promoted. As Philippa Foot has argued, the good needs to be placed before the right.[89] In other words, what is good for a being is prior to and explains how one morally ought to treat that being. 'The way an individual *should be*', Foot explains, 'is determined by what is needed for development, self-maintenance, and reproduction'.[90] For humans, animals, and even plants, Foot points out, there are 'patterns of natural normativity',[91] that is, objective, teleological norms that make individual animals and humans flourish.[92] These norms have a claim on us that it would be irrational to reject.[93] Based on this view, Meritocrats hold that every normative argument about the rights that a being possesses has to be grounded in facts about its good.[94] That is why it 'makes sense' for Meritocrats to ground rights

[86] Rachels, 'Naturalism' (n 84) 78. See also Russ Shafer-Landau, 'The Possibility of Metaethics' (2010) 90 Boston University Law Review 479, 486.
[87] Gary Chartier, 'Natural Law and Animal Rights' (2010) 23 Canadian Journal of Law & Jurisprudence 33, 46.
[88] Jeremy Waldron, *One Another's Equals: The Basis of Human Equality* (Belknap Press of Harvard University Press 2017) 249 (emphasis in original).
[89] Philippa Foot, *Natural Goodness* (Clarendon Press 2001) 24.
[90] ibid 33 (emphasis in original).
[91] ibid 38.
[92] ibid 43–44, 51. On the idea of *telos* in animals, see Aristotle, *Parts of Animals* (AL Peck tr, Harvard University Press 1961) I, 640a37–640b10.
[93] Foot, *Natural Goodness* (n 89) 65. However, Foot herself denied that her argument could carry normative implications for our treatment of animals: see ibid Postscript.
[94] ibid 24.

in beings' characteristics. They do not mean that rights can be logically derived from these characteristics.[95]

Related to the normative assumption of promoting the good is the view that, as John Tasioulas puts it, evaluative considerations about a being's good 'may even be thought of as natural facts, provided we have a suitably expansive understanding of the natural realm, one that does not limit natural facts to those that do explanatory work within the natural sciences'.[96] The suggestion here is that when we are dealing with what is good for a being, we are not simply dealing with an 'is'-matter, but with one that has evaluative connotations; we are, as it is sometimes put, confronted with 'thick concepts', that is, descriptions enriched with evaluations.[97] Bernd Ladwig illustrates this point as follows:

> [T]o say of a human being that he or she would *suffer* if someone took away his or her children implies that it would be *bad* for this person if someone took away their children. This is not a normative proposition by itself, but how would a moral conception look that was wholly indifferent to human suffering and well-being? And someone who insisted on avoiding all thick concepts like 'suffering' would scarcely use a language in which we would continue to recognise our human interests at all.[98]

Ladwig uses an important concept—that of interests—which I have intentionally omitted above when focusing on individuals' characteristics or capacities. However, this discussion of characteristics and capacities was a simplistic picture. For while characteristics are important when it comes to determining which rights a being should have, they alone are not sufficient. Suppose it is one of my characteristics that I am tall. Does that fact entitle me to any rights, for example the right to high ceilings or to bespoke clothing? Or suppose I am jealous. Does that mean I have a right that my wife be loyal? It is unclear why my being tall or jealous should have any palpable connection to fundamental rights. So how exactly can Meritocrats argue that an individual's characteristics are at the basis of fundamental rights? The key to answering this question lies in the concept of 'interests'. Interests play a crucial role in the Meritocratic

[95] To put it in Tasioulas's terms, the Meritocracy is 'foundational', but not 'foundationalist': Tasioulas, 'On the Foundations of Human Rights' (n 83) 45–46.

[96] ibid 46.

[97] See more generally James Griffin, *Value Judgement: Improving Our Ethical Beliefs* (Clarendon Press 1996); Hilary Putnam, *The Collapse of the Fact/Value Dichotomy and Other Essays* (Harvard University Press 2004).

[98] Bernd Ladwig, 'Human Rights and Human Animals' in Marion Albers, Thomas Hoffmann, and Jörn Reinhardt (eds), *Human Rights and Human Nature* (Springer 2014) 32 (emphasis in original).

conception because they bridge the gap between an individual's characteristics or capacities and the rights they deserve. Meritocrats adopt an interest-based approach to rights, according to which a being's rights are determined by the interests they possess. And these interests, in turn, depend on the characteristics that the being has. For instance, a being with the characteristic of being a social animal will generally have an interest in having social affiliations.

There are a number of different formulations of the interest-based approach but one that has become widely known is Joseph Raz's. According to Raz, *X* has a right 'if and only if *X* can have rights, and, other things being equal, an aspect of *X*'s well-being (his interest) is a sufficient reason for holding some other person(s) to be under a duty'.[99] Importantly, as Raz's theory shows, someone's having an interest in something is not sufficient for that interest to deserve rights protection. Rather, the interest must also be sufficiently important to justify holding others duty-bound to respect the right. I will return to this point below when considering the *Objection from Nature Worship*. For our purposes, it is enough to note that Meritocrats have identified criteria, such as sentience, which they consider at least sufficient for having interests.[100]

How exactly can interests serve as a bridge between characteristics (a descriptive concept) and rights (a normative one)? To understand this, we can follow Ladwig's argument that interests such as the interest not to suffer are 'thick concepts'. As he suggests, we commonly use concepts like 'suffering' in a thick sense, that is, we accept that they have a normative claim on us. In fact, it seems so obvious to most of us that the bad ought to be prevented and the good promoted, that it is rarely acknowledged explicitly. Meritocrats, too, often simply take for granted that no one could reasonably reject this assumption.[101] Even the Aristocrats overlook it frequently, which is why they accuse Meritocrats of violating Hume's Law. However, as the discussion above shows, Meritocrats can argue that they make no logically fallacious inferences from an 'is'-premise to an 'ought'-conclusion. Rather, they argue that the interests which ground rights have normative significance because of the normative premise that the good ought to be promoted. Interests, in this reading, are partly normative reasons for why a being ought to have certain rights. It is in this sense that Meritocrats, as James Griffin puts it, are already partly 'within the normative circle'[102] when they ground rights in beings' natural characteristics.

[99] Joseph Raz, *The Morality of Freedom* (Oxford University Press 1988) 166.
[100] See eg Sherry Colb and Michael Dorf, *Beating Hearts: Abortion and Animal Rights* (Columbia University Press 2016) 20.
[101] See Pollmann, 'Human Rights Beyond Naturalism' (n 76) 123.
[102] James Griffin, *On Human Rights* (Oxford University Press 2008) 35.

However, it is important to note that this openness to normative assumptions does not make Meritocrats *Internalists*. True, Meritocrats accept the premise that we ought to promote the good and that, as a result, interests are at least half-normative because they are part of the good. In this respect, Meritocrats appear much like *Internalists*. But Meritocrats can argue that what distinguishes their conception from *Internalists'* is that it is not purely normative, but also partly factual. To Meritocrats, the interests that ground rights, and the capacities from which they arise, are 'features of the world',[103] as Griffin puts it. This is to say that there is a certain factuality about these interests that can be determined objectively, that is, empirically. As Griffin argues, 'these interests' being met or not met are *goings-on in the world*'.[104] As is the case with other goings-on in the world, it is possible to make judgements about interests that can be correct or incorrect 'in the way that statements of natural fact can be'.[105] A judgement about whether a being has a particular interest and whether that interest is violated is therefore not a purely normative assertion. Interests are also partly factual aspects of a being's nature, and can therefore be determined objectively.[106] As Griffin emphasizes, '[p]articularly deeply embedded in us are certain biological aims—for food, health, protection of our capabilities—and certain psycho-biological aims—for example, for companionship, affection, reproduction'.[107] That a being feels pain, for instance, is a matter of fact that everyone can agree on (at least in principle).[108] Because of their partly factual existence, interests are at least partly *external* to our beliefs. They are not mere figments of our imagination, nor mere normative stipulations. Rather, they are part 'of a belief-independent world of empirical fact'[109] that influences our beliefs and concepts. For these reasons, *Externalism*, although receptive to normative considerations, is not imprisoned by them. In contrast to *Internalism*, *Externalism* is not restricted to purely normative decisions, stories, and interpretations. Rather, it can enlist facts about the world to bolster its normative conclusions.

Based on these clarifications about the exact nature of Meritocracy's *Externalism*, we can now see why the *Objection from Hume's Law* fails. Directed as it is against a strawman version of *Externalism*, which does not accept the

[103] ibid.
[104] ibid 35 (emphasis added).
[105] ibid 120.
[106] Others have defended objectivism about normative statements, but there is no need to go that far to follow my argument: see Dwayne H Mulder, 'Objectivity' (*Internet Encyclopedia of Philosophy*) <https://www.iep.utm.edu/objectiv/> accessed 11 June 2023.
[107] Griffin, *On Human Rights* (n 102) 116.
[108] ibid 123.
[109] ibid 121.

premise that the good ought to be promoted and which rejects the normativity of interests that promote the good, it holds no water when set against the more sophisticated version of *Externalism* which I have described above.[110]

With the move to a more sophisticated *Externalism*, Meritocrats can also refute the *Objection from Nature Worship*. *Externalism*, they can point out, does not entail mindless worship of all things natural. Instead, it requires an evaluation of what an individual's good is and what part of it ought to be promoted. To use Nussbaum's words, we can say that Meritocrats do 'not attempt to extract norms directly from some facts about human nature'. Rather, they evaluate 'the innate powers of . . . beings, asking which ones are the good ones, the ones that are central to the notion of a decently flourishing . . . life'.[111] As a result, although it may be in the interest of predators to kill other animals, Meritocrats do not have to promote that interest by giving predators a right to kill others. To put this in Razian terms, not every interest of a being gives rise to a right.[112] Among the conditions the interest needs to meet to ground a right is that it must be a sufficient reason to hold others under a duty to respect the right.[113] If, as in the case of the predators, we come to the conclusion that the predator's interest in killing other animals is not a sufficient reason to hold others duty-bound to respect that right—for instance because that interest is harmful to others—then the predator has no right to kill other animals.

It has now become clear what was tentative about Albers, Hoffman, and Reinhardt's definition of *Externalism* that I provided at the outset of this section. Their definition suggested that *Externalists* are reductivists who infer rights from facts about nature without allowing for an evaluative element. As we saw in this subsection, however, ideal Meritocrats are not reductivists. They accept the simple (yet often unacknowledged) normative assumption that the good ought to be promoted and they see interests that promote the good as being partly normative. As a result, they do not believe that the natural sciences—as important as they are in identifying a being's characteristics and interests—can provide all the information needed to determine who has which rights. Refining our working account, we can thus say that *Externalism* is the attempt to ground moral and legal principles in the interests of beings, which,

[110] See also Ladwig, 'Human Rights and Human Animals' (n 98) 30.

[111] Martha C Nussbaum, 'Beyond "Compassion and Humanity": Justice for Nonhuman Animals' in Cass R Sunstein and Martha Nussbaum (eds), *Animal Rights: Current Debates and New Directions* (Oxford University Press 2005) 310.

[112] See also Neil MacCormick, 'Rights, Claims and Remedies' (1982) 1 Law and Philosophy 337, 338.

[113] For a fuller list of conditions see Tasioulas, 'On the Foundations of Human Rights' (n 83) 57–60.

although forming part of the nature of these beings and therefore of the empirical world, also have a normative side to them.

4.2 *Grounding*

Having analysed how Meritocrats explain rights-holding by drawing on characteristics and interests of individual beings, we can now turn to the question of why they adopt *Externalism*, and whether there are problems with this approach. In this section, I will argue that *Externalism*'s appeal lies in its capacity to *ground* fundamental rights in an individual's objectively determinable characteristics and interests, which gives these rights a firm foothold. However, as I will show, this virtue of *Externalism* is at the same time also its vice.

What exactly do I mean when I say that *grounding* is characteristic of the Meritocratic conception of fundamental rights? The term 'grounding' is used figuratively in philosophical discourse to describe the process of providing normative principles with an empirical, metaphysical, or other foundation. In ordinary discourse, 'grounding' is used in a more literal sense for the process of connecting an electrical device to the earth with the aid of a wire. As I use it, the term draws on both these senses: *Grounding* describes the process of providing rights and similar concepts—and thereby in a metaphorical sense also their holders—with a foundation in their earthly existence. They are 'inserted into nature',[114] to use Justin Smith's words. The process of *grounding* thus contrasts diametrically with the process of *founding* which is characteristic of the Aristocracy. As I discussed in Chapter 3, the Aristocracy's *Internalism* allows it to create its own foundations by drawing exclusively on normative decisions, stories, and interpretations.

Why do Meritocrats *ground* fundamental rights in the interests of beings? The central advantage of this approach is that, by drawing on interests, Meritocrats can provide a solid basis for rights. As we have established in the previous section, interests are at least partly objective (judgements about interests can be correct or incorrect) and external (interests are part of the furniture of the world). In the Meritocracy, whether or not someone deserves a right hinges therefore on whether they possess the relevant characteristics and interests that are sufficiently weighty to impose corresponding duties on others. To establish whether or not a being has such interests, we have to study them.

[114] Justin EH Smith, *Nature, Human Nature, & Human Difference: Race in Early Modern Philosophy* (Princeton University Press 2015) 18.

In other words, there is a fact of the matter as to whether or not someone has an interest. As the legal scholar David Favre has observed, that animals have 'interests is not a matter of philosophy or debate, it is a matter of fact that is derived from the existence and nature of the DNA.'[115] In virtue of this DNA, Favre continues, living beings have 'a package of skills and capabilities that we expect the individual to exercise in pursuing his or her life.'[116] The process of *grounding* thus provides a non-arbitrary foundation for rights; one that is anchored in empirical reality. To be sure, as we saw, evaluations will be required to discern exactly what counts as an interest and whether or not it is weighty enough to establish duties in others. However, the need for such evaluations does not change the fact that *Externalism* allows Meritocrats to root rights in nature. Nature is of course far from inert. Beings evolve, and interests change. Compared to normative principles and assumptions founded by human beings, however, they only change at a snail's pace. For this reason, Meritocracy's *Externalism* provides a much more stable footing for fundamental rights than the more capricious decisions, stories, and interpretations that characterize Aristocracy's *Internalism*.

Externalism has thus become a powerful tool for challenging the Aristocratic orthodoxy, about which I say more in Chapter 6. Applying *Externalism*, Meritocrats have concentrated on the countless nonhuman animals who possess interests that would make them deserving of certain fundamental rights but who have so far been granted no such rights. Animals live in societies that are not based on the idea that they should have fundamental rights, despite their possession of relevant capacities and interests. This explains the appeal of the Meritocracy: a society's reluctance to accept animals' fundamental rights is no impediment to it. Rather, it is the starting point for a *Merit*-based challenge. Meritocrats can point to the fact that individual animals deserve fundamental rights because they possess relevant interests and characteristics. As we saw, these interests and characteristics form part of the furniture of the empirical world, which is why their existence and the degree to which they are (not) fulfilled can be established objectively. The Meritocracy thus provides the tools which are necessary to argue for an extension of fundamental rights to animals in societies which have remained largely ignorant of their interests. In contrast to the Aristocracy, Meritocracy's *Externalism* therefore does not suffer from the problem that it arbitrarily excludes beings from rights-holdership.

[115] David Favre, 'Living Property: A New Status for Animals within the Legal System' (2010) 93 Marquette Law Review 1021, 1048.
[116] ibid 1049.

The Meritocracy's *grounding*-approach also has a grave *downside*, however. In tying fundamental rights to individuals' interests and capacities, it does more than justify granting fundamental rights to animals. It also justifies giving some human beings fewer and weaker fundamental rights if they possess fewer and weaker interests.[117] As we saw above, the Meritocracy is based on *Merit*-based *Gradualism* and *Inclusivity*, meaning that it rejects the ideas that all human beings have a high status simply in virtue of being born human (*Heredity*), that they possess equal rights (*Equality*), and that all nonhumans are excluded from that status and these rights (*Exclusivity*). By undermining the central pillars of the Aristocracy, *Externalism* jeopardizes the idea that no human being should be treated as inferior to other human beings.[118] In an address which discusses the lessons of animal rights, Laurence Tribe describes this problem succinctly:

> [W]hen we insist that rights depend on the individual's possession of certain measurable traits such as self-awareness or the ability to form complex mental representations or to engage in moral reasoning, and when we treat it as a mere matter of grace or optional beneficence whenever a simulacrum of such rights is awarded as a privilege to human beings who lack all of those qualifying traits (like infants or the severely mentally retarded or the profoundly comatose), then it follows that it would be entirely permissible not to award those basic legal protections to such beings.[119]

In fact, according to the Meritocracy's *Merit*-based approach, it would not only be permissible to deny rights to beings who lack the relevant capacities and interests, but *obligatory*. This realization has left some Meritocrats 'profoundly uncomfortable'.[120] As McMahan notes,

> it would be dangerously invidious to give public expression to a view that accords a higher degree of moral inviolability to people with higher psychological capacities or a worthier moral nature. Even if such a view were true, it is virtually certain that if it were widely espoused and recognised as

[117] See also Ngaire Naffine, *Law's Meaning of Life: Philosophy, Religion, Darwin and the Legal Person* (Hart Publishing 2009) 124.

[118] See on the importance of this idea Andrea Sangiovanni, *Humanity Without Dignity: Moral Equality, Respect, and Human Rights* (Harvard University Press 2017) 3.

[119] Laurence H Tribe, 'Ten Lessons Our Constitutional Experience Can Teach Us About the Puzzle of Animal Rights: The Work of Steven M Wise' (2001) 7 Animal Law 1, 7.

[120] See McMahan, 'Challenges to Human Equality' (n 54) 104.

true, it would then be distorted or otherwise abused in efforts to justify the unjustifiable.[121]

The Meritocracy's *Externalism*, in other words, opens the floodgates for a (renewed) division of the human species into individuals, or groups of individuals, who deserve more and stronger rights than others. Tribe is therefore right when he warns that those I call Meritocrats 'are on an awfully steep and slippery slope that we would do well to avoid'.[122] Because of Meritocracy's *Gradualism*, we would have to decide not only about the rights of those humans who entirely lack the capacities necessary for the possession of certain fundamental rights, but, as he warns, also 'about people who are three-quarters of the way to such a condition. I needn't spell it all out, but the possibilities are genocidal and horrific and reminiscent of slavery and of the holocaust.'[123]

4.3 Critical disability studies and the problem of the Meritocracy

This problem of the Meritocracy is also echoed in critical disability studies. Taking aim at Meritocratic thinkers such as Singer and McMahan, some critical disability scholars have developed powerful critiques of the ableist logic that they have identified in this type of animal rights work.[124] Many of their criticisms can be applied not only to Singer's and McMahan's accounts, but to the Meritocracy more generally. I will focus on three prongs of their critique that are particularly relevant for our discussion of the Meritocracy's shortcomings.

First, critical disability scholars have taken issue with the way in which animal rights scholars and others *conceptualize humans with disabilities*: namely, as beings who have certain essential and self-evident characteristics. When Meritocrats talk about humans with disabilities, the complaint goes, these humans are seen as having relatively static characteristics that can be

[121] ibid.
[122] Tribe, 'Ten Lessons' (n 119) 7.
[123] ibid.
[124] Like these scholars, I consider Singer and McMahan to be proponents of 'animal rights' in the broad sense, and more specifically the Meritocratic conception of fundamental rights. This is despite the fact that, as consequentialists, they do not endorse rights in the same way as deontologists do. However, Singer himself has used the term 'rights' as a 'convenient political shorthand': see Singer, *Animal Liberation: A New Ethics for Our Treatment of Animals* (n 26) 8. He has also employed the concept of moral rights in the context of the great ape project: Peter Singer and Paola Cavalieri, 'A Declaration on Great Apes' in Peter Singer and Paola Cavalieri (eds), *The Great Ape Project: Equality Beyond Humanity* (St Martin's Press 1993) 4. For a similarly flexible use of the term 'rights' in McMahan, see eg Jeff McMahan, *The Ethics of Killing: Problems at the Margins of Life* (Oxford University Press 2002) 420.

described using abstract categories such as 'severely disabled person' or 'mentally retarded persons'.[125] This approach is seen as deficient, first of all, because it fails to give a voice to the affected people themselves.[126] For example, rather than allowing an affected person to decide for themselves whether they have an interest in continued existence, it is assumed that, simply because they appear to meet an abstract definition of severe mental disability, they lack the ability to plan for the future and therefore lack an interest in continued existence. Second, the view that humans with disabilities have essential and static characteristics is often based on a medical model of disability, which assumes that disability is an empirically definable trait. According to critical disability scholars, one problem with this model is that it tries to understand disabled persons 'without reference to any historical, political, or social factors that might affect the nature or status of this group of individuals', as Licia Carlson notes.[127] In other words, when animal rights proponents argue that humans with disabilities lack certain characteristics and interests, they run the risk of ignoring the socially contingent—and, according to many, socially constructed—nature of disability. This is particularly dangerous for Meritocrats who, as we saw, make a person's *Merit* of a particular right dependent on that person's characteristics and interests. Medical science has 'repeatedly proven to be extremely bad'[128] at identifying the characteristics and interests of persons with disabilities, as Sunaura Taylor has pointed out. But, further, even if it had a better track record, viewing disability through a medical prism can be problematic because it overlooks disability's socially contingent nature. This means concretely that Meritocrats risk regarding the absence of a particular characteristic or interest in a disabled person as being due to that person's essential nature, rather than being caused by social factors that can be changed. To take a simple example, on the medical model, the fact that a blind person cannot read voting materials could be misinterpreted as suggesting that they lack the ability for and interest in political participation—rather than as showing that society has failed to make voting materials universally accessible, such as by providing materials printed in braille.

Second, and relatedly, when Meritocrats view humans with disabilities through the medical prism, they *reinforce the perception that these human beings are 'abnormal'*. As Taylor argues, on the medical model, disability is 'a negative,

[125] Licia Carlson, *Faces of Intellectual Disability: Philosophical Reflections* (Indiana University Press 2010) 10–11, 142.
[126] See Sunaura Taylor, *Beasts of Burden: Animal and Disability Liberation* (The New Press 2017) 129.
[127] Carlson, *Faces of Intellectual Disability* (n 125) 11.
[128] Taylor, *Beasts of Burden* (n 126) 129.

a biological drawback that needs intervention and should be avoided'.[129] In other words, humans with disabilities tend not only to be seen as different, but as being something lesser: they are not 'normal' human beings, but beings with fewer and weaker interests. Take Singer, for example, who claimed that it would be 'flying in the face of reality to deny that, on average' disabled people have lives that 'are less worth living than the lives of people who are not disabled'.[130] Critical disability scholars resist the notion that disabled lives are less worth living than non-disabled lives.[131] As Carlson warns, once disability is viewed as something 'objectively abnormal', it justifies practices 'ranging from involuntary sterilization, institutionalization, and forced rehabilitation to social marginalization, euthanasia, and "mercy killing"'.[132] But there is also the subtler issue of disregarding disabled persons' unique characteristics and ways of perceiving the world. For example, scholars in the field have developed the concept of 'crip time' to describe the fact that persons with disabilities live at different speeds and may therefore experience time itself differently than other persons.[133] Taylor invokes this point to challenge Singer's and others' argument that, because some disabled persons lack the ability to make plans for the future in the way neurotypical humans do, they must therefore also lack an interest in continued existence.[134] The broader point critical disability scholars like her are making here is that it is dangerous to assume that, simply because humans with disabilities are different, they cannot live lives that are just as meaningful as the lives of non-disabled humans.[135]

Finally, Meritocratic approaches are criticized for *'animalising'*[136] *humans with disabilities*. The concern here is that Meritocrats—in their attempts to break down boundaries between humans and animals that they regard as preventing animals from getting the rights they deserve—bring human beings, especially those with disabilities, closer to animals. According to some critical disability scholars, this is problematic for at least two reasons. First, it ignores crucial differences between disabled humans and animals and the different forms of abuse they are subjected to.[137] Second, they argue that it marginalizes disabled persons, or rather reinforces their existing marginalization. As Carlson puts it, 'in their close association with animals, [humans with

[129] ibid.
[130] Singer, *Practical Ethics* (n 66) 188.
[131] See eg Taylor, *Beasts of Burden* (n 126) 139.
[132] Carlson, *Faces of Intellectual Disability* (n 125) 5.
[133] See eg Alison Kafer, *Feminist, Queer, Crip* (Indiana University Press 2013) 25–46.
[134] Taylor, *Beasts of Burden* (n 126) 131–32.
[135] See ibid 135–36.
[136] Carlson, *Faces of Intellectual Disability* (n 125) 145 (emphasis in original).
[137] ibid 149.

disabilities] are presented as only *marginally human*, reduced to bare fellow-species status, thus placed not only at the margins of the moral community but at the margins of humanity itself'.[138] Paul Spicker goes as far as stating that 'the belief that mentally handicapped people are animals is at the root of many of the abuses they have suffered'.[139] In a critique of the Great Ape Project, which advocates fundamental rights for great apes, Nora Ellen Groce and Jonathan Marks locate the problem with Meritocratic approaches in the fact that comparison between humans and animals is a 'two-way street': 'If animals are significantly like disabled humans, then disabled humans are like animals'.[140] This, they believe, takes us back to the idea of *scala naturae*, that is, the view that there is a natural hierarchy in nature, which we encountered in Chapter 2. According to Groce and Marks, this idea has served as a justification for depriving vulnerable human beings who are placed at the bottom of the ladder of rights that those at the top possess.[141]

For many critical disability scholars, then, Meritocratic theories should be rejected. In their view, Meritocrats' focus on *Gradualism* and individual *Merit* is not just a harmless attempt to protect animals. Rather, it can have 'bone-chilling'[142] implications for the most vulnerable human beings. By *grounding* rights in individuals' *Merit*, one risks giving weaker protection to humans with disabilities because of an insufficient understanding and appreciation of their capacities and interests, thus exposing them to 'continued exploitation' and even 'death'.[143] And, just as dangerously, even when one understands a person's interests, there is the risk that *Gradualism* is misappropriated to justify immoral policies. 'As history shows', Groce and Marks remind us, 'when translated into the political arena, scientific-sounding arguments often serve as rationalisations for doing harm to the most vulnerable elements of society'.[144] For this reason, Groce, Marks, and other scholars have cautioned against 'draw[ing] connections between nonhuman animals and persons with intellectual disabilities'.[145] In the words of the disability rights activist Harriet McBride

[138] ibid 138 (emphasis in original).

[139] Paul Spicker, 'Mental Handicap and Citizenship' (1990) 7 Journal of Applied Philosophy 139, 142. Spicker is drawing on Wolf Wolfensberger, *The Principle of Normalization in Human Services* (National Institute on Mental Retardation 1972).

[140] Nora Ellen Groce and Jonathan Marks, 'The Great Ape Project and Disability Rights: Ominous Undercurrents of Eugenics in Action' (2001) 102 American Anthropologist 818, 819.

[141] ibid.

[142] Harriet McBryde Johnson, 'Unspeakable Conversations' *The New York Times* (16 February 2003) <https://www.nytimes.com/2003/02/16/magazine/unspeakable-conversations.html> accessed 11 June 2023.

[143] Taylor, *Beasts of Burden* (n 126) 146.

[144] Groce and Marks, 'The Great Ape Project and Disability Rights' (n 140) 821.

[145] Carlson, *Faces of Intellectual Disability* (n 125) 145.

Johnson, to these thinkers, animal rights proponents' 'call to get past species seems a luxury way beyond . . . reach'.[146]

Many critical disability scholars not only resist Meritocratic theories. They also actively defend Aristocratic arguments to prevent what they view as the dangerous animalization of human beings caused by the Meritocracy. In particular, many think that only by drawing a sharp line between humans and nonhumans can vulnerable human beings be protected. Temple Grandin, an animal welfare advocate and autism rights activist, has been one of the most explicit champions of this strategy. According to her, the only way to counter Meritocratic threats to vulnerable human beings' rights is to decide that 'human life must be preserved because human life is precious. It has higher moral value because it is our own species.'[147]

It is important to note that not all critical disability scholars agree that we should endorse speciesism or some other form of human exceptionalism. For instance, Taylor herself argues that 'we cannot have disability liberation without animal liberation—they are intimately tied together'[148] because they are connected forms of oppression. In a similar vein, Maneesha Deckha has proposed that putting a 'positive spin' on animalization by 'affirming human proximity and kinship to animals'[149] is the best way forward. Equally, Meritocratic conceptions need not necessarily fall afoul of all the issues critical disability scholars identify in works such as Singer's or McMahan's. For example, if Meritocrats need to go beyond medical assessments of a person's abilities to adequately assess their *Merit*, then they should do so. However, even more nuanced and socially attuned Meritocratic approaches will face the problem that they ultimately require giving fewer and weaker rights to those with fewer and weaker interests. That this may negatively impact humans with disabilities is a necessary by-product of the Meritocratic fundamental rights conception.

Of course, neither this downside of the Meritocracy, nor the remedies people like Grandin have proposed to it, are new. As we saw in Chapter 2, the problematic consequences which critical disability scholars, Grandin, Tribe, and others describe are simply the consequences which the Meritocrats have inherited from the Enlightenment naturalists who adopted monistic accounts of nature that emphasized gradation and thereby eroded the uniqueness and equality of

[146] Johnson, 'Unspeakable Conversations' (n 142).

[147] Grandin Temple, 'Avoid Being Abstract When Making Policies on the Welfare of Animals' in Marianne DeKoven and Michael Lundblad (eds), *Species Matters: Humane Advocacy and Cultural Theory* (Columbia University Press 2011) 214.

[148] Taylor, *Beasts of Burden* (n 126) 146.

[149] Maneesha Deckha, 'Animalization and Dehumanization Concerns: Another Psychological Barrier to Animal Law Reform' (2023) 2 Psychology of Human-Animal Intergroup Relations 1, 4.

human beings.[150] Recall for instance Delamétherie's treatise of 1802, in which he established a hierarchy of human beings, segregating humans into different classes, depending on their characteristics. This was exactly what egalitarians were criticizing about the naturalists. The slippery slope that Tribe and others flag is the same which Salaville warned us about in his 1805 essay. As Salaville urged, to avoid the slope, we need to '*admit* that man and animals differ by their respective nature and that this difference authorises and makes legitimate with respect to them what it prohibits with respect to us'.[151] Put in the language adopted in this book, to protect the equality of all human beings, we need to resort to *founding* humans' special rank and rights independently of their individual capacities and interests.[152] Because *Differential Consideration* and *grounding* work in concert, we can prevent one only by halting the other.

5 Conclusion

This chapter has examined the Meritocratic conception of fundamental rights, which forms the second conception on the spectrum of fundamental rights approaches. As I have shown, Meritocrats conceive of animals as *deserving* of rights if they possess the relevant characteristics and interests which *ground* these rights. Drawing on Vlastos's account of the 'M-system' and Delamétherie's naturalist approach, I have analysed the two characteristic features of the Meritocratic conception. First, it follows *Differential Consideration*, which was shown to mean: that Meritocrats endorse the idea of basing rights on an individual's desert rather than their birth (*Merit*); that they reject the equality of rights in favour of a differentiated approach (*Gradualism*); and that they include nonhuman beings in the category of fundamental rights-holders (*Inclusivity*). In contrast to the Aristocracy, the Meritocracy was thus shown to reject egalitarian ideas in favour of differential ideas, as was the case with the naturalist stream on which it is based. Second, Meritocrats adopt an *Externalist* approach. *Externalism*'s ability to *ground* rights in natural facts was shown to be its strength. At the same time, this also turned out to be an important

[150] See also Ann Thomson, 'Diderot, le matérialisme et la division de l'espèce humaine' (1999) 26 Recherches sur Diderot et sur l'Encyclopédie 197.

[151] Jean-Baptiste Salaville, *De l'homme et des animaux* (Ch Crapelet 1805) 51 (emphasis added; my translation).

[152] See also Mulgan, 'The Ethics of Killing: Problems at the Margins of Life by Jeff McMahan' (n 52) 457.

weakness, yielding the 'shocking'[153] result of promoting different categories of rights-holders.

As we saw, not only utilitarian theories like Singer's and McMahan's[154] but also some rights-based theories such as Delamétherie's are Meritocratic. However, as I noted, there is an emerging strand of sentientist rights theories, which embrace egalitarianism to a greater degree than other Meritocratic theories. Do these sentientist rights theories avoid the above-mentioned problems? And are these theories nevertheless Meritocratic? Or do they represent a third and more attractive conception, one that perhaps even lies outside the spectrum? It is to these questions that we turn in the next chapter.

[153] Alice Crary, *Inside Ethics: On the Demands of Moral Thought* (Harvard University Press 2016) 125.
[154] On McMahan's less straightforwardly utilitarian, Two-Tiered Account, see Chapter 7, Section 1.

5

Sentientist Rights: A Third Conception?

1 Introduction

Chapters 3 and 4 have portrayed the Aristocratic and Meritocratic conceptions of fundamental rights, two antithetical ideal-types located on opposite ends of the spectrum of fundamental rights conceptions. As I will show in the following chapters, important practical lessons can be drawn from the fact that Aristocratic and Meritocratic accounts have opposing strengths and weaknesses. Before I turn to these lessons, however, I need to address whether alternative fundamental rights approaches are available that avoid some, or potentially all of the problems faced by Aristocratic and Meritocratic accounts.

In this chapter, I will focus on one approach that has gained particular traction in animal rights scholarship in the recent past. The approach I have in mind is the sentience-based, or 'sentientist', rights approach.[1] Theories following this approach vary in their nature and focus.[2] For example, on Martha Nussbaum's capabilities approach, sentience is a necessary condition for a being to possess the entitlements required to flourish as a member of their species.[3] According to Gary Francione, sentience gives animals a right not to be property,[4] as well as a right to life.[5] Jane Kotzmann argues that sentience and intrinsic value serve as pluralistic bases for legal animal rights and equality.[6] And on Alasdair Cochrane's account, sentience confers equal moral value (or worth) and rights

[1] I am grateful to an anonymous reviewer for encouraging me to address the sentientist approach separately. Note, however, that the sentientist approach is not the only one available: see eg for a leading vulnerability-based approach Maneesha Deckha, *Animals as Legal Beings: Contesting Anthropocentric Legal Orders* (University of Toronto Press 2021). For a care-ethics-based approach see Carol J Adams, *The Sexual Politics of Meat: A Feminist-Vegetarian Critical Theory* (Bloomsbury 1990).

[2] See eg Sue Donaldson and Will Kymlicka, *Zoopolis: A Political Theory of Animal Rights* (Oxford University Press 2011) 24–25 (who develop a group-differentiated rights approach on sentience); Saskia Stucki, *One Rights: Human and Animal Rights in the Anthropocene* (Springer 2023) 3 (who bases her proposal for One Rights on sentience, but without explicitly addressing the question of equality).

[3] Martha C Nussbaum, *Justice for Animals: Our Collective Responsibility* (Simon & Schuster 2022) 119.

[4] Gary L Francione, *Animals, Property, and the Law* (Temple University Press 1995) 14.

[5] Gary L Francione, *Why Veganism Matters: The Moral Value of Animals* (Columbia University Press 2020) 80–82.

[6] Jane Kotzmann, 'Sentience and Intrinsic Worth as a Pluralist Foundation for Fundamental Animal Rights' (2023) 43(2) Oxford Journal of Legal Studies 405, 425.

More Equal Than Others. Raffael N Fasel, Oxford University Press. © Raffael N Fasel 2024.
DOI: 10.1093/oso/9780198907435.003.0005

on all sentient beings.[7] Some of these accounts were explicitly developed as a response to the comparatively weak protections that marginalized beings have in utilitarian Meritocratic theories such as Peter Singer's, but also in deontological animal rights accounts such as Tom Regan's.[8] Two central features unite sentientist rights accounts: first, they argue that nonhuman animals should have certain fundamental moral and/or legal rights in virtue of their sentience; and, second, they hold that fundamental rights-holders have equal status.

The existence of the sentientist rights approach appears to pose a particular problem for proponents of the Meritocracy. This is because the sentientist rights approach seems to offer an attractive alternative for animal rights advocates who want to argue for animal rights without incurring the costs of the Meritocracy. As we saw in the previous chapter, a key problem with Meritocratic accounts such as Singer's and Jeff McMahan's is that they threaten to introduce moral hierarchies between different beings, undermining the equal status and rights of vulnerable human beings. By arguing for both animal rights and equal status, the sentientist rights approach would thus appear to share in the strength of the Meritocracy, but without suffering from its weakness. As such, the sentientist rights approach would seem to have a promising answer for generations of Aristocrats who worried about the impact of extending rights to animals on human rights and equality. As we saw in Chapter 2, the animal rights sceptic Jean-Baptiste Salaville was one of the first to throw down the gauntlet and argue that it is impossible to grant rights to animals without automatically eroding the status and rights of human beings.[9] This raises the question: Have sentientist rights theorists managed to do the 'impossible' by meeting what we might call *Salaville's Challenge*—that is, developing a fundamental rights approach that extends fundamental rights to animals in a way that does not undermine the high status and equal rights of humans—and that is therefore acceptable to Aristocratic human rights proponents? And, if so, does this mean that the sentientist rights approach is a third fundamental rights conception—one that is not Meritocratic, and more attractive than the Meritocracy?

[7] Alasdair Cochrane, *Sentientist Politics: A Theory of Global Inter-Species Justice* (Oxford University Press 2018) 14.

[8] Tom Regan, *The Case for Animal Rights* (University of California Press 1983). See for a criticism of the exclusionary implications of Regan's subject-of-a-life criterion: Mary Anne Warren, *Moral Status: Obligations to Persons and Other Living Things* (Oxford University Press 2000) 106.

[9] Jean-Baptiste Salaville, *De l'homme et des animaux* (Ch Crapelet 1805) 53. For a contemporary version of the same worry, see eg Richard L Cupp, 'Cognitively Impaired Humans, Intelligent Animals, and Legal Personhood', *Pepperdine University Legal Studies Research Paper No 12* (2016) 501 <http://papers.ssrn.com/abstract=2775288> accessed 11 June 2023.

To answer these questions, we first need to examine whether the sentientist rights approach is indeed a third conception or whether it is in fact a Meritocratic approach. As I will argue, although the sentientist rights approach is *less* Meritocratic than purer instantiations of the Meritocracy such as Singer's and McMahan's theories, it nevertheless bears characteristic marks of the Meritocracy. Specifically, it is *Externalist* and at least partially adopts *Differential Consideration*. As I will show, even if the sentientist rights approach was considered not to be Meritocratic but a separate conception of rights, it comes with its own problems. Although it is in some respects more attractive than the Meritocracy, it does not meet *Salaville's Challenge*. Aristocrats would reject the sentientist rights approach because sentience is probably not an either-or matter but a continuum (I call this the *Spectrum Problem*), and because the sentientist approach in principle allows for some humans to have no rights, and for animals' rights to outweigh humans' rights (I call this the *Indifference Problem*).

To make my case, I will focus on what I take to be the most robust and fully developed sentientist rights approach: Alasdair Cochrane's. Cochrane's theory is of particular interest to us because it is based on an attractive theory of equality, which Cochrane calls 'sentient equality'.[10] In a nutshell, for Cochrane, all sentient beings have equal moral worth. This equality is grounded in sentient beings' possession of interests, which he regards as an either-or matter. I do not have the space to analyse how well other sentientist rights theories defend the idea of equal rights, but Cochrane's can serve as a good test case for whether such theories can meet *Salaville's Challenge* and assuage Aristocrats. For if Cochrane's sophisticated theory cannot meet *Salaville's Challenge*, then we have some reason to be pessimistic that others can.

The chapter is structured as follows. Section 2 begins by outlining Cochrane's sentientist rights approach, with a particular focus on his theory of sentient equality, and I will show how that theory avoids some of the problems of other Meritocratic approaches. Section 3 then considers whether Cochrane's account is representative of a third conception of rights, or whether, as I will argue, it is in fact a Meritocratic account. I will then argue that even if we consider Cochrane's and other sentientist rights theories as being representative of a third conception that is not Meritocratic, they still face problems that would make them unpalatable to Aristocrats. Focusing in particular on the *Spectrum Problem* (Section 4) and the *Indifference Problem* (Section 5), I will show that

[10] Cochrane, *Sentientist Politics: A Theory of Global Inter-Species Justice* (n 7) 14.

the sentientist rights approach does not meet *Salaville's Challenge*. A conclusion will recapitulate the chapter's main insights.

2 Sentient equality: a beginner's guide

The aim of Cochrane's 2018 book *Sentientist Politics: A Theory of Global Inter-Species Justice*, which has already become a classic in the field, is to imagine and defend a political order that takes the interests of all sentient creatures seriously. A central element in Cochrane's theory is the argument that all sentient individuals have ultimate and equal intrinsic moral worth, called 'sentient equality'.[11] To understand the problems of sentientist rights accounts, it is helpful to first get a better sense of what sentient equality is and does.

Building on Singer's work, Cochrane argues that sentience, which he defines as 'the capacity for conscious experience',[12] gives a being intrinsic moral worth. This is because Cochrane views sentience as a necessary and sufficient condition for having interests. Only sentient beings matter 'for their own sakes',[13] and not just because humans have an instrumental interest in them. According to him, sentient beings differ in this crucial respect from plants and inanimate objects such as bikes. For while plants can flourish if they are watered and bikes are better bikes if they are well-oiled, Cochrane argues that plants and bikes cannot *themselves* be benefitted by these actions because they lack inherent interests.[14]

Having established that animals have inherent moral worth, the question Cochrane then addresses is *how much* worth they have. Specifically, he asks whether there are any good reasons for the traditional position that humans have more moral worth than nonhuman animals. After rejecting invocations of the biological criterion of membership in the species *Homo sapiens*, on the grounds that such a criterion is speciesist, he addresses the (*Internalist*) view that we can simply *assume* that only humans have a high and equal status. According to him, this view, too, is deficient, among other reasons because the assumption of human equality has not been a historical constant and needs a more solid foundation.[15]

[11] ibid.
[12] ibid 15.
[13] ibid (emphasis removed).
[14] ibid 17.
[15] ibid 19.

Cochrane thinks we can find such a foundation in empirical characteristics. However, not just any characteristic will do. He considers and rejects the characteristic of moral personhood on the ground that it excludes many humans, or that it can only accommodate them by relying on strained normality and potentiality claims.[16] Cochrane also rejects two-tiered views of Meritocrats like Jeff McMahan who argue that while all sentient beings have some moral worth, sentient beings who are *persons* have more moral worth.[17] Importantly for our purposes, Cochrane rejects this approach by arguing that any attempt at grounding moral worth in 'personhood, or the possession of other complex cognitive capacities' is problematic because 'the simple fact is that these capacities are not all or nothing, but come in degrees'.[18]

Cochrane anticipates a rejoinder that even capacities that come in degrees could serve to ground equal moral worth as long as they are understood as 'range properties'—a notion we have already encountered in the previous chapter. John Rawls, who proposed this solution to reconcile egalitarianism with natural capacities, gives the following illustration of a range property:

> [T]he property of being in the interior of the unit circle is a range property of points in the plane. All points inside this circle have this property although their coordinates vary within a certain range. And they equally have this property, since no point interior to a circle is more or less interior to it than any other interior point.[19]

Cochrane is sceptical of the range property approach because it is 'stipulative and seems to evade rather than confront the problem at hand: for if capacities for personhood count morally, then why not grant more moral worth for more capacities?'.[20] According to him, the logical conclusion of accounts that base moral worth in gradual characteristics such as personhood is that they would yield not only a two-tiered account of moral worth, but 'a highly stratified and hierarchical account'.[21] As he emphasizes, in such an account, the most vulnerable in society—infants, humans with serious disabilities, and so on—would be placed on the lowest rungs, thus having less moral worth than others.

16 ibid 20–21.
17 I say more about McMahan's 'Two-Tiered Account' in Chapter 7, Section 1.
18 Cochrane, *Sentientist Politics: A Theory of Global Inter-Species Justice* (n 7) 22.
19 John Rawls, *A Theory of Justice* (Harvard University Press 1971) 508.
20 Cochrane, *Sentientist Politics: A Theory of Global Inter-Species Justice* (n 7) 22.
21 ibid 23.

Cochrane believes that the characteristic of sentience, that is, the possession of interests, does not run into these problems. '[U]nlike the capacities for personhood or other characteristics based on cognitive complexity', he holds, 'the possession of interests is "binary". That is to say, an individual either possesses interests or does not, making it straightforward to explain why the moral worth of humans does not come in degrees.'[22] To be sure, Cochrane acknowledges that there is some uncertainty as to when sentience begins in foetuses and whether certain types of animals, such as insects, qualify as sentient. Furthermore, not every sentient being has the same interests: 'individuals will often have different *types* and *numbers* of interests; and even when individuals have the same interest, it may vary in *strength* and *complexity*.'[23] However, he argues, this does not stand in the way of a fundamental equality between sentient beings:

> [I]t is impossible for any individual to be more or less *in possession of interests*: an individual either has them, or does not. So grounding moral worth in the possession of interests does conform to aspects of common sense: it is by far the most compelling ground for human equality.[24]

This account of sentient equality is in tune with common sense, Cochrane contends, because it does not require treating all sentient beings alike. Drawing on the distinction between equal treatment and treatment as an equal (also called 'equal concern'), which I discussed in Chapter 4, he emphasizes that sentient equality only requires treating sentient beings as equals, that is, giving them equal concern for interests that are alike. However, it does not require treating all sentient beings identically. For instance, he finds that the toothache of a human being does not necessarily require the same response as the toothache of a rat because this would be 'wildly impractical and burdensome'.[25]

Having established what sentient quality *is*, we can now turn to what it *does* in Cochrane's account. Sentient equality plays a key role because it serves as the foundation for his theory of rights for all sentient animals. Cochrane criticizes utilitarian Meritocrats such as Singer on the ground that their embrace of the principle of *Equal Consideration* does not lead them to impose constraints on what can be done to individuals based on their own sakes, rather than the

22 ibid 24.
23 ibid (emphasis in original).
24 ibid (emphasis in original).
25 ibid 24–25.

sake of overall utility. According to Cochrane, the sentientist rights approach avoids this problem.[26] On Cochrane's own theory, promoting animals' interests matters not because it contributes to overall utility, but because it promotes the well-being of individuals with equal inherent moral worth. Employing a Razian interest-based account of rights (discussed in the previous chapter), Cochrane holds that, as long as interests are all things considered sufficiently important to impose duties on others, they give rise to rights possessed by the holders of those interests. According to him, among the rights that all animals possess at least *prima facie* are the right to life and the right not to be made to suffer.[27] Because these rights are to him best viewed not as being based on humanity, but on sentience, Cochrane proposes that we should call them 'sentient rights' rather than 'human rights'.[28]

Finally, in his theory, sentient equality is not only the basis for individuals' entitlement to equal concern and respect for their rights, but it also serves as the foundation for reordering politics more generally—a point that he explores throughout the book. As he notes,

> the equal moral worth of sentient creatures and the set of sentient rights that they entail ought to replicate and replace the role of human equality and human rights when thinking about politics. In other words, I claim that 'sentient equality' and 'sentient rights' provide the *justification* of our political institutions, and should serve to *shape* and *constrain* their design.[29]

For those who want ethics, politics, and law to be more accommodating of animals' interests, Cochrane's theory of sentient equality is attractive for obvious reasons. But it also has selling points for Aristocratic human rights proponents who are sceptical of animal rights. One strong suit that stands out is that, by grounding animal rights in what Cochrane views as the binary characteristic of sentience, his theory refuses to say that some animals can have more moral worth than some humans. For instance, in contrast to McMahan's and Singer's Meritocratic theories, Cochrane's account does not give more moral worth to socially intelligent animals such as chimpanzees, who may possess moral personhood, than to humans with severe mental disabilities who are

[26] ibid 26.
[27] ibid 27–29.
[28] ibid 30.
[29] ibid (emphasis in original).

thought to lack moral personhood.[30] As such, Cochrane's theory of sentient equality closes at least one avenue that could lead to vulnerable human beings being given lower moral worth.

But could Cochrane's theory be criticized by Aristocrats for adopting a type of rights differentialism? After all, it grants different sentient beings different rights to the extent that they possess different interests. For instance, a being with an interest in family life would potentially qualify for a right to family life, whereas another being (eg a solitary animal) who does not have that interest would not get that right. It could be argued that this would be anathema to Aristocratic human rights thinkers because it imperils the principle of the indivisibility of human rights, which I described in Chapter 3. According to this principle, human beings have—at least conditionally—all human rights. That is, human rights are wholesale. A retail approach like Cochrane's would seem to contradict this principle.

Adherents of sentientist rights accounts could respond to this objection by drawing attention to the ways in which human rights practice already seems to fall short of the Aristocratic ideal of indivisibility. For all intents and purposes, they might argue, human rights practice has adopted the retail approach. Consider, for example, international treaties such as the Convention on the Rights of the Child (CRC).[31] This Convention protects rights that factually belong only to a specific group of humans: children. Article 9 CRC for instance provides for children's right not to be separated from their parents against their will. Of course, it is theoretically possible to argue, as strict Aristocrats would, that an adult human being possesses the right not to be separated from her parents, and that she simply currently fails to meet the conditions of being a child required to exercise this right. However, the response would go, such an argument is stilted and would make little difference on the ground. For all practical purposes, children, women, men, and other groups of human beings have at least partially different rights. The differentialism of Cochrane's theory could therefore hardly be accused of undermining a vital principle of human rights law. However, as we will see in Sections 4 and 5, this does not mean that Cochrane's theory can fully assuage Aristocrats and meet *Salaville's Challenge*.

[30] In Singer's case, the claim is that it is morally worse to take the life of a person than it is to take that of a non-person: Peter Singer, *Practical Ethics* (3rd edn, Cambridge University Press 2011) 80.

[31] Convention on the Rights of the Child (1989, CRC) <https://www.ohchr.org/en/professionalinterest/pages/crc.aspx> accessed 11 June 2023.

3 Is the sentientist rights approach Meritocratic?

Before I discuss why sentientist rights theories like Cochrane's struggle to respond to *Salaville's Challenge*, it is worth considering whether a sentientist rights approach like Cochrane's is a third conception that stands next to or even outside the Aristocratic and Meritocratic fundamental rights conceptions, or whether it is an instantiation of the Meritocracy. As I argue in this section, Cochrane's sentientist rights approach differs from clear-cut instantiations of the Meritocracy like Singer's and McMahan's accounts. Above all, it is closer to the Aristocracy than these accounts because it denies that status can be *Gradualist*. However, like Meritocratic accounts, Cochrane's sentientist rights theory is *Externalist* and at least partly displays the feature of *Differential Consideration*. Hence, the sentientist rights approach does not escape the fundamental rights spectrum. Albeit a less pure instance than accounts like Singer's and McMahan's, it, too, is a Meritocratic theory.

Before unpacking this argument, let us briefly refresh our memory of the nature of the spectrum of fundamental rights conceptions and when it is appropriate to call a theory 'Meritocratic' or 'Aristocratic'. As will be recalled from the Introduction, I propose that individual fundamental rights accounts can be located on the spectrum of fundamental rights conceptions, somewhere between its Aristocratic and Meritocratic ends. The more an account matches the features of *Equal Consideration* and *Internalism*, the more it is an instantiation of the ideal-type of the Aristocracy, and the more it approximates *Differential Consideration* and *Externalism*, the more it is an instance of the Meritocracy. As I noted, while some accounts approximate the ideal-types more than other accounts, there are likely no accounts that are perfect instantiations of either the Aristocracy or Meritocracy. Because we are therefore necessarily dealing with a 'more or less', I proposed that there is a threshold of sufficient compliance with an ideal-type's features that, if met by an account, warrants calling that account a 'Meritocratic' or 'Aristocratic' account. The judgement of where that threshold lies and whether an account meets it necessarily involves some evaluation. The question for us, then, is whether the sentientist rights approach can be said to possess the Meritocracy's features to a sufficient extent as to be categorized as a 'Meritocratic' account. And, if it turns out not to be Meritocratic, is it at least on the spectrum of fundamental rights conceptions? Or does it fall outside of it?

There are compelling reasons for categorizing Cochrane's sentientist rights theory as Meritocratic. Let us start with its *Externalism*. As I explained in Chapter 4, *Externalism* is one of the two characteristic features of the

Meritocracy. *Externalists* reject *Internalism*, favoured by Aristocrats, which *founds* human rights and basic equality in normative decisions, stories, and interpretations. According to *Externalists*, *Internalism* is problematic because it fails to provide a secure and non-arbitrary basis for rights. *Externalism* avoids these problems by *grounding* rights in empirical facts about individuals. These facts include a being's capacities, such as their sentience, agency, or sociability, as well as the interests arising out of these capacities, such as the interest not to suffer, to have autonomy, or to have social contacts. As I discussed in Chapter 4, interests are at least partly factual and non-normative.

Cochrane's theory is plainly *Externalist*. As we saw above, it is firmly anchored in characteristics and interests: according to Cochrane, the characteristic of sentience is a necessary and sufficient condition for possessing interests. Employing a Razian interest-based approach to rights, Cochrane argues that a sentient being's rights are grounded in their interests. That Cochrane's theory is *Externalist* becomes even more evident if we consider that, as we saw above, he explicitly rejects *Internalist* accounts, which maintain that we can simply claim that humans are equal. As Cochrane contends, 'the equal moral worth of humans cannot simply be *assumed*; instead, a robust defence of human equality needs to be grounded in reasons, such as the identification of some positive *characteristic* which humans share'.[32] There is therefore no doubt that, at least in this respect, Cochrane joins the ranks of Meritocratic theories such as McMahan's and Singer's, which are also *Externalist* and ground rights in capacities and interests.[33]

Turning now to *Differential Consideration*, Cochrane's sentientist rights theory manifests this feature at least to some degree. As will be recalled from Chapter 4, *Differential Consideration* is the other characteristic feature of the Meritocracy and consists of three sub-elements: rights are grounded in individuals' possession of certain physical capacities, rather than their birth into a particular species (*Merit*); equality is rejected in favour of a *Gradualist* approach to distributing rights (*Gradualism*); and any type of being is included in the category of rights-holders who deserves it (*Inclusivity*). Cochrane's theory exhibits the features of *Merit* and *Inclusivity* and, to a lesser degree, *Gradualism*.

That Cochrane's theory endorses *Merit* becomes clear from its *Externalist* approach. As we saw above, Cochrane not only rejects *Internalism* but also opposes the view that membership in the species *Homo sapiens* can serve as a

[32] Cochrane, *Sentientist Politics: A Theory of Global Inter-Species Justice* (n 7) 19 (emphasis changed).

[33] See Chapter 4, Section 4.3 (footnote 124) on the fact that, as consequentialists, Singer and McMahan do not endorse rights in the same way as deontological thinkers do, and on why we can nonetheless consider them as proponents of the Meritocratic conception of fundamental rights.

ground for rights. Drawing on Singer, Cochrane points out that making rights dependent on the species a being is 'born into' is 'speciesist'.[34] Cochrane's theory is therefore firmly wedded to the *Merit*-based view that it is an individual's characteristics and interests that should determine what rights they get, not their species membership.

Cochrane's endorsement of *Inclusivity* follows naturally from this. In his theory, any sentient being who possesses the relevant interests has a *prima facie* claim to rights protection, regardless of species. This is why he argues that human rights should be renamed 'sentient rights':[35] to exclude nonhuman sentient animals from rights-holdership simply because they are not human would be arbitrary, so humans need to make room for other sentient animals possessing an interest in rights protection.

The one feature of *Differential Consideration* that Cochrane's theory does not manifest, at least fully, is *Gradualism*. As we saw in Chapter 4, *Gradualism* has two aspects: it views rights as being *justified by merit* (meaning that only those who possess an interest that grounds a particular right can have the right the interest grounds) and *proportioned to merit* (meaning that those who possess the rights-grounding interest to a greater degree will have a stronger right). Cochrane's theory adopts both features, but does not draw the conclusion from it that status itself is gradual.

As we saw above, his account embraces the *justified-by-merit* view that rights are retail, not wholesale. This is why, on his theory, only children can have the right not to be separated from their parents against their will, provided by Article 9 CRC. This is because only children have the interest that grounds that right. Cochrane's theory also accepts that rights are *proportioned to merit*. As we will see in Section 5, Cochrane argues that a being such as a rat, who has a weaker interest in being alive than an adult human being, also has a weaker right to life than the human being.

However, while Cochrane thus applies *Gradualism* to the distribution of rights, he does not apply it to the question of status. Unlike Meritocratic *Gradualists*, he rejects the position that there is little to no room for a principle of equality that treats all interest-holders alike. As we saw above, Cochrane believes that equality is based on sentience and that sentience is a binary characteristic which a being either has or does not have. Because sentience is binary, it does not lend itself to *Gradualism* and a hierarchization of moral or legal status. In this respect, then, Cochrane's and other sentientist

[34] Cochrane, *Sentientist Politics: A Theory of Global Inter-Species Justice* (n 7) 19 (emphasis removed).
[35] ibid 30.

rights theories are decidedly un-Meritocratic. In Cochrane's theory, all sentient beings—regardless of whether they lack the same rights, or rights of the same strength[36]—have equal moral status (or worth). By adopting this idea of equal status, sentientist rights theories like Cochrane's depart from more extreme versions of the Meritocracy and move towards the Aristocracy and its feature of *Equal Consideration*.

However, it would be misguided to think that this makes these theories entirely un-Meritocratic. Considering that Cochrane's sentientist rights theory manifests all but one feature of the Meritocracy clearly, it can plausibly be classified as a Meritocratic theory. True, it is not as pure an instantiation of the Meritocracy as utilitarian theories like Singer's or McMahan's. But, as we saw, even a less pure instantiation of the Meritocracy can still be an instantiation of the Meritocracy.

Suppose, for the sake of argument, that I am wrong in classifying Cochrane's theory as Meritocratic. Does that mean that it automatically falls outside the spectrum of the Aristocracy and Meritocracy, and becomes its own, third conception? One reason speaking in favour of this view might be that the defence of equality that Cochrane puts forward seems quite unique. I noted above that, with its endorsement of the idea of equal moral status, Cochrane's theory approaches the Aristocracy's feature of *Equal Consideration*. While this statement is broadly true, it skated over two important aspects. First, Cochrane's theory rejects key elements of *Equal Consideration*, such as *Heredity* (the idea that humans possess a high status and rights simply in virtue of being born human) and *Exclusivity* (the exclusion of nonhumans from that rank and from rights). His theory also modifies *Equality* (the idea that all humans have equal rights) insofar as it opens equal status to all sentient beings, not just humans. Second, and more importantly, Cochrane's defence of the equality principle is *Externalist*, not *Internalist*. That is, Cochrane does not argue that equal worth is something we explain by drawing on normative decisions, stories, or interpretations. Rather, it is something we can ground in the fact that all sentient beings are equally in possession of interests.

Although notable, the first aspect (Cochrane's rejection of *Heredity* and *Exclusivity* and his modification of *Equality*) would simply be a reason for classifying his theory as a *less* Aristocratic theory than others, but not for viewing it as operating outside the fundamental rights spectrum. By contrast, the second aspect (Cochrane's *Externalist* grounding of equal status) would seem to make his approach special in that it introduces an idea, foreign to the

[36] ie even if they lack 'equal rights' as defined in Chapter 3, Section 3.

spectrum, that one can explain equality of status while employing a purely *Externalist* approach grounded in characteristics and interests. If this approach was successful, then we might have reason to classify Cochrane's theory—and potentially other sentientist rights theories—as a third conception operating outside the spectrum, rather than being located somewhere in-between the Meritocracy and Aristocracy.

As I will show in the next section, the problem with this conclusion is that Cochrane's claim that sentience serves as a binary ground for equal status is more problematic than appears at first sight. As I will argue, we have reason to believe that sentience is not, after all, a binary criterion, but one that comes in degrees. This means that while Cochrane and other sentientist rights theorists may still have a good justification for arguing for equal status (or worth), that argument is not *Externalist* but, to be successful, must be based on other, *Internalist* reasons. And, as such, even the ostensibly unique egalitarianism of Cochrane's theory can be captured using the terminology offered by the fundamental rights spectrum. Put differently, sentientist rights theories like Cochrane's are best placed not outside the spectrum, but somewhere closer to the middle of the spectrum.

4 More or less sentient: the *Spectrum Problem*

Assume that I am wrong that Cochrane's sentientist rights account is Meritocratic, and that I am also wrong that it does not escape the fundamental rights spectrum. Cochrane's sentientist rights account, as well as potentially other such accounts, would thus appear to represent an attractive third conception that avoids some of the shortcomings of the Meritocracy. Does this mean that a theory like Cochrane's can meet *Salaville's Challenge*, that is, present a fundamental rights account for animals that does not erode the high status and equal rights of humans? In other words, can Cochrane assuage Aristocratic human rights proponents?

As we saw in Section 2, Cochrane may believe that his theory can meet *Salaville's Challenge*, for he contended that 'the arguments which support the idea of equality for all sentient creatures are in fact in tune with, as opposed to in tension with, many people's understanding of common sense'.[37] In this section, I address the first respect in which his theory and, in particular, his account of sentient equality is not as compelling to human rights proponents

[37] Cochrane, *Sentientist Politics: A Theory of Global Inter-Species Justice* (n 7) 23.

as he seems to believe. This is because it faces the *Spectrum Problem*, that is, the problem that sentience may not be a binary property but may instead come in degrees. In other words, it is not clear that Cochrane's theory of sentient equality can establish equal moral worth on a stable foundation that is not susceptible to undermining the moral status and interests of vulnerable human beings, as Aristocrats would require. It is worth recalling here that the need to avoid gradation is paramount according to Aristocratic thinkers. As Anne Phillips has put it,

> when it comes to the equality I have represented as at the heart of the notion of the human, there is no room for gradations. We cannot have a continuum in which some of the lesser humans sheer off into being 'more equal' to some of the greater animals, and we cannot have some humans more equal than others. Where equality is concerned, there is no getting away from the boundary dilemma: we are either in or out.[38]

So, the question is whether the sentientist rights approach can meet this demanding standard of avoiding all continuums and gradations when it comes to equal status and rights. In my view, it cannot because it runs into the *Spectrum Problem*.

To understand this problem, recall Cochrane's arguments against the views of authors who ground equality in personhood and similar characteristics. Cochrane rejects these views on the basis that characteristics such as personhood, which are not binary but rather come in degrees, would serve to introduce a stratified account of morality on which vulnerable humans (and animals) come out on the short end. By contrast, Cochrane believes that although beings' interests can differ in degree, their sentience is an either-or matter.[39] Sentience, to him, is like a light that is either turned on or off. And because we can know whether the switch is on or off and because it cannot be 'more on' in one case than in another, sentience provides a stable foundation for equal moral status.

Compelling as it may seem, it is not as obvious as Cochrane argues that sentience does not run afoul of the same problem as personhood. After all, sentience is also an empirical characteristic. We must therefore take seriously the possibility that it, too, could be on a spectrum. In other words, we must

[38] Anne Phillips, *The Politics of the Human* (Cambridge University Press 2015) 131.

[39] Cochrane is not alone in believing that sentience is a binary property. Gary Francione, for instance, holds that '[t]o talk about degrees of sentience makes no sense': Francione, *Why Veganism Matters: The Moral Value of Animals* (n 5) 96.

consider the possibility that some beings may be *more sentient* than others, and as such would seem to have more moral worth.

To see why this possibility should not be dismissed, consider Cochrane's definition of sentience as 'the capacity for conscious experience'.[40] Sentient beings, he elaborates, 'can experience the world and their place in it [and] . . . have the ability to feel and respond to those experiences—to "enjoy" or to "suffer"'.[41] How can one measure these abilities? Because a being's conscious experience is internal to that being and thus cannot be directly observed, one can only measure sentience indirectly.[42] In a recent study on pain in fish, Lynne Sneddon identifies some of the central properties that scientists can look for to find out whether an animal is sentient. These properties include: 'the presence of a nociceptive system similar to that of mammals, relevant brain areas to process pain or nociceptive information, pathways from the periphery to these brain areas, and the existence of opioid receptors and endogenous opioids'.[43] A brief consideration of three of these features will help cast doubt on the view that it is self-evident that sentience is a binary property.

Take first the nociceptive system, which we can define for our purposes as a set of biological processes that allows a body to transmit information to the brain about stimuli that are injurious or potentially injurious to the organism.[44] For example, when a hot plate is touched, nociceptors transmit the relevant information about tissue damage to the brain. The response to such noxious stimuli occurs, among other ways, through two different types of fibres, which transmit the information at significantly different speeds.[45] As studies have shown, not all potentially sentient animals have both types of fibres.[46] And not all nociceptors are receptive to the same stimuli. For instance, some animals, such as squids, respond to mechanical stimuli but not thermal stimuli.[47]

[40] See for a different interpretation of sentience (though one that is sympathetic to Cochrane's binary view) as the capacity to feel: Donald M Broom and Ken G Johnson, *Stress and Animal Welfare: Key Issues in the Biology of Humans and Other Animals* (2nd edn, Springer 2019) 18.

[41] Cochrane, *Sentientist Politics: A Theory of Global Inter-Species Justice* (n 7) 15.

[42] Helen Proctor, 'Animal Sentience: Where Are We and Where Are We Heading?' (2012) 2 Animals 628, 630.

[43] Lynne U Sneddon, 'Pain Perception in Fish: Indicators and Endpoints' (2009) 50 Institute for Laboratory Animal Research Journal 338, 338.

[44] See Lynne U Sneddon, 'Evolution of Nociception in Vertebrates: Comparative Analysis of Lower Vertebrates' (2004) 46 Brain Research Reviews 123, 124; Ulf Baumgärtner, 'Nozizeptives System' (2010) 24 Der Schmerz 105.

[45] Sneddon, 'Evolution of Nociception in Vertebrates: Comparative Analysis of Lower Vertebrates' (n 44) 124.

[46] ibid.

[47] Robyn J Crook, Roger T Hanlon, and Edgar T Walters, 'Squid Have Nociceptors that Display Widespread Long-Term Sensitization and Spontaneous Activity after Bodily Injury' (2013) 33 The Journal of Neuroscience 10021.

Without needing to delve into detail, the important point to note here is that not all sentient animals have an identical nociceptive system. Rather, they possess systems that work in different ways, with some that transmit information faster and others that convey it more slowly. The possession of a nociceptive system, in other words, is not a binary matter.

Consider now the presence of relevant brain areas to process the nociceptive or pain information. A developed cortex and, more generally, the possession of a central nervous system are often mentioned as relevant in this context.[48] The difficulty, again, is that these phenomena come in many different shapes, and in different degrees of complexity, lending no support to the view that sentience is an either-or phenomenon. The cortex is more developed in some sentient animals than it is in others, and some animals (mammals) also have a neocortex.[49] The centralization of the nervous system, too, is different in different sentient animals. One particularly striking example is cephalopods. These creatures possess a basic central nervous system but, in contrast to mammals, they also have neurons in their arms.[50] For these reasons, this second element of sentience does not seem like a light switch either.

Finally, opioid receptors and endogenous opioids. The latter are chemical substances released by the body which function among other ways as analgesics, that is, to relieve pain. Such relief occurs at the receptors. Again, without losing ourselves in detail, we can note that there are not only different opioid receptor types,[51] but also different endogenous opioids.[52] Different sentient beings can thus possess different receptor types and employ different opioids.

All this suggests that it is difficult to regard sentience as something that a being either has or does not have. Rather, it seems that there may be different kinds of sentience, that is, different ways of being conscious in the world. Some kinds of sentience may be more elaborate than others, and beings that have those types of sentience may be more receptive than others to certain sensations. What is more, certain types of sentience may lead to more intense sensations and stronger interests than others. For example, one species may be more sensitive to mechanically inflicted pain than another, whereas that other

[48] Sneddon, 'Evolution of Nociception in Vertebrates: Comparative Analysis of Lower Vertebrates' (n 44) 125; see on the central nervous system Proctor, 'Animal Sentience: Where Are We and Where Are We Heading?' (n 42) 632.

[49] Sneddon, 'Pain Perception in Fish: Indicators and Endpoints' (n 43) 339.

[50] Shuichi Shigeno and others, 'Cephalopod Brains: An Overview of Current Knowledge to Facilitate Comparison With Vertebrates' (2018) 9 Frontiers in Physiology 1. See also the very accessible Peter Godfrey-Smith, *Other Minds: The Octopus and the Evolution of Intelligent Life* (Williams Collins 2016).

[51] Eduardo E Benarroch, 'Endogenous Opioid Systems: Current Concepts and Clinical Correlations' (2012) 79 Neurology 807.

[52] ibid.

species might feel thermal differences more vividly than the first; and a third might be more sensitive to both than the previous two.

At this stage, a proponent of Cochrane's theory could respond that the diversity and complexity of the phenomena that constitute sentience are neither here nor there. After all, Cochrane explicitly allows that interests will come in different 'types and numbers' and may vary in 'strength and complexity'.[53] Different nociceptive processes, nervous systems, receptors, and opioids may simply express different types, strengths, and degrees of complexity of interests. But, the response goes, that does not mean that sentience is not itself a binary phenomenon on which we can ground equality. This is because we can distinguish between the *capacity for sentience*, which comes in degree, and *sentience itself*, which does not.[54] Put differently, just because different beings acquire their sentience in different ways does not mean that they are not equally sentient.

The first problem with this response is that it assumes that different ways of experiencing the world can all be translated into a single currency of sentience: one that allows us to view being 'in possession of interests' as an either-or matter. However, it is not clear whether this really is the case.[55] Kristin Andrews, for example, has pointed out that there are 'innumerable types of sentience', with pain being only one type:

> Pleasure, temperature sensation, perception, color experience, dream experience, imagination, smell, hunger, touch, nostalgia for the past, self-awareness, guilt, etc. are other forms of sentient experience, and these too only begin to scratch the surface when it comes to the varieties of sentience we can already identify.[56]

According to Andrews, these different types of sentience cannot all be measured by the same yardstick, but rather each require different measurement criteria. This seems to make it difficult to translate the different types of sentience into a common currency of sentience. And, if sentience is heterogeneous rather

[53] Cochrane, *Sentientist Politics: A Theory of Global Inter-Species Justice* (n 7) 24 (emphasis removed).

[54] See on this distinction Andrew Lee, 'Does Sentience Come in Degrees?' (2020) 29(20) Animal Sentience 1. In private correspondence, Don Broom suggested to me a similar distinction between *structure* (which he views as non-binary) and *function* (which he views as binary) of sentience.

[55] See also Federico Zuolo, 'Misadventures of Sentience: Animals and the Basis of Equality' (2019) 9 Animals 1, 9.

[56] Kristin Andrews, 'Does the Sentience Framework Imply All Animals Are Sentient?' (2022) 32(17) Animal Sentience 2. See also Cecilia de Souza Valente, 'Decapod Sentience: Broadening the Framework' (2022) 7 Animal Sentience 2.

than homogenous, proponents of sentient equality have a harder time arguing that there are only different types of interests, not different types of sentience.

To be sure, this is an empirical question that cannot be answered without more research. Let us therefore assume, again for the sake of argument, that sentience is a homogenous phenomenon. Even under this assumption, however, sentient equality would not be on a secure foundation because there is a second problem: some sentient beings may have more intense ways of experiencing the world, that is, more intense ways of feeling. Some, in other words, may be *more* sentient than others. As Federico Zuolo argues, this is possible 'because sentience is a property that supervenes upon other physical properties that come in degrees such as the capacity to feel pain, complexity of the nervous system, etc'.[57] That sentience may come in degrees is not a far-fetched claim. It is a possibility that is taken seriously in contemporary studies on sentience. For example, Jonathan Birch proposes a 'sliding-scale of sentience, with organisms higher up the scale requiring more stringent levels of protection than those further down'.[58] And Andrew Lee in a recent piece considers whether sentience may be more like a 'dimmer switch'[59] than a switch that is either on or off.

Both authors ultimately suggest that we need more evidence to reach a final verdict on the matter. However, the sheer fact that they consider it a possibility that sentience is not binary should worry sentientist theorists. For the success of sentient equality—and therefore the success of sentient rights and sentientist politics—is staked on sentience delivering a binary foundation for equal moral worth. But if sentience turns out to be a matter of degree, then the obvious question for sentientist thinkers becomes: Should more sentience not matter *more*? If sentience is the only moral currency, is it not better to have more rather than less of it? As Cochrane himself puts it in the context of capacities for personhood: If such capacities matter, 'then why not grant more moral worth for more capacities?'.[60] Zuolo reaches the same conclusion when noting that, 'sentience has the same kinds of problems as personhood'.[61] Hence, far from having a robust foundation, sentient equality may turn out to be built on sand. And this, in turn, provides ammunition to the sceptics who fear that animal rights would lead to undermining vulnerable human beings' equal moral worth.

[57] Zuolo, 'Misadventures of Sentience: Animals and the Basis of Equality' (n 55) 9.
[58] Jonathan Birch, 'Degrees of Sentience?' (2018) 21(11) Animal Sentience 2.
[59] Lee, 'Does Sentience Come in Degrees?' (n 54) 1.
[60] Cochrane, *Sentientist Politics: A Theory of Global Inter-Species Justice* (n 7) 22.
[61] Zuolo, 'Misadventures of Sentience: Animals and the Basis of Equality' (n 55) 5.

To be clear, there is nothing preventing sentientist rights accounts like Cochrane's from accommodating the different forms and shapes and—possibly—degrees of sentience, by introducing a minimum threshold to salvage the idea of equal moral worth. That is, proponents of such accounts could argue that as long as a being is minimally sentient, they can be said to be 'in possession of interests',[62] and therefore have the same inherent equality as a being with more (or different) sentience. As I will show in Chapter 7 when presenting my proposal for the Species Membership Approach, good reasons speak for such a threshold. However, Cochrane explicitly rejects the idea of a threshold when discussing the notion of a range property. According to him, range properties are ultimately stipulative and do not provide a stable enough foundation for a status of equality. Yet, if his theory is to avoid giving more moral worth to beings with more—or more developed forms of—sentience, he would seem to have no choice but to treat sentience as a range property. As Cochrane himself notes regarding theories that ground equality in empirical characteristics such as personhood, their logical conclusion is a stratified, hierarchical account of moral worth. We can go even further and say that such theories may do away with the idea of moral status altogether. Allen Buchanan made this observation when discussing accounts that ground moral status in interests: 'the interest-based view, properly understood, seems to be a kind of debunking of the idea of different moral statuses, properly speaking, and a recommendation to replace it with something more like a continuum or gradient of moral considerability'.[63] To avoid such a continuum of moral worth on which vulnerable human beings will likely come out on the short end, sentientist rights theories would have to embrace a threshold of equality.

However, it is crucial to note that such a threshold-based solution to the *Spectrum Problem* goes beyond a pure sentientist approach in which only sentience matters morally. This is because the reason for having a threshold in the first place cannot be derived from sentience itself. After all, if sentience is all that matters for moral worth, then, as we saw above, it follows that the more sentient a creature is, the greater is their moral worth. If sentience is what matters, then it does not stop mattering above the threshold.[64] The threshold of equality would thus have to be based on some other reason than sentience.

[62] Cochrane, *Sentientist Politics: A Theory of Global Inter-Species Justice* (n 7) 24.

[63] Allen Buchanan, *Beyond Humanity? The Ethics of Biomedical Enhancement* (Oxford University Press 2011) 218.

[64] See Tim Mulgan, 'The Ethics of Killing: Problems at the Margins of Life by Jeff McMahan' (2004) 34 Canadian Journal of Philosophy 443, 458–59. See also Zuolo, 'Misadventures of Sentience: Animals and the Basis of Equality' (n 55) 3 (calling this the 'variability above the threshold' problem).

Aristocrats, of course, have a readily available *Internalist* reason for thresholds of equality: they are politically necessary to avoid introducing dangerous hierarchies between rights-holders. As long as sentientist rights theorists take sentience to be the sole ground for having interests and for mattering morally, however, that Aristocratic reason is unavailable to them. Sentientist rights proponents are thus faced with a choice: either they insist that only sentience matters morally, in which case they are at risk of introducing a hierarchy of rights-holders, or they adopt an Aristocratic threshold of equality.

This explains why—at the end of the previous section—I said that, despite initial appearances, Cochrane's defence of equal status does not escape the fundamental rights spectrum. To defend the idea of the threshold, he will have to rely on *Internalist* reasons, which is why his theory can, after all, be captured by the framework of the spectrum. Whatever choice sentientist rights proponents make, their approach therefore reveals itself to be no magical third conception that stands outside the Aristocracy and Meritocracy and that can secure the rights of vulnerable human beings without raising some of the same issues that plague the two ideal-types.

To recapitulate, sentientist rights theories such as Cochrane's run into the *Spectrum Problem*. Because sentience may well not be a binary characteristic but one of degree, it is not a stable foundation upon which equal moral worth should be built. If sentience is all that matters morally, then beings with less sentience matter less morally. Sentientist theorists could avoid the *Spectrum Problem* by declaring that variations of sentience do not matter if a being meets a certain threshold of sentience. However, adopting such a threshold approach means departing from a pure sentientist account and incorporating an Aristocratic element, thus remaining within the spectrum of fundamental rights.

5 Your life or the rat's: the *Indifference Problem*

Suppose, for the sake of argument, that sentient equality was based on a stable foundation; perhaps because sentience turns out to be binary after all, or because sentientist rights accounts can adopt a threshold notion of sentience that does not diverge from strictly sentientist commitments. Would this show that Cochrane's theory can meet *Salaville's Challenge*? I believe not. As I will show in this section, even if Cochrane's theory succeeded in giving equal moral worth to all sentient beings, it nevertheless has implications for some human beings that would be considered equality violations according to orthodox human rights doctrine, and would thus be rejected by Aristocratic human rights proponents. Specifically, Cochrane's sentientist theory does not pay attention to the species a being belongs to and therefore in principle allows that some (non-sentient) humans lack equal worth and rights altogether, and that the rights of animals can sometimes outweigh the rights of humans. This is the *Indifference Problem*.

The first and most obvious way in which the *Indifference Problem* makes it difficult for sentientist rights theorists to meet *Salaville's Challenge* is the fact that not all human beings are sentient.[65] For example, as Donald Broom has pointed out, humans with permanent brain damage caused by trauma or insufficient blood supply to the brain can fail to be sentient.[66] Equally, there may be periods at the beginning and the end of human life during which humans are not sentient.[67] On sentientist rights accounts, these humans do not qualify for rights because they lack sentience which, in Cochrane's and others' accounts, is viewed as a necessary condition for the possession of rights-grounding interests. Moreover, because sentientist rights theories take sentience to be the basis for equal moral worth, it follows that humans who lack sentience lack equal moral worth. Since the sentientist rights approach is indifferent to the species of these beings, and only considers whether they are sentient, they cannot be saved by their membership in the human species. While the case of foetuses is a special one to which I will return in Chapter 7, the fact that sentientist rights theories fail to confer equal moral worth and rights to some human beings, such as those with permanent brain damage, would be an obvious reason for condemnation by Aristocratic human rights proponents. As a result, the sentientist rights approach fails to meet *Salaville's Challenge*.

However, there is also a second and less obvious way in which the *Indifference Problem* gets sentientist rights accounts into trouble with Aristocratic human rights advocates. To understand this, recall Cochrane's point that not all sentient beings have the same interests, and that even where the interests are the same, these interests need not have the same strength. Because Cochrane adopts an interest-based approach to rights, it follows that sentient beings with stronger interests—say in liberty—have a stronger right to liberty than those with a weaker interest in liberty.[68] In his discussions of the principle of equal concern, Cochrane generally uses this point to show that humans' rights in

[65] I am thankful to Saskia Stucki for recommending that I raise this issue.
[66] Donald M Broom, *Sentience and Animal Welfare* (CABI 2014) 113–14.
[67] ibid 114–15.
[68] Assuming that this interest is important enough to ground duties in others and therefore to give rise to a right, see Chapter 4, Section 4.1.

certain things would outweigh animals' rights in those same things because, in most cases, humans' interests would be stronger. Consider the following example, which is worth citing in full to understand Cochrane's reasoning.

> [I]magine a situation in which the *prima facie* right to life of a human being comes into conflict with the *prima facie* right to life of a rat. Under a principle of equal consideration [ie equal concern], would we just have to toss a coin to see who wins out? Certainly not. The interests of both should be weighed fairly and equitably against each other. Since human beings have a mental complexity and an emotional life that far outstrips that of rats, and since human beings also have the ability to make plans for and have desires about the future, it is perfectly reasonable to state that the human interest in continued life is ordinarily much stronger than that of rats. If this is correct, then in the case of such a clash, and all else being equal, the right of the human would certainly win out. But it would win out not because it belongs to a member of a particular species that must always take priority, but because it protects an interest that is stronger and more compelling.[69]

From the perspective of a sceptic who is worried that animal rights could undermine human rights, the fact that the human's right to life wins out against the rat's *in this particular instance* is not going to be particularly comforting. After all, this outcome is entirely dependent on contingent facts—with the beings' species playing no role. Granted, in many cases, humans' interests may be stronger than animals' interests. But many cases are not all cases. And it is especially the cases in which humans' interests are not obviously weightier than animals' interests that concern the sceptic, since these cases are likely to involve vulnerable human beings whose interests in some rights—for example, liberty or life—are sometimes considered to be weaker than other humans' interests in these rights. Even more problematically from the sceptic's perspective, the vulnerable humans' interests may be weaker than those of some animals.

Take the above example, but assume that we are dealing with an extraordinary rat who, due to genetic enhancement, has significant mental complexity and the ability to make plans for and have desires about the future. Supposing that this ability grounds the right to life, this would imply that the rat has a strong right to life. Assume now that the rat's strong right does not clash with

[69] Alasdair Cochrane, 'From Human Rights to Sentient Rights' (2013) 16 Critical Review of International Social and Political Philosophy 655, 671 (emphasis in original and internal quotation marks omitted).

an ordinary human's right to life, but with that of a human with severe mental disabilities who is found to have only little, if any, ability to plan for and have desires about the future. In this case, the human's right to life would be considered weaker than the rat's and would therefore lose out.[70] Although seemingly far-fetched, this is a pressing problem in the eyes of the sceptic because there are many animals—for example, great apes, cetaceans, and elephants—who even without genetic enhancement have a mental complexity and ability to plan for the future that may outmatch that of some human beings.

Cochrane's theory in principle allows—indeed requires—that the rights of these animals outweigh the rights of vulnerable humans in cases of inevitable conflicts. It does not matter that direct conflicts between the rights of humans and animals of the sort envisaged above may only seldom arise. The mere possibility that an animal's right could outweigh a human's will be sufficient for some sceptics to reject the sentientist rights approach. We can reasonably infer this from the fact that large parts of human rights scholarship are Aristocratic and harbour aversion to approaches that make the possession and strength of rights dependent on empirical facts. As we saw in Chapter 3, building on the experience of the Holocaust, these Aristocratic thinkers argue that it is too dangerous to ground human rights in empirical contingencies. Instead, they argue, we must simply assume that humans have these rights, and not ask whether they have the relevant interests to deserve them. Recall how Phillips, who defends this approach most forcefully, puts the point:

> If we link the entitlement to human rights to characteristics like vulnerability to pain or capacity for conscious planning, the empirical evidence may well lead to the conclusion that some of the great apes qualify for at least some of the so-called human rights. But it may also lead . . . to the conclusion that some humans who currently qualify—day-old infants who have not yet developed consciousness; those in a coma who have lost it—are not entitled.[71]

Of course, as we saw above, Cochrane rejects basing equality and rights on mere stipulations. What is more, it could be retorted that the whole point of the

[70] The same point also applies to other rights-grounding interests such as the interest in liberty or in family life—a fact that can be used to counter the potential objection by some sentientist rights thinkers such as Francione who believe that the mere fact of being sentient gives all animals and humans the same interest in being alive: Francione, *Why Veganism Matters: The Moral Value of Animals* (n 5) 81.

[71] Phillips, *The Politics of the Human* (n 38) 40. See Chapter 3, Section 4.2. See also Cupp, 'Cognitively Impaired Humans, Intelligent Animals, and Legal Personhood' (n 9) 500–03; Laurence H Tribe, 'Ten Lessons Our Constitutional Experience Can Teach Us About the Puzzle of Animal Rights: The Work of Steven M Wise' (2001) 7 Animal Law 1, 7.

sentientist rights approach is to be 'indifferent' to the question of species membership.[72] After all, Cochrane and others explicitly reject the species membership criterion on the grounds that it is an arbitrary yardstick for moral worth. Hence, far from being a flaw in Cochrane's theory, it could be argued that its indifference to whose rights are being weighed is a strength. One man's trash is another man's treasure.

However, while this may explain why sentientist rights accounts have been particularly appealing to animal rights proponents, it also explains why human rights proponents have remained sceptical. The consequence that non-sentient humans lack equal worth and rights and that a human right—especially a vital one such as the right to life—could be traded off against an animal right in certain circumstances will likely not be acceptable to many. In other words, to the sceptic, indifference to species membership is a vice, not a virtue, of the sentientist rights approach. Because it withholds equal status and rights from non-sentient humans and allows animal rights to override human rights in certain situations, it puts vulnerable human beings' rights at particular risk. That is why the sentientist rights approach does not meet *Salaville's Challenge*. Hence, even if a sentientist rights theory such as Cochrane's overcame the *Spectrum Problem*, the *Indifference Problem* it faces means it will have a hard time finding favour with Aristocrats.

6 Conclusion

This chapter has focused on the increasingly popular sentientist rights approach to examine whether it constitutes a third conception outside the Meritocracy and Aristocracy that can meet what I called *Salaville's Challenge*: allowing for the extension of fundamental rights to nonhuman animals without undermining the high status and equal rights of humans. To answer this question, I used Cochrane's theory of sentient rights and sentient equality as a test case.

As I pointed out, we have first of all reason to be sceptical that sentientist rights theories such as Cochrane's are not Meritocratic. As I demonstrated, Cochrane's theory is Meritocratic in all but one respect (*Gradualism* as applied to status). Hence, simply because it is less Meritocratic than theories such as Singer's or McMahan's does not mean that it lacks the features of the

[72] As Zuolo has pointed out, this idea of indifference (or, as he puts it, 'nondiscrimination') also lies at the heart of Singer's equal consideration of interests principle: Zuolo, 'Misadventures of Sentience: Animals and the Basis of Equality' (n 55) 7.

Meritocracy to a sufficient degree to be called a 'Meritocratic' theory. Second, I argued that even if Cochrane's theory is not seen as Meritocratic, it nevertheless does not escape the spectrum of fundamental rights between the Aristocracy and Meritocracy. It, too, has its place on the spectrum: namely, somewhere closer to the middle than purer Meritocratic theories like Singer's.

I then argued that even if we consider Cochrane's theory as representative of a third conception that is more attractive than Meritocratic theories, that does not mean that it meets *Salaville's Challenge*. This is because it runs into the *Spectrum Problem* (it explains equal status on the basis of the criterion of sentience whose potential gradual nature can invite hierarchization) and the *Indifference Problem* (it withholds equal status and rights from non-sentient humans and allows for animal rights to outweigh human rights). Both these problems would be unpalatable to Aristocratic human rights proponents, which is why Cochrane's theory does not meet *Salaville's Challenge*.

It is worth emphasizing here that I did *not* argue that sentientist rights theories such as Cochrane's are in any way less appealing than purer instantiations of the Meritocracy. In fact, their endorsement of an egalitarian principle is attractive because it helps curb the problems of purer Meritocratic conceptions. However, importantly, Cochrane's theory does not succeed in explaining that principle in a way that transcends the fundamental rights spectrum. Quite the contrary, as we saw, if Cochrane wants to maintain the idea of a binary threshold, he likely needs to resort to *Internalist* explanations for it. And that is simply to say that he would move closer to the Aristocracy. As such, he remains within the framework of the spectrum of fundamental rights, which provides us with all the tools we need to understand the sentientist rights approach, its problems, and how it attempts to address them.

Finally, while I take the insights of this chapter to be applicable to many sentientist rights theories, I should emphasize again that I do not mean to exclude the possibility that there are theories that operate differently from Cochrane's and that may therefore avoid some of the problems it faces. However, because Cochrane's is the most sophisticated sentientist rights theory to date, we have reason to believe that the sentientist rights approach is not the silver bullet that some make it out to be. Despite its appeal, it is unlikely to fully put the minds of human rights proponents at ease who, following Salaville, regard the recognition of animal rights as a threat to human rights.

6

Meritocratizing the Aristocracy

1 Introduction

In this and the next chapter, I will show that the theory of the spectrum of fundamental rights conceptions is not only insightful from an intellectual-historical and analytical point of view, but also useful in practice. After Chapter 2, which dealt with the history of Aristocratic and Meritocratic ideas, and Chapters 3, 4, and 5, devoted to a detailed theoretical analysis of these two conceptions as well as a possible third conception, the present chapter focuses on politics and practical decision-making. It demonstrates why a move towards more Meritocratic legal systems is called for and how it could be achieved practically.

A legal system, to be sure, consists of more than just fundamental rights. For this reason, we need to be careful when drawing conclusions from what Aristocratic and Meritocratic conceptions of *fundamental rights* tell us, to what an entire *legal system* should look like. However, as I noted in the Introduction of this book, the concept of rights has taken on a singularly important role in modern legal discourse and practice. For better or worse, many legal systems have witnessed a 'rights revolution' characterized by an ever-increasing importance of rights claims in virtually all domains of law, and a concomitant growth in the power of courts to interpret these rights.[1] In this chapter, I will focus on two concrete ways in which legal systems can be made more Meritocratic: undoing the property status of non-human animals, which some see as a necessary step for animal rights, and granting certain fundamental rights to animals. Neither of these measures would change legal systems wholesale. However, considering the importance of rights today, I nevertheless consider them sufficient to change a legal system in a way that warrants calling it 'more Meritocratic'. Equally, given the importance of rights and rights-holders, I propose to call legal systems

[1] See, for a critical account, Martin Loughlin, *Against Constitutionalism* (Harvard University Press 2022) 130–35.

More Equal Than Others. Raffael N Fasel, Oxford University Press. © Raffael N Fasel 2024.
DOI: 10.1093/oso/9780198907435.003.0006

'Aristocratic' that largely follow the Aristocratic conception of fundamental rights.[2]

The chapter unfolds as follows. In Section 2, I say more about the exact relationship between the Aristocracy and the Meritocracy. Because their opposing features present us with antithetical options, I will propose that finding a practical middle ground—an equilibrium between the two ideal-types—is the best way forward. I will then argue that new scientific findings and a recent shift in people's perceptions indicate that current legal systems are overly Aristocratic. They exclude from fundamental rights and legal personhood every being who was not born a member of the human species, despite overwhelming evidence that many nonhuman animals also possess capacities—such as sentience, autonomy, and self-consciousness—that are otherwise considered relevant for rights-holding. I will therefore argue that in order to reach an equilibrium, we need to move away from the prevailing Aristocratic conception. In other words, we need to *Meritocratize the Aristocracy*. Section 3 shows how exactly such a Meritocratization of current legal systems can be accomplished in practice by exploring changes to animals' current status as legal property and by discussing certain fundamental rights that could be extended to some animals. A brief conclusion will summarize my findings.

2 Meritocratizing the Aristocracy

Animals today live in the age of the human rights Aristocracy. The purpose of this section is to substantiate this claim by showing that current legal systems are too Aristocratic, and that we therefore have reason to make them more Meritocratic. Section 2.1 makes the case that the best practical position is a middle ground between the Aristocracy and the Meritocracy. In Section 2.2, I will show that despite growing awareness of the similarity between the capacities and interests of human and other animals, laws have not kept pace with these developments and have remained largely wedded to the Aristocracy. I will argue that in order to reach an equilibrium, it is therefore necessary to Meritocratize the Aristocracy. Section 2.3 then contextualizes this argument by showing how the same logic underlay past extensions of Aristocratic rank and rights to formerly excluded groups such as women.

Three points before we begin. First, my proposal to Meritocratize the Aristocracy is a practical, not a theoretical proposal. In other words, I do not

[2] I am grateful to Saskia Stucki for pressing me on this.

claim that we should merge the two ideal-types or alter them in some other way to develop a new conception. Max Weber referred to such merging of ideal-types as 'syncretism',[3] and opposed it for the reason that, instead of resolving the tensions described by ideal-types, it would lead to their concealment. The result of this, he argued, would be that the task of practical decision-makers and politicians, who have to mediate between the conflicting extremes, would become harder.[4] Second, and relatedly, my claim is not that scientific evidence can directly challenge the validity of Aristocratic accounts of fundamental rights. These accounts remain valid in theory insofar as they are internally coherent. However, I will show that these accounts can be challenged indirectly be questioning their founding assumptions. I will argue that if these assumptions cease to be justifiable on non-arbitrary grounds—that is, grounds that have a meaningful connection to reality[5]—then it makes no sense to uphold the accounts. This is what I mean when I say that Aristocratic accounts are practically undesirable, but not theoretically invalid. Finally, I will not discuss the sentientist rights approach as a potential third conception standing outside the fundamental rights spectrum. As I demonstrated in the last chapter, even if sentientist rights theories such as Alasdair Cochrane's are not categorized as less extreme forms of the Meritocracy (as I argued they should), they nevertheless do not escape the fundamental rights spectrum.

2.1 Steering a middle course

When confronted with a choice between two evenly matched extremes, one often fares best by opting for a practical middle ground. The same holds true for the choice that the Aristocracy and the Meritocracy present us with. In order to be able to develop the argument for an equilibrium between the Aristocracy and the Meritocracy, it will be helpful to briefly recall the main strengths and deficiencies of these ideal-types.

As I have argued in Chapter 3, the Aristocracy's strength is its ability to *found* a group's high rank and the equal rights that come with it. Due to its *Internalism*, the Aristocracy relies entirely on normative principles and assumptions that are internal to society. In so doing, it can immunize the status

[3] Max Weber, *The Methodology of the Social Sciences* (Edward A Shils and Henry A Finch trs, Free Press 1949) 57.

[4] This is why Weber argued that scientists have a duty to remain ethically neutral with respect to the ideal-types they are painting: ibid 11, 57–58.

[5] See for this definition of 'arbitrariness' Chapter 3, Section 4.2.

and rights against external criticism. The Aristocracy was thus shown to be able to protect marginalized human beings' equal rights and status against potential attacks from Meritocrats who contend that these humans lack the necessary capacities for some of these rights or for the high status. However, this strength was at the same time also revealed to be the main weakness of the Aristocracy. The Aristocracy's 'immunization' against facts becomes problematic when the normative principles it has *founded* bear little or no correspondence with the actual world, that is, when they become arbitrary. Not only would it make little sense for us to adopt such principles,[6] but they may even give us cause for active resistance.[7] For this reason, David Bilchitz rightly implores that we should only withhold fundamental rights from beings if we have non-arbitrary reasons for doing so. If we fail to provide such reasons, he suggested, then we commit an injustice akin to that of 'apartheid'.[8]

Because the Aristocracy and the Meritocracy are negative images of each other, one shines where the other pales. By adopting an *Externalist* approach to *ground* fundamental rights in a being's actual properties, the Meritocracy avoids the Aristocracy's problem of creating a normative status that becomes too detached from reality. As I have shown in Chapter 4, we can conceive of a being's interests at least partly as objective and external facts about the world. This means that we can determine these interests largely independently of our beliefs about whether or not that being deserves certain fundamental rights. This dependence on external facts is the Meritocracy's strength, but also its greatest liability. As I explained, the Meritocracy has no room for *Equal Consideration.* It has no problem with—indeed, it requires—withholding fundamental rights from humans or other beings who can be shown empirically not to deserve them. As I have cautioned, the Meritocracy thereby risks opening the floodgates for a (renewed) division of the human species into individuals, or groups of humans, who deserve more and stronger rights than others, thus justifying the kind of discrimination and ableism that disability scholars and activists have been warning against.[9] As Laurence Tribe has rightly emphasized, a Meritocratic approach would require us to decide not only on the fundamental rights of humans who entirely lack the relevant capacities, but also on the rights of those who have these capacities to a lesser

[6] See Jeremy Waldron, *One Another's Equals: The Basis of Human Equality* (Belknap Press of Harvard University Press 2017) 59.

[7] See Jeff McMahan, 'Our Fellow Creatures' (2005) 9 The Journal of Ethics 353, 361.

[8] David Bilchitz, 'Moving Beyond Arbitrariness: The Legal Personhood and Dignity of Non-Human Animals' (2009) 23 South African Journal on Human Rights 38, 52. See also Chapter 3, Section 4.2.

[9] For a definition and critique of ableism, see Jennifer Scuro, *Addressing Ableism: Philosophical Questions via Disability Studies* (Lexington Books 2018) 9–29. See also Chapter 4, Section 4.3.

degree—which could take us back to some of the darkest chapters in human history.[10]

With dire consequences looming on either side of the spectrum, what should one do? Between Scylla and Charybdis, the most reasonable course of action is to steer a middle course that avoids the weaknesses of the two extreme conceptions while retaining as many of their strengths as possible.[11] Things would be different, of course, if our two ideal-types were not evenly matched. Were we confronted with a choice between two extremes where one extreme is clearly favourable, it would be foolish to choose the worse extreme. However, the choice between the Aristocracy and the Meritocracy is not of this kind. Both have strengths, and both have weaknesses. In fact, the strength of one *is* the weakness of the other, and vice versa. It therefore seems reasonable, in practice, to adopt a middle ground that minimizes as far as possible the downsides of these approaches while maximizing their benefits.

I should emphasize that while there are good *practical* reasons for adopting an equilibrium between the two ideal-types, there is no reason for thinking that their abovementioned deficiencies in any way reduce the *theoretical* validity of the Aristocracy or Meritocracy in their pure forms. A fully Aristocratic account that is entirely out of touch with reality is as valid in theory as is a fully Meritocratic account that entirely abolishes equal status and equal rights. Such accounts are practically undesirable, but not theoretically invalid.

The fact that adopting a middle ground is the most advisable approach in practice may be partly responsible for the existence of the wide variety of fundamental rights theories that are scattered across the spectrum between the two ideal-types. Concrete accounts have, since the Enlightenment, tended to be more moderate than what their ideal-type in its pristine form would have required. In other words, the ideal-types have been just that: *ideal*-types. Some, in fact, have been quite explicit about their motives for shying away from adopting a more extreme form of their respective ideal-type. The animal rights theorist Tom Regan, for instance, distanced himself from the *Differential Consideration* that the Meritocracy entails because of the 'unsavory implications' he believed the rejection of *Equal Consideration* would have.[12]

[10] See Laurence H Tribe, 'Ten Lessons Our Constitutional Experience Can Teach Us About the Puzzle of Animal Rights: The Work of Steven M. Wise' (2001) 7 Animal Law 1, 7.

[11] cf also Aristotle, *Nicomachean Ethics* (H Rackham tr, Harvard University Press 1926) Book II, 1106–1107a13–17.

[12] Tom Regan, *The Case for Animal Rights* (University of California Press 1983) 263. See also Alasdair Cochrane, *Sentientist Politics: A Theory of Global Inter-Species Justice* (Oxford University Press 2018) 24–25.

I propose that the middle ground we should aspire to in practice constitutes an equilibrium between the two ideal-types. In order to arrive at this equilibrium, we need to go back and forth between the two extremes. This allows us to approximate and eventually reach a balance that combines the strengths of the ideal-types, while minimizing their weaknesses as much as possible. This is no easy task. Ngaire Naffine rightly points out that choosing what to do with different ideal-types—or, as she calls them, 'myths we live by'[13]—involves a 'delicate balancing act'.[14] However, as she highlights, simply because every ideal-type (or 'myth') has its downsides does not mean 'that the myths are false or meaningless or ineffectual or without social and moral value. We live our legal lives according to them and they may well be doing very good work for us.'[15] The key lies in finding the right mixture of these different and conflicting values.

To be sure, for Aristocrats, such a mixture, or equilibrium, will be too Meritocratic. And for Meritocrats, it will be too Aristocratic. However, there is always an opportunity cost involved when we decide which fundamental rights conception we should adopt. We cannot have the best of both worlds. The reason for this is that the Aristocracy and the Meritocracy are antithetical normative positions. Another way of putting this is to say that Meritocrats and Aristocrats are playing a zero-sum game. No gains can be made on one side without inflicting an equivalent loss on the other side (see Figure 1.1 in the Introduction). This also helps explain why no winner has emerged from the debate between Meritocrats and Aristocrats since it surfaced in the Enlightenment. In fact, the antithetical nature of these conceptions explains why no resolution of the debate is possible. As demonstrated by the striking similarity between Salaville's and Delamétherie's theories and those of contemporary theorists, any progress that has been made on these issues has mostly been one of refinement and increasing sophistication of the arguments on either side. The core dispute, however, remains unresolved.

2.2 Keeping pace with scientific advances

Since Salaville's and Delamétherie's debate at the turn of the nineteenth century, dramatic advances have been made in our knowledge about the nature of humans and other animals. Perhaps the most crucial development in this

[13] Ngaire Naffine, *Law's Meaning of Life: Philosophy, Religion, Darwin and the Legal Person* (Hart Publishing 2009) 181.
[14] ibid.
[15] ibid.

regard was the publication of Charles Darwin's *On the Origin of Species* in 1859. Darwin's theory of evolution, accepted by an overwhelming majority of scientists today, effectively dethroned the human species. As James Rachels has put it, '[a]fter Darwin, we can no longer think of ourselves as occupying a special place in creation—instead, we must realise that we are products of the same evolutionary forces, working blindly and without purpose, that shaped the rest of the animal kingdom.'[16]

Numerous other discoveries have since revealed that there is even less of a gap between humans and other animals than Darwin could have imagined. In 2005, for example, a consortium of scientists was able to sequence the chimpanzee genome, discovering that the DNA of humans and chimpanzees is 96 per cent identical.[17] Frans de Waal, a leading primatologist, pointed out in response to this study that 'Darwin wasn't just provocative in saying that we descend from the apes—he didn't go far enough. We are apes in every way, from our long arms and tailless bodies to our habits and temperament.'[18] De Waal's own work on primate ethology is part of yet another burgeoning field that has played an important part in changing our understanding and perception of animals. Ethologists have found out that many types of behaviour that were once believed to be uniquely human are also exhibited by non-human animals. For example, humans have been shown not to be the only species able to recognize themselves in mirrors,[19] to make and use tools,[20] to think about the past and to plan for the future,[21] to use medicine,[22] to have a sense of empathy and fairness,[23] and to have culture.[24] These and more

[16] James Rachels, *Created From Animals: The Moral Implications of Darwinism* (Oxford University Press 1999) 1.

[17] The Chimpanzee Sequencing and Analysis Consortium, 'Initial Sequence of the Chimpanzee Genome and Comparison with the Human Genome' (2005) 437 Nature 69.

[18] Cited in Stefan Lovgren, 'Chimps, Humans 96 Percent the Same, Gene Study Finds' (*National Geographic News*, 29 May 2018) <https://www.nationalgeographic.com/science/article/chimps-humans-96-percent-the-same-gene-study-finds> accessed 11 June 2023.

[19] Koji Toda and Michael L Platt, 'Animal Cognition: Monkeys Pass the Mirror Test' (2015) 25 Current Biology R64.

[20] See eg Robert W Shumaker, Kristina R Walkup, and Benjamin B Beck, *Animal Tool Behavior: The Use and Manufacture of Tools by Animals* (Johns Hopkins University Press 2011).

[21] William A Roberts, 'Mental Time Travel: Animals Anticipate the Future' (2007) 17 Current Biology R418.

[22] Jacobus C de Roode, Thierry Lefèvre, and Mark D Hunter, 'Self-Medication in Animals' (2013) 340 Science 150.

[23] On empathy see eg Frans de Waal, 'The Evolution of Empathy' (*Greater Good*, 1 September 2005) <http://greatergood.berkeley.edu/article/item/the_evolution_of_empathy> accessed 11 June 2023. On fairness see eg Sarah F Brosnan and Frans de Waal, 'Evolution of Responses to (Un)Fairness' (2014) 346 Science 1251776.

[24] Michael Balter, 'Strongest Evidence of Animal Culture Seen in Monkeys and Whales' (*Science*, 25 April 2013) <http://www.sciencemag.org/news/2013/04/strongest-evidence-animal-culture-seen-monkeys-and-whales> accessed 11 June 2023.

discoveries have been chiselling away at the notion that the human species is completely distinct from other animals. We are now more certain than ever that, although interesting and special in its own ways, the human species tops no hierarchy of animals, is no principal link in a chain of beings, and is no summit of creation. In fact, if the theory of evolution has taught us anything, then it is precisely that such hierarchical thinking—of 'higher' and 'lower' animals—is misplaced.

To be sure, there is reason to be careful with the invocation of scientific evidence in support of a legal right or other entitlement. As I discussed in Chapter 4, critical disability scholars have criticized the ways in which scientific 'facts' have historically been and continue to be invoked to undermine the legal protections of humans with disabilities without acknowledging how socially contingent views of disability can be. In the context of race, too, history is replete with problematic invocations of 'science' to justify the attribution of lower status of marginalized ethnicities.[25] In the context of animal rights, there is the particular problem that capacities are interpreted in narrow, anthropocentric ways that fail to do justice to what animals are actually capable of.[26] What is more, there is the risk of overemphasizing similarities with human beings and neglecting the different and unique capacities of animals. However, these are not reasons to forgo scientific evidence. Rather, they are reasons to use such evidence in a more careful way that is cognizant of how history and social context can tinge what we perceive as an objective fact in any given moment.

Despite the abovementioned empirical evidence, relatively little has changed legally for animals since the Enlightenment. Legal systems across the world have failed to protect animals' most basic interests in ways that are too numerous to list here. We would have to consult the whole body of animal (rights) law scholarship to get a full picture of the diverse respects in which current laws are failing animals. Only such an overview would allow us to appreciate the breadth and depth of the ways in which, for example, animals of most species can be killed with few to no limitations, how they can be kept and treated in ways that would likely be considered severe human rights violations if imposed on a human being, or how high the bar often is for recognizing a treatment as inflicting 'unnecessary' suffering on an animal.[27]

[25] See Justin EH Smith, *Nature, Human Nature, & Human Difference: Race in Early Modern Philosophy* (Princeton University Press 2015).

[26] See eg on the problem of 'anthropodenial' Frans de Waal, 'Anthropomorphism and Anthropodenial: Consistency in Our Thinking about Humans and Other Animals' (1999) 27 Philosophical Topics 255.

[27] See for an overview Raffael N Fasel and Sean C Butler, *Animal Rights Law* (Hart Publishing 2023).

For our purposes here, it will be sufficient to note the following: while numerous jurisdictions have enacted animal welfare statutes that recognize animals as sentient beings worthy of protection for their own sake, virtually no legal system (I list the few exceptions in Section 3) has extended to them any of the fundamental rights that human beings possess.[28] As will be illustrated in some more detail below, animals' legal status is thus considerably less favourable than that of human beings. Animals are in many respects still treated in law as if they belonged to an entirely different, and much lower, caste than human beings. This is what I mean when I say that animals today live in the age of the human rights Aristocracy. But can it really be that, to quote Rachels, evidence 'which overturns all our former ideas about man and nature, has no unsettling consequences?'[29]

Of course, ardent advocates of the Aristocracy will not be impressed by such claims. For is not the whole point of the Aristocracy that it is immune to external facts? After all, as we saw, it can have dangerous consequences for the rights of human beings if we start to listen to natural scientists to help us decide who should become a fundamental rights-holder and who should not. At this stage, however, we need to recall that while the Aristocracy cannot be directly contested on empirical grounds, it is still *indirectly* vulnerable to such challenges.[30] The Aristocracy's weakness, as I have pointed out in Chapter 3, is that it risks founding principles that lose touch with external reality. It would make little sense for us to adopt such arbitrary principles, which is why they are not practically viable. Once the detachment from external facts becomes too great, the Aristocracy loses its appeal.

For this reason, it should not come as a surprise that animal rights theories aiming for a more Meritocratic system have at their core claims about the arbitrariness of the current legal status quo. For example, Steven Wise, the director of the Nonhuman Rights Project (NhRP), argues that we should give fundamental rights to nonhuman animals who possess the capacities for autonomy and self-determination 'in order to avoid arbitrary, irrational, and perverse results from disqualifying these nonhuman animals from eligibility for . . . rights that are granted to humans who entirely lack autonomy'.[31] As Alexia Staker has observed, the lawsuits that the NhRP and

[28] cf World Animal Protection, 'Animal Protection Index' <https://api.worldanimalprotection.org/> accessed 11 June 2023.

[29] Rachels, *Created From Animals: The Moral Implications of Darwinism* (n 16) 3.

[30] See Chapter 3, Section 4.2.

[31] Steven M Wise, 'Hardly a Revolution—The Eligibility of Nonhuman Animals for Dignity-Rights in a Liberal Democracy' (1998) 22 Vermont Law Review 793, 910.

other animal rights organizations have filed 'rel[y] heavily on scientific evidence and place[] great faith in the ability of such evidence to convince the courts that legal boundaries should be shifted'.[32] Indeed, Meritocrats often appear to accept axiomatically that there is a connection between growing scientific knowledge and the need to change the legal status quo. For instance, Daniel Davison-Vecchione and Kate Pambos transition without further argument from the finding that '[a]dvancements in science have revealed much of the intelligence, sentience and autonomy possessed by other species' to the claim that '[t]here are strong reasons to cast doubt on the traditional status of nonhumans as property with which we may do as we please'.[33] This view is widespread. In an *amici curiae* brief in support of one of the NhRP's *habeas corpus* lawsuits, seventeen philosophers maintained that the 'biological sciences must inform legal practice',[34] and that we need to 'keep[] pace with both scientific and moral progress'.[35]

As a 2018 decision on the NhRP's Tommy and Kiko cases by the State of New York Court of Appeals shows, this way of thinking also seems to resonate with some judges. In his opinion, Judge Eugene Fahey acknowledged that

> [t]he evolving nature of life makes clear that chimpanzees and humans exist on a continuum of living beings. Chimpanzees share at least 96% of their DNA with humans. They are autonomous, intelligent creatures. To solve this dilemma, we have to recognise its complexity and confront it.[36]

Judge Fahey's opinion appears to confirm a recent shift in society' perception of animals, and what appears to be people's increasing discontent with the legal status quo concerning animals. For example, a survey conducted in 2018 showed that 46.9 per cent of Americans agree with the statement that '[a]nimals deserve the exact same rights as people to be free from harm and exploitation', while 47.5 per cent agreed that '[a]nimals deserve some protection from harm and exploitation, but it is still appropriate to use them for the benefit

[32] Alexia Staker, 'Should Chimpanzees Have Standing? The Case for Pursuing Legal Personhood for Non-Human Animals' (2017) 6 Transnational Environmental Law 485, 499.

[33] Daniel Davison-Vecchione and Kate Pambos, 'Steven M. Wise and the Common Law Case for Animal Rights: Full Steam Ahead' (2017) 30 Canadian Journal of Law & Jurisprudence 287, 290.

[34] *Nonhuman Rights Project, Inc v Patrick C Lavery et al and Nonhuman Rights Project, Inc* v *Carmen Presti et al* (23 February 2018) Proposed Brief by Amici Curiae Philosophers, 8 <https://www.nonhumanrights.org/content/uploads/In-re-Nonhuman-Rights-v.-Lavery-Proposed-Brief-by-PHILOSOPHERS-74435.pdf> accessed 11 June 2023.

[35] ibid 7.

[36] *Nonhuman Rights Project, Inc v Patrick C Lavery et al and Nonhuman Rights Project, Inc v Carmen Presti et al* [2018] State of New York, Court of Appeals No 2018-268, 6, Fahey J, concurring.

of humans'.[37] The survey also revealed that about half would vote in favour of a law that grants the right to bodily liberty to great apes, elephants, and cetaceans, or support a politician who introduced such a law.[38] This is an increase from 2015, when a Gallup poll suggested that almost a third of Americans agree with the (same) statement that 'animals deserve the exact same rights as people to be free from harm and exploitation', and two-thirds agree that they 'deserve some protection from harm and exploitation'. Only 3 per cent agreed with the statement that 'animals don't need much protection from harm and exploitation *since they are just animals*'.[39] Other, more specific surveys have shown for example that, in 2021, 44 per cent of Americans stated they would support a policy to immediately halt creation of new or expansion of existing 'large industrial cattle, swine or poultry operations'[40] and phase out the same by 2040. As regards animals used in research, in 2022, in Gallup's annual survey concerning the moral acceptability of a range of social issues, 43 per cent of Americans found medical testing on animals to be morally unacceptable, a significant increase from 26 per cent in 2001.[41] A similar trend can be observed in the United Kingdom, where in 2018 39 per cent disagreed with the idea that it was acceptable to use animals in all types of research and 66 per cent said that the use of animals in research bothers them.[42] Although the data are limited, other countries seem to be undergoing a similar change in attitude towards a more favourable legal status for animals.[43]

[37] Garrett M Broad, 'Public Support for Animal Rights Goes Beyond Keeping Dogs out of Overhead Bins' (*The Conversation*) <http://theconversation.com/public-support-for-animal-rights-goes-beyond-keeping-dogs-out-of-overhead-bins-93410> accessed 11 June 2023.

[38] ibid.

[39] Rebecca Riffkin, 'In U.S., More Say Animals Should Have Same Rights as People' (*Gallup*, 18 May 2015) <http://news.gallup.com/poll/183275/say-animals-rights-people.aspx> accessed 11 June 2023 (emphasis added).

[40] Rethink Priorities, 'Rethink Priorities Poll: US Farming Policy' (2021) 21, 8–10 <https://docs.google.com/document/d/1UZKrC80YqohyNgc6erUN_xzxMQxExGz9StY9hkFqK-w/edit#> accessed 11 June 2023.

[41] Gallup Inc, 'Americans Say Birth Control, Divorce Most "Morally Acceptable"' (*Gallup.com*, 9 June 2022) <https://news.gallup.com/poll/393515/americans-say-birth-control-divorce-morally-acceptable.aspx> accessed 11 June 2023.

[42] Ipsos MORI, 'Public Attitudes to Animal Research in 2018' (2018) 20, 22 <https://www.ipsos.com/sites/default/files/ct/news/documents/2019-05/18-040753-01_ols_public_attitudes_to_animal_research_report_v3_191118_public.pdf> accessed 11 June 2023.

[43] See on the opposition in EU countries to use of animals in research Eurogroup for Animals, 'Use of Animals in Research, Testing and Education' (2023) <https://savanta.com/knowledge-centre/published-polls/animal-research-poll-eurogroup-for-animals-31-march-2023/> accessed 11 June 2023. On the global opposition to animal testing for cosmetics see Humane Society International, 'Global Polls Reveal Consumers Worldwide Want an End to Animal Testing for Cosmetics: Humane Society International' (27 January 2016) <https://web.archive.org/web/20190317211059/http://www.hsi.org/news/news/2016/01/global_cosmetics_polling_012716.html> accessed 11 June 2023. On a recent study on the support in France of more protective legislation and rights for animals see Harris Interactive, 'Enquête 1/3: la prise en compte du bien-être animal, un tournant dans la société?' (2021) 17 <http://har

This trend in public opinion on the status of animals also has an offshoot in the academic world where an 'animal turn' has led to a shift in scholarly thinking.[44] The animal turn describes a trend in the social sciences and the humanities to study animals as subjects rather than mere objects.[45] According to Jessica Eisen, this turn is 'characterised by both an increasing subject-matter interest in animals and human–animal relationships, and a qualitative shift toward viewing animals as "selves" whose lived experiences are morally, socially, politically, and even legally significant'.[46] Indeed, many of the Meritocratic works discussed in this book are part of the animal turn.

2.3 Expanding the circle of rights-holders

Before we consider, in Section 3 and the next chapter, some of the concrete ways in which a Meritocratization of the Aristocracy can be brought about, it will be illuminating first to contextualize that argument and help us understand how it compares with other fundamental rights expansions. In what follows, I will suggest that the case for Meritocratizing animals' current legal situation should be interpreted as the same sort of project as the women's rights movement and other rights movements. In the case of all these movements, the central aim of the project was (and often still is) to expand the circle of rights-holders to include some formerly excluded categories of deserving beings.

Of course, the claim that we should include at least some animals in the community of rights-holders is an old chestnut in the animal rights literature.[47] What is novel about my proposal to Meritocratize the Aristocracy is its ability to shed light not only on why such a Meritocratic expansion is necessary, but also on the Aristocratic reasons—often overlooked in animal rights scholarship—that speak against an overly radical expansion of the circle. I will first consider the reasons for a Meritocratic extension of the circle of

ris-interactive.fr/wp-content/uploads/sites/6/2021/09/Rapport_Harris_-_Animaux_et_societe_Cetelem.pdf> accessed 11 June 2023. On recent opinion shifts on farmed animals in Australia see Futureye, 'Australia's Shifting Mindset on Farm Animal Welfare' (2018) 39.

[44] See eg Harriet Ritvo, 'On the Animal Turn' (2007) 136 Daedalus 118.

[45] Anne Peters, Saskia Stucki, and Livia Boscardin, 'The Animal Turn: What Is It and Why Now?' (*Verfassungsblog*, 14 April 2014) <https://verfassungsblog.de/the-animal-turn-what-is-it-and-why-now/> accessed 11 June 2023.

[46] Jessica Eisen, 'Animals in the Constitutional State' (2017) 15 International Journal of Constitutional Law 909, 912.

[47] See Keith Thomas, *Man and the Natural World: Changing Attitudes in England 1500–1800* (Penguin Books 1983) 185.

rights-holders to animals before showing that the extension has in all cases been justified by pointing to the arbitrariness of the existing circle.

As I argued in the previous section, we have good reasons for abandoning an Aristocratic status if, from a practical perspective, it makes little sense to retain it. In other words, if the membership of a specific circle of rights-holders becomes indefensible on non-arbitrary grounds, we should no longer maintain it. In such a case, we have to redraw the circle to make it defensible again. The point I want to make now is that, in the history of fundamental rights, the circle of fundamental rights-holders had to be expanded several times because previously drawn circles became indefensible. As is well-known, it took centuries for the current circle of fundamental rights-holders to form. Today, this circle includes humans of any class, gender, ethnicity, age, or bodily ability. Of course, this is unfortunately true only if we consider human rights on paper, not in practice. For we should not neglect the shortcomings and outright violations of rights that many humans, especially those belonging to marginalized groups, face. What is more, simply because a group has been included in the circle of rights-holders does not mean that it will forever remain there, as recent regresses in the domain of women's health and reproductive rights in countries such as the United States illustrate.[48] Notwithstanding these challenges, it is difficult to disagree with Jeremy Waldron's claim, which we encountered in Chapter 3, that equal rights and equal status have, at least in theory, been universalized to 'all men and women'.[49]

However, Waldron's claim overlooks something important: this extension of rights and equal status did not happen overnight. Not everyone suddenly became an 'aristocrat'. Rather, it took time and many struggles for the circle to be drawn the way it is today. While Waldron is, in my view, correct to say that a universalization from noblemen to all members of the human species has occurred, he passes over the long and arduous history of smaller expansions of the circle of rights-holders that were required to bring about (and maintain) this universalization. For example, he makes no mention of the struggle of women and black people to be recognized as rights-holders.[50] This is problematic not only because it skips crucial chapters in the history of human rights, but also because it leads him to fail to notice the mechanism that is behind expansions of the circle. I propose that these expansions occurred whenever the

[48] See eg Risa Kaufman and others, 'Global Impacts of Dobbs v. Jackson Women's Health Organization and Abortion Regression in the United States' (2022) 30 Sexual and Reproductive Health Matters 22, 22–23.

[49] Jeremy Waldron, *Dignity, Rank, and Rights* (Meir Dan-Cohen ed, Oxford University Press 2012) 35.

[50] See Lynn Hunt, *Inventing Human Rights: A History* (Norton 2007) 149–75.

current Aristocracy—that is, the way the circle was drawn—could no longer be defended on non-arbitrary grounds. These expansions of the circle are therefore best interpreted as *Meritocratizations of the Aristocracy*.

Consider the example of women's rights. In 1790—only one year after the adoption of the French Declaration of the Rights of Man and the Citizen—the Marquis de Condorcet published an essay entitled *Sur l'admission des femmes au droit de cité*. In his essay, Condorcet proposed an expansion of political rights to women. The argumentative strategy he adopted is a now familiar one: he pointed out that women possess the same capacities that support men's possession of such rights, yet are granted none of these rights: '[t]he rights of men are based uniquely on the fact that they are sentient beings, capable of acquiring moral ideas, and to reason about these ideas. Because women have these same qualities, they must necessarily also have equal rights.'[51] Condorcet's challenge was thus essentially one of arbitrariness. As he put it, it is simply 'absurd'[52] to 'quietly deprive half of the human race'[53] of their rights. No one had succeeded in providing plausible reasons for thinking that there is a relevant difference between men and women with respect to these rights, which is why Condorcet concluded that it is unacceptable to deprive women of theirs.[54]

Petitions to extend rights protection to previously excluded beings such as women have often been met with the criticism that including more beings would lead to a slippery slope that would ultimately undermine the protections of existing rights-holders.[55] As Claire Jean Kim has observed in the context of the United States, for example, slippery slope arguments—'What's Next?'[56] objections, as she calls them—were a common response to attempted extensions of the circle of rights-holders to black people, Native Americans, and Chinese immigrants. It goes without saying that in the case of these groups of people, as well as in the case of many other previously excluded human groups, the 'What's Next?' objection falsely suggested that an extension of the circle of rights-holders to members of these groups could not be based on good reasons. In other words, the 'What's Next?' objection is often used as an excuse to guard the privileges of more powerful groups.

[51] Marquis de Condorcet, 'Sur l'admission des femmes au droit de cité', *Œuvres de Condorcet*, vol 10 (Firmin Didot Frères 1847) 122.
[52] ibid 121.
[53] ibid.
[54] ibid 129.
[55] See eg the infamous Thomas Taylor, *A Vindication of the Rights of Brutes* (Scholars' Facsimiles & Reprints 1966).
[56] Claire Jean Kim, *Dangerous Crossings: Race, Species, and Nature in a Multicultural Age* (Cambridge University Press 2015) 29.

However, the 'What's Next?' objection can still contain a grain of truth if we take it to refer to the weakness of the Meritocracy. The more moral and legal attention we devote to factual similarities and differences between beings to expand the circle of rights-holders, the more reason we have for relinquishing equal rights and granting rights solely based on the possession of the relevant rights-grounding capacities. It is in this sense that a heedless pursuit of the Meritocracy can be problematic. The Aristocracy's commitment to basic equality and its ability to detach rights from empirical properties give it important advantages over pure Meritocratic accounts. As we saw in Chapter 3, the Aristocracy's uncompromising rejection of views that threaten to undermine equality was certainly one of the reasons why Aristocratic proclamations were in full vogue after the Holocaust. As Naffine points out, 'the Second World War, and its immediate aftermath, served to consolidate the species divide in the name of natural human rights and to affirm a strong legal metaphysical stance: that law is for humans essentially understood as non-animals'.[57] If we reject wholesale 'What's Next?' objections, we ignore that the Aristocracy has something going for it, namely that there are good reasons for drawing a circle in the first place. Many animal rights proponents overlook this when critiquing Aristocratic human rights accounts.

However—and this is where opponents of expansions of the circle go wrong—rights activists are correct to argue that the circle should be extended if it cannot be defended anymore on non-arbitrary grounds.[58] With animal rights we seem to have arrived at precisely such a juncture where the current Aristocracy as I described it in Chapter 3—however justified it may have been in 1945—has today become indefensible on non-arbitrary grounds. As Peder Anker puts it, '[t]oday the idea of animal rights or liberation is not a joke anymore'.[59]

These considerations also reveal the interconnectedness of the animal rights project and other rights projects. For example, Henry Salt, one of the first animal rights advocates in the United Kingdom, argued that '[t]he emancipation of men from cruelty and injustice will bring with it in due course the emancipation of animals also. The two reforms are inseparably connected, and neither can be fully realised alone'.[60] My theory of the spectrum explains

[57] Naffine, *Law's Meaning of Life: Philosophy, Religion, Darwin and the Legal Person* (n 13) 122. Christian ideals were particularly influential in cementing this view of human sanctity post 1945, see Samuel Moyn, *Christian Human Rights* (University of Pennsylvania Press 2015).

[58] See also Thomas Benedikt Schmidt, *Das Tier—ein Rechtssubjekt? Eine rechtsphilosophische Kritik der Tierrechtsidee* (Roderer 1996) 41–42.

[59] Peder Anker, 'A Vindication of the Rights of Brutes' (2004) 7 Philosophy & Geography 259, 261.

[60] Cited in Thomas, *Man and the Natural World: Changing Attitudes in England 1500–1800* (n 47) 185; see also his Henry S Salt, *Animals' Rights: Considered in Relation to Social Progress* (MacMillan 1894).

this interconnectedness. All these movements can be interpreted as being rebellions against an Aristocratic conception that excluded groups on arbitrary grounds, and as having therefore fought for a Meritocratic extension of the circle of rights-holders. Indeed, any reform towards a more *Merit*-based system is not complete as long as there are groups left who deserve rights but are not granted any. This is why the struggles for fundamental rights that different groups have been leading are not unrelated.

Because Waldron neglects the successive nature of 'universalisation', he also seems to miss this connection between different rights movements. He fails to see that in all these instances, the expansion is based on the reason that the existing Aristocracy could no longer be defended on non-arbitrary grounds. In fact, because Waldron's universalization from the nobility to all of humanity is itself simply the product of all these smaller expansions, it, too, can be explained in the same way. Waldron's universalization was a Meritocratic expansion that became necessary because the special status and rights of the nobility were increasingly seen as indefensible. By focusing solely on the larger extension from the nobility to all of humanity, Waldron ignores the reasons that have brought about the smaller extensions, and therefore ultimately also the reason for the larger extension. To put this another way: he fails to see that the Aristocracy is not the only fundamental rights conception; on its opposite side, there is another conception, namely the Meritocracy. Seemingly unaware of this fact, Waldron overlooks that the reasons for universalizing high status and rights from the nobility to all human beings were of the same Meritocratic nature as the reasons for fundamental rights for animals.

Let me emphasize one final point. Some authors have suggested that the expansion of the circle of rights-holders is a one-way street: rights are or should continually be extended to more and more beings.[61] According to Roderick Nash, for example, history demonstrates that rights radiate: they have extended from the nobility to whites, slaves, women, indigenous peoples, and may, in the not too distant future, also be extended to animals, and the environment more generally.[62] Lynn Hunt seems to subscribe to a similar view. According to her, the expansive tendency is inherent to rights; it is, as she puts it, part of '[t]he bulldozer force of the revolutionary logic of rights'.[63] The view I defend in this book does not adhere to Nash and Hunt's expansivism. Not only is it implausible to suggest that, historically, rights only expand but never contract.

[61] See Anker, 'A Vindication of the Rights of Brutes' (n 59) 262.

[62] Roderick Frazier Nash, *The Rights of Nature: A History of Environmental Ethics* (University of Wisconsin Press 1989) 6–8.

[63] Hunt, *Inventing Human Rights: A History* (n 50) 160.

But Meritocratic expansions are not always called for either. A Meritocratic expansion, on my account, is only justified up to the extent that we reach an equilibrium between the Meritocracy and the Aristocracy. It cannot be ruled out that a society may one day overstep the equilibrium and lean too much towards the Meritocracy. For example, a society may decide to jettison equal status entirely and grant differentiated rights to all individual animals. In such a case, we would have reason to scale back the Meritocracy. That is, we would have reason to Aristocratize the Meritocracy.

3 How to realize the middle ground

In the previous section, I have argued that decision-makers should aim for an equilibrium between the Aristocracy and the Meritocracy and I have shown that, because current legal systems have come to lean too heavily towards the Aristocratic side, we should change course and approach the Meritocratic side in order to reach the equilibrium. In this section, I will show how a move towards the Meritocracy can be concretely realized. To do so, I address two of the most pressing regards in which animals' treatment in the law is overly Aristocratic. The two issues I will focus on are the treatment of animals as property, and the denial of fundamental rights to animals.[64]

I should make it clear at the outset that I will not argue in favour of any particular way of Meritocratizing animals' legal status. My aim is simply to present a range of possible approaches that could be taken to move in the right direction. As I see it, all of these approaches are useful in working towards achieving an equilibrium. It is also worth noting that the two aforementioned issues intersect in some respects: ceasing to treat animals as property is likely going to be a key step in granting them fundamental rights. However, there are also respects in which these issues diverge, which is why I discuss them separately.

3.1 Overcoming animals' property status

The first respect in which the current treatment of animals is increasingly arbitrary is that legal systems generally consider animals to have the status of property.[65] Animals are legal things, not legal persons. As Gary Francione, one of the

[64] Other potential paths include conferring legal standing, dignity, or citizenship on animals.
[65] See Fasel and Butler, *Animal Rights Law* (n 27) 10–14.

most vocal foes of animals' property status, puts it, 'the law at present regards animals as the property of their owners and institutionally regards animals only as means to human ends'.[66] Like tables and cars, animals are commodities that can be bought, used, sold, or destroyed—often without meaningful legal constraints.[67] This has significant consequences for animals. In the billions, they are bred, branded, herded, fattened, and milked. They are trapped, tamed, trained, neutered, and forcibly impregnated. They are sheared and skinned, caged and confined. And they are killed. The very existence of these terms is testament to the myriad uses to which animals are subjected. Humans, on the other hand, cannot normally be lawfully subjected to such treatment. This is mainly because, in contrast to animals, they are considered to be legal persons. The law thus exhibits a yawning gap between the legal status of animals and that of humans.

To be sure, many legal systems impose restrictions on the use of animal property that do not apply to the ownership of tables and cars. These restrictions are generally to be found in animal protection acts and ordinances.[68] More often than not, however, these restrictions fail to provide sufficient protection of animals' interests. According to Francione, the reason for this is that, even in legal systems with such protections for animals, they are subjected to a legal paradigm in which they occupy a significantly less attractive status than humans. Even to the extent that there are laws that recognize animals' inherent interests, their protection will naturally be limited because they are still considered the property of humans.[69] As Francione notes, the rights of property owners 'are paramount in determining the ambit of protection accorded to animals by law'.[70]

Considering the overwhelming evidence that we have today showing that many animals share many of the same or similar capacities that human beings possess,[71] it seems surprising that the gap between humans as legal persons and animals as property has not yet been closed, or at least significantly narrowed.[72] To narrow that gap, it is pressing to overcome animals' property status.[73] This is one important way in which the current Aristocratic system

[66] Gary L Francione, 'Animals—Property or Persons?' in Cass R Sunstein and Martha C Nussbaum (eds), *Animal Rights: Current Debates and New Directions* (Oxford University Press 2005) 11.

[67] Fasel and Butler, *Animal Rights Law* (n 27) 10–25, 30–31.

[68] ibid 18–22.

[69] Francione, 'Animals—Property or Persons?' (n 66) 122; Gary L Francione, *Animals as Persons: Essays on the Abolition of Animal Exploitation* (Columbia University Press 2008) 19.

[70] Gary L Francione, *Animals, Property, and the Law* (Temple University Press 1995) 24.

[71] See Section 2.2.

[72] See also Naffine, *Law's Meaning of Life: Philosophy, Religion, Darwin and the Legal Person* (n 13) 122.

[73] For a different perspective see Visa AJ Kurki, *A Theory of Legal Personhood* (Oxford University Press 2019).

can be made more Meritocratic. There are, roughly speaking, two paths that lead in this direction.

First, one could try to overcome animals' property status by removing them from the category of simple property which they co-habit with inanimate legal objects in many jurisdictions. Under this approach, animals would not be recognized as full legal persons in the same way that humans are. Rather, animals would come to occupy a middle position: not mere things, but not legal persons either. David Favre, who has put forward a proposal of this sort, argues that animals should be conceived of as 'living property'.[74] Living property, according to Favre, differs from other kinds of property (ie real, personal, and intellectual property) in that it is property with an inherent interest in well-being. This means that, in order to guarantee the protection of animals' well-being, the rights of the owners of living property are more limited than those of other kinds of property. For example, ownership title of 'living property' could be transferred only when it is in the best interest of the animal.[75] Likewise, the use of an owned animal for specific purposes (eg food, fur, or scientific research) and the conditions in which these animals are kept could be subject to specific limitations and prohibitions.[76] As Favre notes, the relationship between owners and 'living property' would in certain respects become like that of parent and child.[77]

Some countries have already taken steps in the direction of transforming animals' legal status along these lines.[78] Section 90a of the German Civil Code, for example, was amended in 1980 to provide that '(1) Animals are not things; (2) They are protected by special statutes.'[79]

Although important Meritocratic milestones in their own right, these legal changes (and kindred ones in other jurisdictions)[80] have so far been of largely symbolic importance.[81] The reason for this is that animals, although not

[74] David Favre, 'Living Property: A New Status for Animals within the Legal System' (2010) 93 Marquette Law Review 1021. See also Richard L Cupp, 'Animals as More Than "Mere Things", But Still Property: A Call for Continuing Evolution of the Animal Welfare Paradigm', *Pepperdine University School of Law, Legal Studies Research Paper Series* (2016) <https://papers.ssrn.com/sol3/papers.cfm?abstract_id=2788309> accessed 11 June 2023.

[75] Favre, 'Living Property: A New Status for Animals within the Legal System' (n 74) 1056.

[76] ibid 1057–58.

[77] ibid 1059, 1071.

[78] See also *Nonhuman Rights Project, Inc v Patrick C Lavery and Nonhuman Rights Project, Inc v Carmen Presti* (n 36) 7.

[79] Section 90a of the German Civil Code (1896, Bürgerliches Gesetzbuch, BGB), Schöning Carmen V (tr), <https://www.gesetze-im-internet.de/englisch_bgb/englisch_bgb.pdf> accessed 11 June 2023.

[80] See eg Swiss Civil Code (1907, Zivilgesetzbuch, ZGB) Article 641a <https://www.admin.ch/opc/en/classified-compilation/19070042/index.html#a641a> accessed 11 June 2023; Austrian Civil Code (1811, Allgemeines bürgerliches Gesetzbuch, ABGB) section 285a <www.ris.bka.gv.at/GeltendeFassung.wxe?Abfrage=Bundesnormen&Gesetzesnummer=10001622> accessed 11 June 2023.

[81] See eg Janneke Vink, *The Open Society and Its Animals* (Palgrave Macmillan 2020) 87.

considered to be mere property anymore, are for the most part still subject to property rules in these jurisdictions. Section 90a of the German Civil Code, for instance, also includes a third paragraph stating that '[t]hey [animals] are governed by the provisions that apply to things, with the necessary modifications, except insofar as otherwise provided'. Although the laws protecting animals have in certain instances managed to impose important restrictions on the treatment of animals (notably for companion animals), even ardent defenders of animal welfarism often acknowledge that how the law treats animals is far from ideal.[82]

Dissatisfied with what they see as a lack of palpable change, some have argued that the first, tiered way of overcoming animals' property status is doomed to failure. As mere 'property plus',[83] they argue, animals cannot be guaranteed sufficient protection of their interests. This is because this hybrid position between property and personhood exists in a system whose core premise is that animals are ours to use. Animals necessarily end up getting sucked back into the old dichotomy.[84] For opponents of the tiered system, turning animals into 'property plus' will have little positive effect. To be truly able to close the gap between the legal status of humans and animals, they argue, we need to extend legal personhood to animals.[85] Among the proponents of this approach, two main camps can be distinguished. The first proposes to confer on animals a *sui generis* legal personhood that is different from human legal personhood; the second wants to put animals in the same category as human legal persons.

An illustrative example of the first camp is Saskia Stucki's account. Stucki proposes that animals should be categorized as 'animal persons' (*tierliche Personen*).[86] Every sentient animal, she argues, should be included in this category of persons, which would come to complement the two other categories generally recognized in law: natural persons and legal persons.[87] According to Stucki, this approach is preferable to including animals in the category of (human) natural persons because practical considerations, including fears of devaluing human legal status, militate against the latter strategy.[88]

[82] See eg Robert Garner, 'Animal Welfare: A Political Defense' (2006) 1 Journal of Animal Law and Ethics 161, 167.
[83] cf Angela Fernandez, 'Animals as Property, Quasi-Property or Quasi-Person' (2022) <https://thebrooksinstitute.org/sites/default/files/presentations/Animal%20Law%20Fundamentals%20-%20Angela%20Fernandez_1.pdf> accessed 11 June 2023.
[84] Francione, *Animals, Property, and the Law* (n 70) 5.
[85] See Taimie L Bryant, 'Sacrificing the Sacrifice of Animals: Legal Personhood for Animals, the Status of Animals as Property, and the Presumed Primacy of Humans' (2008) 39 Rutgers Law Journal 247, 264.
[86] Saskia Stucki, *Grundrechte für Tiere: Eine Kritik des geltenden Tierschutzrechts und rechtstheoretische Grundlegung von Tierrechten im Rahmen einer Neupositionierung des Tieres als Rechtssubjekt* (Nomos 2016) 305.
[87] ibid 304–05, 321.
[88] ibid 304.

The second camp in the legal personhood debate argues that animals should be given the same legal status as natural persons that human beings possess. One proponent of this second approach is Francione.[89] According to him, the reason why humans cannot be treated as another's resource is that humans possess what he calls 'a basic right not to be treated as property'.[90] This right, he argues, is 'a minimal prerequisite to being a . . . legal person'.[91] It ensures that its holders are taken seriously and that their interests do not generally have to give way to the greater good. According to Francione, animals should share in the same status of legal personhood because they, too, have basic interests worthy of protection against trade-offs. That not all humans and animals possess the same interests is inconsequential for their status as legal persons, he holds, because they all share an interest in continued existence.[92]

Practically, animals' legal personhood could function with a guardianship model similar to that which exists for human beings who cannot represent their own interests in court, such as children or persons with certain mental disabilities. As Martha Nussbaum proposes, animals 'may be treated as we currently treat children and many people with mental disabilities, who have a large menu of rights and are in that sense far from being "mere property", although those rights must be exercised through human guardianship'.[93] According to Christopher Stone, one of the central advantages of the guardianship model is that it prevents the flood of litigation some believe could potentially arise from extending standing on behalf of animals to anyone with an interest in the protection of animals.[94] While there would almost certainly be an increase in litigation also under the guardianship model—after all, legal personhood is conferred on animals precisely to effect change—it would ensure that only specific guardians can be responsible for an animal and thereby prevent many different people from bringing claims on behalf of the same animal.[95] Also, guardians will generally have a better understanding of the needs of the ward and therefore be better positioned to defend their ward's interests in court.[96]

[89] Francione, 'Animals—Property or Persons?' (n 66). For another example, see Bilchitz, 'Moving Beyond Arbitrariness: The Legal Personhood and Dignity of Non-Human Animals' (n 8) 68.
[90] Francione, 'Animals—Property or Persons?' (n 66) 124.
[91] ibid 125 (emphasis removed).
[92] Francione, *Animals as Persons: Essays on the Abolition of Animal Exploitation* (n 69) 193.
[93] Martha C Nussbaum, *Frontiers of Justice: Disability, Nationality, Species Membership* (Harvard University Press 2006) 376–77.
[94] See Christopher D Stone, 'Should Trees Have Standing—Toward Legal Rights for Natural Objects' (1972) 45 Southern California Law Review 450, 470.
[95] ibid 470–71.
[96] ibid 471.

Perhaps unsurprisingly, this second way of overcoming animals' property status is even further from being realized than the first way. As pointed out above, the closest most legal systems have come to overcoming animals' property status is to extend to them a special, but largely symbolic status as 'property plus'. This has certainly to do with the far-reaching practical implications a Meritocratization of the second kind would have. As Francione points out, including animals in the category of legal persons may impose an obligation on us 'to stop using animals for food, biomedical experiments, entertainment, or clothing, or any other uses that assume that animals are merely resources, and that we prohibit the ownership of animals'.[97]

But things are changing also in this regard. In 2016, the Third Court of Guarantees in Mendoza, Argentina, granted a writ of *habeas corpus* that the Association of Officials and Advocates for Animal Rights (AFADA) had filed on behalf of Cecilia, a chimpanzee held at the zoo of Mendoza.[98] The Court rejected the state attorney's argument that the case should be dismissed on the grounds that Cecilia is an animal and therefore 'still a thing', and it ordered Cecilia's transfer to a great ape sanctuary.[99] Highlighting the genetic proximity between human beings and chimpanzees, and their shared capabilities, the Court reasoned that '[a] chimpanzee is not a thing, he is not an object that can [be] disposed of like a car or a building. Great apes are legal persons, with legal capacity.'[100] Confronted with the question of how Cecilia would exercise her personhood, the Court pointed out that a similar incompetence on the part of many human beings does not prevent them from being legal persons for the simple reason that representatives can exercise the rights on their behalf.[101]

In 2022, the Constitutional Court of Ecuador made a similar finding when it decided a *habeas corpus* petition filed for the woolly monkey Estrellita, who had been kept by a private individual until government authorities seized Estrellita. Even though Estrellita died before the Constitutional Court could decide the petition, the Court used the case to clarify its interpretation of Article 83(6) of Ecuador's Constitution, pursuant to which Ecuadorians have the duty and

[97] Francione, 'Animals—Property or Persons?' (n 66) 132.

[98] Lauren Choplin, 'Chimpanzee Cecilia Finds Sanctuary: An Interview with GAP Brazil' (*Nonhuman Rights Project*, 20 April 2017) <https://www.nonhumanrights.org/blog/chimpanzee-cecilia/> accessed 11 June 2023.

[99] *'Cecilia'* [2016] Tercer Juzgado de Garantías Mendoza P-72.254/15 (Ana María Hernández tr <https://www.nonhumanrights.org/content/uploads/2016/12/Chimpanzee-Cecilia_translation-FINAL-for-website.pdf> accessed 11 June 2023), 5.

[100] ibid 24.

[101] ibid 27.

obligation to, among other things, 'respect the rights of nature'. Drawing attention to the Constitution's non-anthropocentric approach, the Court argued that Article 83(6) does not only confer rights on nature as a collective entity, but also to individual wild animals. Using the terms 'legal person' and 'subject of law' roughly synonymously, the Court found that, although different from human beings, animals are also subjects of law.[102] As subjects of law, it reasoned, wild animals have numerous fundamental rights, including the right to life, to bodily integrity, to food, and not to be hunted.[103]

Cases such as these are significant because of the improvements of living conditions that they can bring about for the animals themselves. But in addition, these cases are of great symbolic importance because they show that legal personhood for animals is not a mere pipe dream. These cases provide us with a rare glimpse into what a world would look like in which animals cease to be property. And cases such as these can inspire other animal rights advocates around the world to push for similar Meritocratizations in their legal systems.

3.2 Fundamental rights for animals

The second regard in which the current legal treatment of animals appears to be increasingly difficult to justify on non-arbitrary grounds is their wholesale exclusion from fundamental rights-holdership. Whilst human beings possess such fundamental legal rights as the right to life, the right to bodily and mental integrity, or the right to family life, nonhuman animals possess no equivalent rights. This is the case despite the fact that, as has been pointed out, many animals today demonstrably possess similar capacities and interests to those that would seem relevant for humans' possession of these rights. Because animals lack such rights, the law allows infringements of their most basic interests with few constraints. Another way to Meritocratize the current status of animals would therefore be to grant at least some fundamental rights to some other animals.

As may have become evident in the previous section, the issue of fundamental rights is closely related to the question of legal personhood. According

[102] *'Estrellita'* [2022] Constitutional Court of Ecuador, No 253-20-JH, translation available at <animal.law.harvard.edu/wp-content/uploads/Final-Judgment-Estrellita-w-Translation-Certification.pdf> accessed 11 June 2023, para 81 and footnotes 86–87.

[103] ibid, paras 119, 124, 132–33.

to a dominant view in the literature, legal personhood is a *conditio sine qua non* for fundamental rights-holdership.[104] Wise, for example, invites us to think of legal personhood as an 'empty "rights container"'.[105] Into this container, we can 'drip' different rights, depending on the interests of the relevant person. On this view, legal personhood is simply the 'capacity for possessing any legal right'.[106] According to Wise, this conceptualization can also explain how humans and animals may share some but not all fundamental rights ('drips'). Francione adopts a similar view, arguing that '[t]he right not to be treated as the property of others is basic and different from any other rights we might have because it is the grounding for those other rights; it is a prelegal right'.[107] In contrast to Wise, however, Francione admits that it is conceptually possible to sever the question of fundamental rights from legal personhood.[108] But while animals may be able to possess some legal rights despite remaining property, Francione argues that they could not possess any meaningful rights—or fundamental rights, as I have been calling them.[109]

Other scholars disagree with this view.[110] Alasdair Cochrane, for instance, finds that as owners, humans do not have absolute control over the animals they possess. Instead, their ownership rights are limited, in the same way as they are for other kinds of property: 'if I own a barrel of beer, I cannot simply sell glasses of it to passers-by on the street; if I own a house, I cannot refuse entry to all other people in all circumstances; and if I own a piece of land, I cannot simply build what I like upon it'.[111] Property, Cochrane argues, consists of a range of different relations which the owner can have towards her property: she can possess it, use it, manage it, transfer it, derive income from it, be protected against expropriation, etc. Because not all of these relations need to be present for property ownership to exist,[112] Cochrane infers that it is possible for someone to be the owner of, say, a cow without being allowed to use or transfer her in ways that would cause her suffering or to bring about her

[104] See eg Steven M Wise, 'The Legal Thinghood of Nonhuman Animals' (1996) 23 Boston College Environmental Affairs Law Review 471. For an overview of the two main approaches, see Fasel and Butler, *Animal Rights Law* (n 27) 92–97.
[105] Steven M Wise, 'Nonhuman Rights to Personhood' (2013) 30 Pace Environmental Law Review 1278, 1281.
[106] See for a similar view Bilchitz, 'Moving Beyond Arbitrariness: The Legal Personhood and Dignity of Non-Human Animals' (n 8).
[107] Francione, 'Animals—Property or Persons?' (n 66) 124.
[108] Francione, *Animals, Property, and the Law* (n 70) 14.
[109] See Francione, 'Animals—Property or Persons?' (n 66) 125; Francione, *Animals, Property, and the Law* (n 70) 14.
[110] See eg Favre, 'Living Property: A New Status for Animals within the Legal System' (n 74) 1053–70.
[111] Alasdair Cochrane, 'Ownership and Justice for Animals' (2009) 21 Utilitas 424, 426.
[112] ibid 427.

death.[113] On Cochrane's view, then, a cow can have rights (such as rights to bodily integrity and to life) despite being property.[114]

Because our main focus lies on the practical implementation of fundamental rights for animals rather than its conceptual requirements, it is sufficient to simply flag the existence of this debate. We do not need to take sides in it. To the extent that—given the scarcity of decisions dealing with animals' fundamental rights—a pattern can be discerned in case law, courts seem so far to have largely avoided answering the question of whether legal personhood is a precondition for fundamental rights—unless the petition explicitly required them to address the issue, as in the *habeas corpus* cases.[115] For example, in *Nair v Union of India*, the High Court in the Indian state of Kerala, dealing with the question as to whether the treatment of circus animals was in compliance with the Prevention of Cruelty to Animals Act (1960) and the Constitution of India, raised the issue of animals' fundamental rights without once discussing their property status.[116]

Setting aside the question of legal personhood, we can now turn to the question of *which* fundamental rights could be conferred on nonhuman animals. Jean-Claude Delamétherie made a good start in answering this question when, in 1787, he proposed that all animals who are capable of having sensations should possess three fundamental rights: the right to life, the right to health, and the right to enjoyments (*plaisirs*).[117] His short catalogue of fundamental rights is deficient in two regards, however. First, it is just that: *short*. Unless one interprets the three rights in a broad way, one will struggle to capture other fundamental rights which seem applicable to at least some animals. Second, by focusing solely on the question of whether an animal is sensitive, Delamétherie ignored other capacities which allow allocating fundamental rights in a more Meritocratic way. Now, because the number of fundamental rights and especially that of animals who have interests grounding such rights is far too large for the limited space of this section, I will focus on just a few proposals.[118]

Among the rights that are missing from Delamétherie's list is the *right to bodily integrity*. This is a right that, in the human context, protects its holders

[113] See ibid 438, 441.
[114] See, for a similar view, Kurki, *A Theory of Legal Personhood* (n 73) 86–87.
[115] See eg *'Cecilia'* (n 99) 22–25.
[116] *NR Nair et al v Union of India et al* [2000] Kerala High Court 2000(3)RCR(Civil)650, para 13. See also *Narayan Dutt Bhatt v Union of India et al* [2018] High Court of Uttarakhand 2018(3) RCR(Civil)544, para 99A.
[117] See Chapter 2, Section 5.
[118] For an example of a broader set of rights see eg Finnish Animal Rights Law Society, 'Proposal: Fundamental Rights for Animals' <https://www.elaintenvuoro.fi/english/> accessed 11 June 2023.

from 'physical assaults, torture, medical or other experimentation, immunisation and compelled eugenic or social sterilisation, and cruel or degrading treatment or punishment'.[119] The right imposes corresponding duties on the state to protect the rights-holders against such interference. The right to bodily integrity is in principle applicable to all animals who are sentient, and proposals have emerged to turn this right into a reality. For instance, a citizens' initiative launched in 2016 in the Swiss Canton of Basel-Stadt proposed to amend the canton's Constitution to guarantee *inter alia* the right to bodily and mental integrity for nonhuman primates.[120] Although the initiative limited the right to nonhuman primates for practical reasons, the drafters argued that this 'does not exclude the possibility that other animals presenting the relevant characteristics might also come to enjoy the same (or other) fundamental rights'.[121]

Another fundamental right that is being tipped as a right that can be extended beyond the human species is the *right to life*.[122] There is widespread acceptance that an interest in continued existence is a necessary condition for the right to life. However, opinions are divided on what makes an animal have an interest in continued existence. According to a more demanding view, to have an interest in continued existence, an animal needs to be autonomous, that is, to be able to make plans for the future.[123] On this view, only animals who have this ability are considered to possess a real interest in continuing to exist. A less demanding view sets the bar lower and holds that every sentient animal—autonomous or not—possesses an interest in continued existence.[124] This latter view was endorsed by the Indian Supreme Court in *Animal Welfare Board of India v A Nagaraja* (2014). In this case, the Court had to adjudicate the legality of '*Jallikattu*' events in which crowds of people attempt to tame

[119] David Feldman, *Civil Liberties and Human Rights in England and Wales* (2nd edn, Oxford University Press 2002) 241.

[120] See Sentience Politics, 'Cantonal Initiative "Basic Rights for Primates"' (2022) <https://sentience-politics.org/politics/fundamental-rights-basel-ch/> accessed 11 June 2023.

[121] Sentience Politics, 'Fundamental Rights for Primates: Policy Paper' (2016) <https://ea-foundation.org/files/Fundamental-Rights-for-Primates.pdf> accessed 11 June 2023 (I was one of the drafters). The initiative was rejected by the citizens of Basel-Stadt in February 2022: Staatskanzlei Basel-Stadt, 'Wahl- und Abstimmungsergebnisse (Archiv)' <https://www.staatskanzlei.bs.ch/politische-rechte/wahlen-abstimmungen/resultate-archiv.html> 11 June 2023. See also Charlotte E Blattner and Raffael N Fasel, 'The Swiss Primate Case: How Courts Have Paved the Way for the First Direct Democratic Vote on Animal Rights' (2021) 11 Transnational Environmental Law 201.

[122] See also Paola Cavalieri and Peter Singer, 'A Declaration on Great Apes' in Paola Cavalieri and Peter Singer (eds), *The Great Ape Project: Equality Beyond Humanity* (St Martin's Griffin 1993) 5; James Rachels, 'Do Animals Have a Right to Life?' in Harlan B Miller and William H Williams (eds), *Ethics and Animals* (Humana Press 1983) 275.

[123] See eg Peter Singer, *Animal Liberation: A New Ethics for Our Treatment of Animals* (HarperCollins 1975) 18–20; Peter Singer, *Practical Ethics* (3rd edn, Cambridge University Press 2011) 97–98.

[124] See eg Gary L Francione, 'Equal Consideration and the Interest of Nonhuman Animals in Continued Existence: A Response to Professor Sunstein' (2006) 2006 University of Chicago Legal Forum 1, 231, 239–40.

bulls and bullocks. Because the animals used in the events are not only subjected to a host of distressful and painful practices,[125] but sometimes also suffer fatal injuries, the Court considered whether they are protected by a right to life similar to that which human beings possess. The Court held that '[e]very species has a right to life and security, subject to the law of the land, which includes depriving its life, out of human necessity'.[126] In its more recent decision *Animal Welfare Board of India v Union of India* (2023), the Indian Supreme Court partially walked this back. In this case, the Court faced challenges brought against several state laws that had been introduced in *Nagaraja*'s wake to sanction *Jallikattu* and similar races, albeit with stricter regulations. On the question of animals' right to life, the Court held that, in *Nagaraja*, the finding that animals could have fundamental rights under the Indian Constitution had only ever been made at an 'advisory level' or as a 'judicial suggestion'.[127] Such a decision, it argued, would have to be made by the legislator.[128] The Court's change of course notwithstanding, *Nagaraja* helps to illustrate how a right to life for animals could be incorporated into an existing constitution, and it has inspired similar rulings in other jurisdictions.[129]

Finally, it can be pointed out that irrespective of whether one adopts the more or the less demanding view of what an interest in continued existence requires, the right to life is itself seen as a necessary condition for other fundamental rights. It could thus be argued that this aspect of the right to life may make animals eligible for it simply in virtue of being eligible for other fundamental rights.[130]

While the rights to bodily integrity and life would form an important subset of fundamental rights for many animals, they do not exhaust the list of rights that could be extended. Most importantly, a range of what are sometimes known as socio-economic rights could be meaningfully applied to animals, too. An important example of such a right is the *right to health*, which Delamétherie included on his list.[131] Other potential candidates which he does

[125] See *Animal Welfare Board of India v A Nagaraja et al* [2014] Supreme Court of India 2014 (5) SCJ 614, paras 16–17.

[126] ibid para 62. I am grateful to Kelly Dhru for advice on this judgment. See also *Narayan Dutt Bhatt v Union of India* (n 116) para 98.

[127] *Animal Welfare Board of India et al v Union of India et al* [2023] Supreme Court of India, Writ Petition (Civil) No 23 of 2016, para 24.

[128] ibid.

[129] See eg *'Kaavan'* [2020] *Islamabad Wildlife Management Board v Metropolitan Corporation Islamabad*, Islamabad High Court, WP No 1155/2019, 36–37.

[130] See Sentience Politics, 'Fundamental Rights for Primates: Policy Paper' (2016) 8 <https://ea-foundation.org/files/Fundamental-Rights-for-Primates.pdf>. See also Cochrane, *Sentientist Politics: A Theory of Global Inter-Species Justice* (n 12) 29.

[131] See also Alasdair Cochrane, 'Cosmozoopolis: The Case against Group-Differentiated Animal Rights' (2013) 1 Law, Ethics and Philosophy 127, 135.

not mention are the *right to food*, the *right to shelter*, and the *right to an adequate standard of living*. In the human rights context, such socio-economic rights are commonly referred to as 'positive' rights,[132] to contrast them with 'negative' rights not to be interfered with. Several courts have taken steps towards extending such positive rights to animals. Perhaps the best example is the Estrellita case, which I discussed in Section 3.1. Interpreting Article 83(6) of the Ecuadorian Constitution, which protects 'the rights of nature', the Ecuadorian Constitutional Court found that this provision also protects individual wild animals' rights, including numerous positive rights. Among the rights that wild animals have are the 'rights to food in accordance with the nutritional requirements of their species, to live in harmony, to health, to habitat, [and] to the free development of their animal behaviour'.[133] In a similar vein, the Cecilia judgment, which I mentioned in Section 3.1, held that animals have a 'right to live in an environment and conditions appropriate for [their] species'.[134]

The idea that animals should have fundamental rights to receive positive protection of their most basic capacities and needs also seems to be reflected in cases from India. In *People for Animals v Mohazzim* (2015), the Delhi High Court held that 'all the birds have fundamental rights to fly in the sky'[135]—a finding that was also reached in a different case before the Gujarat High Court, in *Abdulkadar v State of Gujarat* (2011), in which that Court held that birds 'have [the] right to move freely in the open sky'.[136] While such a right would have a negative component—prohibiting interferences with birds' ability to fly—it could also have a positive component, such as the requirement to create an environment that enables birds to fly.

As I have pointed out above, the list of rights which could reasonably be extended to other animals will be longer and more complex than what I could present here. Because my goal was merely to provide a sneak peek into what a Meritocratic extension of fundamental rights to animals could look like, I will not consider any further examples and distinctions. Instead, I want to close by drawing attention to the fact that there may also be numerous fundamental rights that will *not* be applicable to animals. This is because no nonhuman animal can likely be shown to have an interest grounding these rights. As the

[132] For criticism see Sandra Fredman, *Human Rights Transformed: Positive Rights and Positive Duties* (Oxford University Press 2008) 1.

[133] *'Estrellita'* (n 102) para 119.

[134] *'Cecilia'* (n 99) 32.

[135] *People for Animals v Md Mohazzim et al* [2015] Delhi High Court 2015(3)RCR(Criminal)94, para 5.

[136] *Abdulkadar Mohamad Azam Sheikh v State of Gujarat et al* [2011] Gujarat High Court No 1635/2010, para 8.11.

Court of Mendoza made clear in the Cecilia ruling, animal rights 'is not about granting [animals] the same rights humans have'.[137] Examples of rights that are unlikely candidates for extension to most, if not all, nonhuman animals are rights such as the right to a fair criminal trial, freedom of the press, or the right to vote. As Cass Sunstein puts it,

> [t]he legal protection to be accorded to animals does, of course, depend on the kind of creatures that they are. Dogs and horses should not have the right to vote; but they should have a right to good lives for dogs and horses. Animals with less developed cognitive capacities deserve rights of a different sort. There is no blueprint here. My suggestion is only that the rights that animals deserve should be related to their capacities.[138]

4 Conclusion

This chapter has demonstrated that the theory of the spectrum of fundamental rights conceptions, which I developed in the previous chapters, is not only theoretically illuminating but also practically useful. More specifically, I have argued that because the Aristocracy and the Meritocracy are antithetical ideal-types that present us with equally good reasons for and against adopting them, the best practical solution is to steer a middle ground between these extremes. Because current legal systems are too wedded to the Aristocratic extreme, I proposed that we ought to 'Meritocratize the Aristocracy' to reach this middle ground. I have explored two concrete ways in which such a Meritocratization could be achieved: by transforming animals' property status and by extending fundamental rights to them.

My aim was to show that animals' legal status quo is changing and that the tide is turning away from Aristocratic legal systems that subject animals to human whim. At the same time, however, I have emphasized what is generally neglected in discourse about expanding rights: that there are virtuous elements in Aristocratic systems that should not be swept away entirely by the tide. In the next chapter, I argue that these virtuous elements counsel in favour of adopting a practical approach to extending rights and legal personhood to animals which focuses on their species membership, not their individual characteristics.

[137] *'Cecilia'* (n 99) 27.

[138] Cass R Sunstein, 'The Rights of Animals' (2003) 70 The University of Chicago Law Review 387, 401.

7

The Species Membership Approach

1 Introduction

The previous chapter has argued that most legal systems exclude all nonhuman animals from fundamental rights protections, and consider them to be property. To remedy this situation, the chapter made the case for a Meritocratization of this Aristocratic state of the law. I discussed two different legal strategies to achieve such a Meritocratization: changing animals' status as property, and conferring certain fundamental rights on them. My suggestion was that, by adopting these strategies, we can work towards reaching an equilibrium between the Aristocratic and the Meritocratic conceptions. But what if these strategies overshoot the mark, and simply result in the pendulum swinging too far in the Meritocratic direction?

To accommodate this legitimate worry, the present chapter adds an important caveat to the abovementioned strategies. I propose that extensions of fundamental legal rights, legal personhood status, and other potential legal protections to animals should occur *based on species membership*, not individual abilities or interests. I call this approach the Species Membership Approach, or the SMA for short. According to the SMA, we should be Meritocrats in extending fundamental legal rights and cognate legal protections to other animals. However, in doing so, we should follow Aristocrats by focusing on the species of the fundamental rights-holder rather than on their individual capacities. As I will explain in this chapter, the SMA is an unconventional approach because it challenges a belief that has become an article of faith among animal rights proponents: that species membership is an arbitrary criterion that should be abandoned in favour of considering the needs of individual animals. Against this orthodoxy, I will argue that, in law, granting rights, personhood, and other entitlements based on individual capacities is neither feasible nor desirable. Extending these legal positions to all members of the same species, by contrast, is a more pragmatic and politically prudent way forward: one that allows attaining a Meritocratic expansion of the circle of rights-holders while at the same time taking on board key Aristocratic insights.

More Equal Than Others. Raffael N Fasel, Oxford University Press. © Raffael N Fasel 2024.
DOI: 10.1093/oso/9780198907435.003.0007

While I believe the SMA to make an important contribution to current debates by showing what a practical middle ground between the Aristocracy and Meritocracy can look like, I do not claim that it is the only way of having nonhuman animals recognized as holders of fundamental legal rights and similar entitlements in a broadly egalitarian way. As I will point out below, there are other legal proposals that are akin to the SMA.[1] In the domain of ethics, too, there are approaches that resemble the SMA. For example, according to Jeff McMahan's 'Two-Tiered Account',[2] the killing of persons (beings who are autonomous) should be considered equally morally wrong, regardless of how strong a person's interests are, because killing a person means failing to respect them. By contrast, the wrongness of killing beings who are not persons is assessed on a scale, making the killing of those with stronger or more interests in remaining alive worse than the killing of those with weaker or fewer such interests.[3] On the face of it, McMahan's account seems to combine the Aristocratic idea of equal worth (for persons) with the Meritocratic idea of a scale of moral considerability (for non-persons). However, it is worth flagging two key differences that help bring out what makes the SMA distinctive.

First, in contrast to McMahan's and other accounts, the SMA does not attempt to merge Aristocratic and Meritocratic elements. As I noted in the previous chapter, I follow Max Weber in rejecting syncretic approaches that blend elements from different ideal-types. The problem with such merging, I explained, is that it tends to conceal the underlying characteristics of the ideal-types that are being melded. As a result, the task of decision-makers to mediate between the conflicting ideal-types becomes harder.[4] That is why the SMA does not propose a *theoretical* resolution of the tension between the Aristocracy and the Meritocracy. Instead, it pursues a *practical* middle ground that aims to make clear what choice decision-makers and politicians face, and how they can pursue conflicting values underlying both ideal-types.

Second, and relatedly, the SMA is not about the *moral* rightness or wrongness of killing or other types of harm. Rather, it is about how fundamental *legal* rights, *legal* personhood, and other *legal* entitlements can be extended to nonhuman beings in a way that is compatible with core egalitarian

[1] See Section 2.3.
[2] Jeff McMahan, *The Ethics of Killing: Problems at the Margins of Life* (Oxford University Press 2002) 245. See for another account that is similar to the SMA Shelly Kagan, *How to Count Animals, More or Less* (Oxford University Press 2019) 294–97.
[3] McMahan, *The Ethics of Killing: Problems at the Margins of Life* (n 2) 245, 256.
[4] See Chapter 6, Section 2.

assumptions. This legal and practical focus explains why, in contrast to ethical theories such as McMahan's,[5] the SMA is open to embracing species membership as a necessary condition for the extension of rights protections and legal status.

The chapter is structured as follows. I will begin, in Section 2, by proposing that the species membership criterion should be rehabilitated among animal rights lawyers. To make the case for the SMA, I will shed light on the pragmatic and political reasons for using species membership rather than individual interests as a criterion for legal entitlements. I will then point out some of the important differences between law and philosophy—differences that show why species membership can be a helpful legal criterion, even if it is problematic to use as a philosophical one. The section ends by explaining the rationale behind choosing species as a criterion for extending legal rights and other protections to animals. In Section 3, I will demonstrate the viability of the SMA by showing how it fares in three test cases—the cases of Sesha the human being, Minnie the elephant, and Knuckles the chimpanzee. In Section 4, finally, I will outline how the SMA can be operationalized, focusing on the questions as to which species should come first (and which last), who counts as a member of a species, who gets to decide which species deserve protection, and how to deal with conflicts arising between the rights of humans and nonhumans. A brief conclusion will summarize the chapter's findings.

2 Rehabilitating species membership as a criterion

The SMA is the view that fundamental rights (and cognate concepts such as legal personhood) should be extended, in law, on the basis of a being's *species membership*. It proposes that every member of the same species should receive equal status and equal rights.[6] While this may be reminiscent of the Aristocracy, there is an important difference here. In contrast to the Aristocracy's anthropocentric speciesism, the SMA does not restrict fundamental rights to the human species. Instead, it is open to extending these rights, and cognate entitlements, to other species. Despite its openness to granting such entitlements to other species, however, the SMA is an unorthodox position to hold in the animal rights community. To understand why this is so, it is necessary to consider the

[5] Jeff McMahan, 'Killing and Equality' (1995) 7 Utilitas 1, 15, 24; McMahan, *The Ethics of Killing: Problems at the Margins of Life* (n 2) 211.

[6] As a reminder, see for the definition of these terms Chapter 3, Section 3.

aversion animal rights proponents have to basing their claims on a being's species rather than their individual capacities or interests.

The species membership criterion has been a bogeyman in the animal rights literature ever since Peter Singer's forceful critique of speciesism.[7] As we saw in Chapter 4, Singer criticized species membership for being a morally irrelevant criterion when it comes to determining whether a creature has moral considerability. Species membership, Singer argues, is on par with other arbitrary criteria, such as membership in a specific race or sex. As he emphasizes, '[i]t should be obvious that the fundamental objections to racism and sexism . . . apply equally to speciesism'.[8] Singer's position has gained a large following over the years. Today, the species membership criterion is rejected by virtually all animal rights advocates. Alasdair Cochrane, for example, finds that '[p]icking species membership . . . is entirely arbitrary',[9] adding that at 'the heart of many traditional theories of animal ethics has been . . . a general scepticism about the moral relevance of group-based distinctions'.[10] In a similar vein, Gary Francione charges that 'species is not a justification for treating animals as property any more than is race a justification for human slavery'.[11] In a recent *amici curiae* brief in support of the Nonhuman Rights Project's (NhRP's) *habeas corpus* petitions on behalf of chimpanzees, a consortium of seventeen philosophers adopted the same view when arguing 'that species membership alone cannot rationally be used to determine who is a person or a rights holder'.[12]

My aim is not to challenge this criticism wholesale: some of it is entirely warranted. Rather, I submit that despite the legitimate aspects of the criticism of speciesism, we would do well not to toss the species membership criterion overboard completely. More specifically, I propose that the rejection of that criterion by moral philosophers should not be adopted blindly by lawyers. Philosophy is not the same as law: what holds there does not necessarily

[7] Peter Singer, *Animal Liberation: A New Ethics for Our Treatment of Animals* (HarperCollins 1975) 6; see on the term 'speciesism' Richard D Ryder, 'Speciesism Again: The Original Leaflet' (2010) 2 Critical Society 1.

[8] Singer, *Animal Liberation: A New Ethics for Our Treatment of Animals* (n 7) 6.

[9] Alasdair Cochrane, 'From Human Rights to Sentient Rights' (2013) 16 Critical Review of International Social and Political Philosophy 655, 661.

[10] Alasdair Cochrane, *Sentientist Politics: A Theory of Global Inter-Species Justice* (Oxford University Press 2018) 5.

[11] Gary L Francione, 'Animals—Property or Persons?' in Cass R Sunstein and Martha C Nussbaum (eds), *Animal Rights: Current Debates and New Directions* (Oxford University Press 2005) 131.

[12] *Nonhuman Rights Project, Inc v Patrick C Lavery et al and Nonhuman Rights Project, Inc v Carmen Presti et al* (23 February 2018) Proposed Brief by Amici Curiae Philosophers, 8 <https://www.nonhumanrights.org/content/uploads/In-re-Nonhuman-Rights-v.-Lavery-Proposed-Brief-by-PHILOSOPHERS-74435.pdf> accessed 11 June 2023.

hold here. Species membership may not be a *morally* relevant criterion: but, as I will argue in the following, it is a pragmatically and politically useful criterion in *law*.

2.1 The case for the SMA

Let us begin with the *pragmatic* reasons that speak in favour of the SMA, and against extending legal rights and personhood on the basis of individual capacities or interests. The first pragmatic reason relates to judicial competence and administrability, that is, the need for a criterion that judges are qualified to apply and that is workable.[13] The SMA is pragmatically preferable to individualistic approaches because it saves judges from having to determine whether the particular animal before them possesses the capacities and interests that are relevant for the right whose extension is under consideration. Such a determination will be difficult not only because judges are not zoologists, but also because such data are generally not collected on individual animals. Judges will generally have to rely on the scientific data that are presented to them by the parties. These will in most instances be data about specific groups within an animal species, or data about the species more generally. Hence, when the NhRP filed the first *habeas corpus* petitions on behalf of four chimpanzees in 2013, its president Steven Wise acknowledged in a public debate that '[w]e don't have access to the four chimpanzees who are in captivity . . . and right now we're talking indeed about your *average chimpanzee*, and we don't have a reason for thinking that they are not your average chimpanzee'.[14]

Second, the SMA is a useful tool for reasons of judicial economy. Judges will generally lack the time to study the characteristics of an individual animal before them. Courts are busy places, and judges have only limited time for each case. This problem is amplified in cases that are deemed to be less important, as is common in cases that involve nonhuman animals. From a pragmatic point of view, it will therefore be more efficient for judges to rely on general studies about the species of the relevant animal, allowing them to decide more cases in less time.

[13] On administrability see eg Anthony J Bellia, 'Establishment and Judicial Administrability' (2008) 25 Constitutional Commentary 259.

[14] David Grimm, 'Live Chat: Should Animals Be Granted Legal Rights?' (*Science*, 2 December 2013) at 38:58 <http://www.sciencemag.org/news/2013/12/live-chat-should-animals-be-granted-legal-rights> accessed 11 June 2023 (emphasis added).

Third, reasons of prudence speak for the SMA. Basing their reasoning on an animal's species allows judges to err on the safe side when the animal at hand does not appear to be a 'normal' adult member of its species. Perhaps the animal is an adolescent with less than fully developed capacities and interests. Or the animal is cognitively disabled and appears to have some capacities and interests to a lesser extent. In such cases, it will be even more difficult for judges to decide whether the individual animal before them qualifies for a specific right. In contrast to philosophers and scientists, however, they 'lack the luxury of deferring judgement until data are more complete', as Wise points out. 'In the face of uncertainty and chance of error', he notes, judges 'must decide and content themselves with deciding on which side they wish to err'.[15] Given their duty to render a decision, it would be more prudent for judges to err on the side of extending the relevant rights to the animal by relying on their species membership. The stakes are high in cases of this sort: if a judge chooses not to grant certain fundamental rights to an animal and it turns out, based on Meritocratic considerations, that the animal deserved these rights then the animal's basic interests have been unjustifiably violated.

Of course, erring in favour of extending rights protection is not without its costs—quite literally: requiring the state to protect rights involves a financial commitment that the state must be able to bear to enforce the right effectively. This is true for more traditional rights, such as the right to bodily integrity, which primarily require states to prosecute violations and refrain from infringing the right themselves. And it is even more true for rights, such as the right to adequate health, which require large investments in infrastructure such as hospitals.[16] Finally, in addition to being a potential financial burden, erring in favour of extending rights protection can imperil a court's legitimacy in the eyes of the public if doing so is viewed as a step too far by a majority of people. However, judges will need to balance these costs against the consequences suffered by the animals if rights are not extended to them. The more serious the harm that would be inflicted, the more reason judges have to be overinclusive rather than underinclusive—that is, to be safe rather than sorry.[17]

This is not to say that, even when the benefits outweigh the costs, judges or other officials can never deviate from applying the species standard. Many legal

[15] Steven M Wise, *Drawing the Line: Science and the Case for Animal Rights* (Perseus Publishing 2002) 39.

[16] See OHCHR, 'Key Concepts on ESCRs—Are Economic, Social and Cultural Rights Fundamentally Different from Civil and Political Rights?' <https://www.ohchr.org/en/human-rights/economic-social-cultural-rights/escr-vs-civil-political-rights> accessed 11 June 2023.

[17] See also Wise, *Drawing the Line: Science and the Case for Animal Rights* (n 15) 40.

presumptions can be rebutted, and it may also be possible—and sometimes necessary—to rebut the presumption that an animal deserves the same legal entitlements as other members of its species. Defeasibility of that presumption could be indispensable, for instance, in cases where it is obvious that the relevant being will not benefit from having certain rights that other members of their species possess.[18] Assume, for example, that chimpanzees deserve a right to liberty. For most chimpanzees, it will make sense to presume that they possess the relevant capacities—for example, the capacity to live autonomously—to benefit from that right. In the cases of infant chimpanzees and some chimpanzees with severe mental disabilities, however, having such a right could be to their detriment. This is because, if their liberty was not restricted, these beings could inflict harm on themselves or others. In such cases, judges need to be able to rebut the presumption and refuse certain rights to a being. This kind of defeasibility is also at work in the context of legal rights where humans are concerned. For example, the presumption that a human being can enter into contracts can be rebutted in the case of persons who lack the necessary power of judgement. As in the case of the SMA, this defeasibility serves to prevent harm to the party who lacks the relevant capacities to conclude valid agreements, as well as to the party contracting with them.

A sceptic of the SMA might want to raise an objection at this stage: by allowing for the SMA's presumption to be rebutted, do I not allow Meritocratic considerations to return through the back door? And would this not ultimately undermine the effort to save the principle of equality by moving away from individual capacities-based considerations? The sceptic is right in one respect: the presumption that an animal deserves the same entitlements as their conspecifics would indeed be rebutted based on Meritocratic considerations. However, as in the case of defeasibility in human rights, this does not mean that the underlying egalitarian principle is abandoned. As argued above, officials could only rebut the general presumption in exceptional circumstances: cases where it is obvious that upholding the presumption could result in harm to that being or others. Even when such exceptions are granted, the presumption itself—and with it the Aristocratic egalitarian principle—will remain unaffected.

Critical disability scholars' warning calls about the Meritocracy, discussed in Chapter 4, reverberate in the context of defeasible presumptions. By allowing

[18] Defeasibility may also be required in cases where large groups of individuals have different needs despite belonging to the same species. An example for this could be domesticated horses who, despite belonging to the same species (*Equus ferus*), lead lives that are quite different from the lives of Mongolian wild horses.

for rights protections to be removed on Meritocratic grounds, one runs the risk of undermining the equal status and equal rights of vulnerable beings, especially of humans with disabilities. However, as before, I believe this to be a reason to be careful, not to abandon Meritocratic thinking altogether.[19] Presumptions would be rebuttable only where the existence of a right has a harmful effect on its holder or on other rights-holders, not on grounds of political convenience or economic efficiency, let alone malicious motives. Whether a right has a harmful impact on its holder should be determined in ways that are informed by, and sensitive to, historical and social contingencies colouring such assessments, and that do not reinforce perceptions of vulnerable beings as something 'lesser'.[20]

Let us now turn to the second type of reasons that speak for the SMA: *political* reasons. It is not only pragmatically advisable to extend (or refuse to extend) fundamental rights on the grounds of species membership rather than individual characteristics. It is also politically desirable. The first reason for this is that it allows us to uphold our commitment to egalitarianism. This commitment, as we saw in Chapter 3, is a key tenet of modern society. Extending legal personhood or fundamental rights to animals based on their species rather than their individual merit leaves the core of the Aristocracy's *Equal Consideration* intact. The SMA thus takes up the egalitarian baton by taking seriously the political desirability of not making an individual's rights dependent on the particular attributes they possess or fail to possess. As we saw above, even McMahan, who otherwise does not flinch from adopting Meritocratic positions, seems to concede the political need for a practical device such as the SMA which allows for more Meritocracy whilst not giving up fully on Aristocracy's commitment to *Equal Consideration*—a commitment he considers 'virtually unthinkable to abandon'.[21]

Second, the SMA is politically desirable because it manages to accommodate these reasons for avoiding an extension of rights based on individual capacities, while at the same time allowing for the promotion of a more Meritocratic system by facilitating the extension of fundamental rights, legal personhood, and other protections to nonhuman beings. Pointing to advances in our understanding of the capacities and interests of nonhuman animals, I have argued in

[19] See, on the need to be attentive to difference, also David Bilchitz, 'Dignity, Fundamental Rights and Legal Capacity: Moving beyond the Paradigm Set by the General Comment on Article 12 of the Convention on the Rights of Persons with Disabilities' (2016) 32 South African Journal on Human Rights 410.

[20] See Chapter 4, Section 4.3.

[21] Jeff McMahan, 'Challenges to Human Equality' (2008) 12 The Journal of Ethics 81, 104. See also Cochrane, *Sentientist Politics: A Theory of Global Inter-Species Justice* (n 10) 23.

Chapter 6 that there is a need to steer legal systems away from protecting only human beings with fundamental rights and cognate entitlements, and towards a middle-ground position that confers on animals some similar protections. The SMA is politically desirable because it manages to adopt such a middle-ground position that accommodates the claims for animal rights. Although it is itself equality-preserving and Aristocratic to a certain extent, it moves beyond the current Aristocracy by opening up rights-holdership and similar protections to other beings on Meritocratic grounds. As a result, the SMA incorporates virtuous elements of both the Meritocracy and the Aristocracy while keeping their liabilities at a minimum.

2.2 Legal practice is not moral philosophy

Underlying the abovementioned pragmatic and political reasons for rehabilitating the species criterion is the obvious (though often neglected) fact that legal practice works differently from moral philosophy. This is important to highlight, especially in the debate about fundamental legal rights for animals. Although great strides have been made, this debate is still to some extent dominated by questions about fundamental *moral* rights and thus influenced by moral and political philosophers at least as much as by lawyers and legal philosophers. Given the scarcity of institutionalized animal rights to work with, it may be natural that the animal rights discussion was launched from a more abstract, philosophical perspective. However, because of the predominance of this perspective, the fact is often overlooked that some criteria and factors that play a role from a philosophical point of view do not—and often cannot—play the same role in law. Wise puts this thought succinctly when defending the NhRP's legal strategy to focus on autonomous animals who are relatively few in number:

> If I were Chief Justice of the Universe, I might make the simpler capacity to suffer, rather than practical autonomy, sufficient for personhood and dignity-rights . . . But the capacity to suffer appears irrelevant to common-law judges in their consideration of who is entitled to basic rights. What is at least sufficient is practical autonomy. This may be anathema to disciples of Bentham and Singer. I may not like it much myself. *But philosophers argue moral rights; judges decide legal rights.*[22]

[22] Wise, *Drawing the Line: Science and the Case for Animal Rights* (n 15) 34 (emphasis changed).

What exactly is different about law, and fundamental legal rights more specifically?[23] Fundamental legal rights are special, first of all, because they are based on *legal fictions*—a device that cannot be found in the toolbox of philosophers. Legal fictions allow the law to assume that a certain state of affairs *S* is the case, and to draw legal conclusions from it, regardless of whether or not *S* is actually the case. By employing legal fictions, law creates its own reality. For this reason, law can in principle attribute fundamental rights to any kind of entity. Most importantly for our purposes, law can attribute rights to beings who lack the capacities that would be required on strictly Meritocratic grounds. Courts, as Wise points out, 'employ a legal fiction that attributes the capacities for autonomy and self-determination to humans—normal infants, profoundly retarded adults, anencephalic infants, and those who lie in persistent vegetative states—who, it can be empirically demonstrated, lack them'.[24] The SMA makes use of a similar legal fiction to extend fundamental rights based on an animal's species, even if it can be empirically demonstrated that the concrete individual lacks the relevant capacities and interests.

Legal fictions are a double-edged sword, however. As Wise cautions, the same capacity to 'controvert[] empirical evidence' can also serve to exclude from rights-holdership beings who would deserve it.[25] Legal fictions can be used to achieve underinclusiveness as much as overinclusiveness.[26] Whether we choose to tailor legal fictions in a way that Meritocratizes animals' legal status quo, or in a way that entrenches the current Aristocracy is a matter of choice, and therefore highly political.[27]

This brings us to the second way in which law is special: law is subject to the vicissitudes of politics in a way that philosophy is not. This has to do with the unique role law has to fulfil in society. As Ngaire Naffine explains, law is charged with the 'highly practical and diverse tasks of social regulation and dispute resolution'.[28] To be able to fulfil these tasks, the law needs to be responsive at least to some extent to what is regarded as valuable in the community.[29] This holds especially for decisions of major importance, like the decision to

[23] For other differences see eg Tomasz Pietrzykowski, *Personhood Beyond Humanism: Animals, Chimeras, Autonomous Agents and the Law* (Springer 2018) 91–92.

[24] Steven M Wise, 'Hardly a Revolution—The Eligibility of Nonhuman Animals for Dignity-Rights in a Liberal Democracy' (1998) 22 Vermont Law Review 793, 909.

[25] ibid 882.

[26] See ibid 882–83; Ngaire Naffine, *Law's Meaning of Life: Philosophy, Religion, Darwin and the Legal Person* (Hart Publishing 2009) 165.

[27] Ngaire Naffine, 'Legal Personality and the Natural World: On the Persistence of the Human Measure of Value' (2012) 3 Journal of Human Rights and the Environment 68, 82.

[28] Naffine, *Law's Meaning of Life: Philosophy, Religion, Darwin and the Legal Person* (n 26) 175.

[29] ibid 181.

include nonhuman beings in the categories of rights-holders or legal persons, which 'sends a message to the community and expresses, on behalf of the community, who or what is to count—who matters', as Naffine points out.[30]

While this does not mean that non-political (such as moral or scientific) considerations play no role in the decision to take steps in the Meritocratic direction, it would be naive to approach fundamental rights legally in the same way as one would approach them philosophically. In other words, when deciding on who should be recognized as a fundamental rights-holder, we cannot simply copy and paste moral rights into the legal domain. Instead, we have to factor in and weigh a multitude of considerations in our decision whether, to whom, and how to extend rights and other entitlements (I say more about this in Section 4).[31] That this decision often does not reflect the ideal conceptions of many philosophers becomes apparent in the fact that, historically, legal personhood and fundamental rights were only extended gradually—and often only after arduous social and legal battles—to formerly excluded groups of beings, such as women, children, foreigners, black people, indigenous peoples, or people with disabilities.[32]

Awareness of the factors that make law and legal rights special explains why the scepticism of philosophers (and lawyers!) about the species criterion is misplaced in law. For example, as noted above, in an *amici curiae* brief in support of the NhRP, seventeen philosophers argued that '[s]pecies membership is at best a heuristic that aids a superficial assessment of moral status'. The philosophers base their conclusion on the finding that 'understood as a biological classification', species membership bears no 'moral weight'.[33] While this may be true, the philosophers seem to overlook that, in law, species membership can be more than an aid in the assessment of moral status. As I have argued here, species membership can be a pragmatically and politically useful criterion for determining holdership of legal rights and other legal entitlements.

2.3 The suitability of the SMA

The suitability of the SMA for legal animal rights is so evident, I believe, that it is at least implicitly accepted also by animal rights proponents such as Wise. I say

[30] ibid.
[31] Wise, 'Hardly a Revolution—The Eligibility of Nonhuman Animals for Dignity-Rights in a Liberal Democracy' (n 24) 797.
[32] Christopher D Stone, 'Should Trees Have Standing—Toward Legal Rights for Natural Objects' (1972) 45 Southern California Law Review 450, 451.
[33] Proposed Brief by Amici Curiae Philosophers (n 13) 11.

'implicitly' because Wise's scholarly work also contains passages which seem to suggest that he is adopting an uncompromising Meritocratic approach.[34] However, a closer look at the *habeas corpus* cases which Wise filed with the NhRP reveals that he is not committed to a strictly Meritocratic view. This assessment is based on two observations. First, there is the abovementioned fact that Wise himself conceded that at least the first cases which the NhRP filed on behalf of chimpanzees were based not on data about the capacities of these individual chimpanzees, but rather on data about 'your average chimpanzee'.[35] Second, and more importantly, one of the NhRP's key arguments would fail if it did not implicitly endorse something like the SMA.[36] The argument in question is the 'equality argument', which the NhRP summarizes as follows: '[h]umans who have never been sentient or conscious or possessed of a brain *should* have basic legal rights. But *if* humans bereft even of sentience are entitled to personhood, *then* this Court must either recognise Tommy's just equality claim to bodily liberty or reject equality.'[37] As Richard Cupp has noted, for the equality argument to work, the NhRP needs to recognize the personhood and rights of severely disabled human beings, despite the fact that they lack the relevant capacities for these legal positions. Otherwise, its argument that the same personhood and rights should be extended to chimpanzees with similar or greater autonomy would collapse.[38]

Once the equality argument collapses, the NhRP would be left only with the 'autonomy argument', according to which any being with the required levels of autonomy and self-determination deserves to be a legal person entitled to bodily liberty and integrity.[39] However, as is obvious, this argument can accommodate neither the rights and personhood of severely mentally disabled human beings, nor those of severely mentally disabled chimpanzees. For the equality argument to work, and for the NhRP to avoid denying severely mentally disabled human beings' personhood and rights, it therefore has to distance itself from a strict Meritocratic approach. One way of doing so is to adopt

[34] See eg Wise, 'Hardly a Revolution—The Eligibility of Nonhuman Animals for Dignity-Rights in a Liberal Democracy' (n 24) 884.

[35] Grimm, 'Live Chat: Should Animals Be Granted Legal Rights?' (n 14) at 38:58 (emphasis added).

[36] For a similar observation see Naffine, *Law's Meaning of Life: Philosophy, Religion, Darwin and the Legal Person* (n 26) 177.

[37] *Nonhuman Rights Project, Inc v Patrick C Lavery et al*, Memorandum of Law in Support of Petition for Habeas Corpus (2 December 2015) Supreme Court of the State of New York, County of New York, 109 <https://www.nonhumanrights.org/content/uploads/Tommy-Memo-of-Law-Dec-2-2015.pdf> accessed 11 June 2023 (emphasis in original).

[38] Richard L Cupp, 'Cognitively Impaired Humans, Intelligent Animals, and Legal Personhood', *Pepperdine University Legal Studies Research Paper No 12* (2016) 52–53 <http://papers.ssrn.com/abstract=2775288> accessed 11 June 2023.

[39] cf Memorandum of Law in Support of Petition for Habeas Corpus (n 37) 100–02.

something like the SMA. In fact, Wise himself has acknowledged the usefulness of legal fictions insofar as 'they represent a groping towards just and equitable results that may lie beyond the reach of a strict adherence to the law. The attribution of legal personhood to entities that might not strictly be entitled to it [under a purely Meritocratic approach], such as incompetent humans, . . . is one example.'[40] For these reasons, I believe that Wise's and the NhRP's approach is best interpreted as one that implicitly accepts the SMA.

The central idea behind the SMA was best captured by Laurence Tribe. In a commentary on the NhRP's litigation, he challenged Wise's ostensibly strict Meritocratic approach, by pointing out that this approach would be in discord with how the law works:

> When Steve, who condemns assigning rights purely on the basis of where the group we call 'human' begins and ends, would extend rights to chimps and bonobos . . . he wouldn't administer a battery of IQ tests to each individual chimp before declaring it eligible for these newly proclaimed rights. *He, like all of us, would make decisions on a group basis even as he purports to condemn doing so.* So those people who say we all have rights just because we are human, including the infant who can't solve equations, and including the comatose person, are not necessarily guilty of some form of species megalomania or of group think. That's the way our legal system works.[41]

As noted above, the SMA is not the only species-based proposal. According to Martha Nussbaum's theory, for instance, 'the appropriate benchmark . . . for judging whether a given creature has decent opportunities for flourishing'[42] is what is 'normal' for that species. Nussbaum calls this the 'species norm.'[43] On her account, 'atypical' members of a species, such as disabled members, are to be measured by what is considered 'normal' for the species, and not by their own individual capacities. The species norm is required by justice, according to Nussbaum, because 'atypical' members of a species normally still live with members of their own species. This creates a duty on society to help integrate them as far as possible. For instance, as she argues, humans with cognitive

[40] Wise, 'Hardly a Revolution—The Eligibility of Nonhuman Animals for Dignity-Rights in a Liberal Democracy' (n 24) 882.

[41] Laurence H Tribe, 'Ten Lessons Our Constitutional Experience Can Teach Us About the Puzzle of Animal Rights: The Work of Steven M. Wise' (2001) 7 Animal Law 1, 6–7 (emphasis added).

[42] Martha C Nussbaum, *Frontiers of Justice: Disability, Nationality, Species Membership* (Harvard University Press 2006) 365.

[43] ibid 347; Martha C Nussbaum, *Justice for Animals: Our Collective Responsibility* (Simon & Schuster 2022) 108, 140.

disabilities 'can flourish only as a human being. They have no option of flourishing as happy chimpanzees',[44] even though their capacities might be more similar to chimpanzees' than to those of 'typical' human beings. As Nussbaum points out, focusing on species rather than individual capacities is 'strategically'[45] important because it avoids 'practically dangerous'[46] outcomes such as the allocation of fewer resources to humans with disabilities.

Other authors have also explicitly focused on species membership criteria. Alexia Staker, for instance, submits that '[a]n incremental approach, initially focused on securing personhood for certain *species*, may be more viable, both legally and politically'.[47] In a similar vein, Tomasz Pietrzykowski, noticing the problems that an approach based on individual capacities creates for the equal status of human beings, has argued for what he calls 'modest (minimised) speciesism'.[48] On this approach, human beings receive their status and rights based on their biological humanity, rather than individual capacities or interests. Nonhuman beings, by contrast, should be recognized as legal subjects if they possess the required 'individual *or generic* psychological capacities'.[49]

Finally, not only scholars, but also many courts seem to adopt approaches akin to the SMA. Consider, for example, that although the courts mentioned in the previous chapter had to adjudicate on the legality of the treatment of *individual* bulls, birds, chimpanzees, or monkeys, they focused for the most part not on the individual animals themselves. Instead, they based their reasoning on the animals' *species*, or even broader categories such as 'animals', as was the case in the judgments of the Indian Supreme Court and the Court of Mendoza. In an opinion on the NhRP's petitions on behalf of the chimpanzees Tommy and Kiko, Judge Fahey of the State of New York Court of Appeals stated expressly that the answer to the question 'whether *a chimpanzee* . . . has the right to liberty protected by habeas corpus . . . will depend on our assessment of the intrinsic nature of *chimpanzees as a species*'.[50] As this illustrates, judges find it useful to work with more abstract, group-based categories rather than with individual animals. It therefore seems likely that, far from rejecting the

[44] Nussbaum, *Frontiers of Justice: Disability, Nationality, Species Membership* (n 42) 364.
[45] ibid 190.
[46] ibid.
[47] Alexia Staker, 'Should Chimpanzees Have Standing? The Case for Pursuing Legal Personhood for Non-Human Animals' (2017) 6 Transnational Environmental Law 485, 506 (emphasis added).
[48] Pietrzykowski, *Personhood Beyond Humanism: Animals, Chimeras, Autonomous Agents and the Law* (n 23) 107.
[49] ibid 102 (emphasis added).
[50] *Nonhuman Rights Project, Inc v Patrick C Lavery et al and Nonhuman Rights Project, Inc v Carmen Presti et al* [2018] State of New York, Court of Appeals No 2018-268, 4, Fahey J, concurring (emphasis added).

SMA, many judges may welcome it as a confirmation of their current way of approaching the rights and personhood of animals.

2.4 Why species?

For the reasons discussed above, species membership should no longer be considered as a criterion that is off-limits to animal rights lawyers. But why precisely does the SMA focus on *species* rather than some other group-based category? Why does it not take population or *genus*, or even some entirely non-biological category, such as geographic or purpose-based community (eg the category of animals used in scientific experimentation) as a criterion? A sceptic of the SMA could argue that privileging species over any of these other categories is arbitrary. The concept of 'species', she might add, is a construct which scientists use to better understand nature, but which has no independent reality.[51]

The sceptic's challenge is not entirely misguided: the SMA's privileging of the species membership criterion may at first glance appear arbitrary as there is, in fact, some disagreement among biologists on what exactly a 'species' is. As Richard Richards puts it, 'there are multiple, inconsistent ways to divide biodiversity into species on the basis of multiple, conflicting species concepts'.[52] This 'species problem' has led some biologists to embrace the nominalist view that 'species' are fictions: arbitrary divisions of the natural continuum that have no basis in objective fact.[53] If the species concept was indeed an illusion, then the SMA, which is built on that concept, would itself be no more than a pipe dream.

As we saw in Chapters 2 and 4, the sceptic's intuition about nature's resistance to simple categorization was shared by naturalists as far back as the seventeenth and eighteenth centuries. To describe nature accurately, Denis Diderot pointed out, 'there would have to be as many different denominations as there are individuals'.[54] But while the sceptic is correct that it is difficult to draw lines in nature, she is incorrect in suggesting that *no* lines can be drawn. As the evolutionary biologist Ernst Mayr has emphasized, 'species is a biological phenomenon that

[51] See eg Benjamin H Burma, 'The Species Concept: A Semantic Review' (1949) 3 Evolution 369, 369.

[52] Richard A Richards, *The Species Problem: A Philosophical Analysis* (Cambridge University Press 2010) 5.

[53] See eg Burma, 'The Species Concept' (n 51); Brent D Mishler, 'The Advantages of Rank-Free Classification for Teaching and Research' (2003) 19 Cladistics 157.

[54] Denis Diderot, 'Animal', *Encyclopédie, ou Dictionnaire raisonné des sciences, des arts et des métiers* (1770) 683 (my translation).

cannot be ignored'.[55] This is because, while the species category may be an organizational tool that scientists have constructed to make sense of nature, that does not mean that species themselves are artificial constructs. Rather, as Mark Ellis has pointed out, 'the species category remains a class defined by a valid concept with a membership of objectively real individuals'.[56] In other words, species capture objective natural patterns, allowing scientists to organize the continuum of nature in meaningful ways.[57] Importantly for our purposes, the species category permits an explanation of the central features which certain groupings of animals possess but others lack. The specific characteristics of individual animals, Mayr has emphasized, 'can often best be interpreted in terms of this relationship [of species]'.[58] There is necessarily some messiness and vagueness with emerging species and organisms that do not seem to fit existing species concepts.[59] However, that does not change the fact that there are many clear cases of species that can be—and often are—established as beneficiaries of legal protection. This is true, for example, of existing endangered species legislation.[60] The sceptic's worries thus prove unfounded.

Still, the fact that species membership is a useful category does not mean that my argument for Meritocratizing the Aristocracy *necessarily* requires using biological species as the relevant criterion for extending fundamental rights to nonhuman animals. Other group-based criteria might also provide a means of avoiding the arbitrary,[61] anthropocentric approach of the Aristocracy, while steering clear of the ableist dangers of the Meritocratic conception.[62]

[55] Ernst Mayr, 'Preface' in Ernst Mayr (ed), *The Species Problem: A Symposium Presented at the Atlanta Meeting of the American Association for the Advancement of Science* (American Association for the Advancement of Science 1957) iii.

[56] Mark W Ellis, 'The Problem With the Species Problem' (2011) 33 History and Philosophy of the Life Sciences 343, 347.

[57] ibid 358.

[58] Ernst Mayr, 'Difficulties and Importance of the Biological Species Concept' in Ernst Mayr (ed), *The Species Problem: A Symposium Presented at the Atlanta Meeting of the American Association for the Advancement of Science* (American Association for the Advancement of Science 1957) 371. See also Elizabeth Martin and Robert Hine (eds), 'Species', *A Dictionary of Biology* (7th edn, Oxford University Press 2015) 555.

[59] See Ellis, 'The Problem With the Species Problem' (n 56) 356.

[60] See eg J Peyton Doub, *The Endangered Species Act: History, Implementation, Successes and Controversies* (CRC Press 2013) 29.

[61] As a reminder, I define 'arbitrariness' in this context as losing a meaningful connection to reality, understood as compatibility with empirical facts. See Chapter 3, Section 4.2.

[62] Adopting other group-based criteria would be a way of responding to Sue Donaldson and Will Kymlicka's objection that a focus on species risks neglecting 'ties across species and diversity within species': Sue Donaldson and Will Kymlicka, *Zoopolis: A Political Theory of Animal Rights* (Oxford University Press 2011) 99. However, it is not the only possible response. As Nussbaum's theory shows, a particular species' capabilities can include 'interspecies relationships', which is why even a species-focused account does not have to neglect inter- and intraspecies ties. See Nussbaum, *Frontiers of Justice: Disability, Nationality, Species Membership* (n 42) 365.

For instance, it is possible that some designation other than 'species' may become necessary if nonhuman beings other than animals—such as robots or enhanced beings—develop in ways that make them deserving of some fundamental rights protection. For the time being, however, species membership is one of the best standards we have at our disposal to distribute legal rights, legal personhood, and other legal entitlements to deserving animals.

3 Sesha, Minnie, and Knuckles

Let me now illustrate the practical viability of the SMA. I will do so by showing how it fares in what can be described as three concrete *test cases*: the cases of Sesha, Minnie, and Knuckles. I propose that all three cases call for some fundamental rights protection and a legal status such as legal personhood. However, as we will see, each of these beings has some feature that makes them ineligible for rights-protection under Aristocratic or Meritocratic accounts. For the purposes of this discussion, I will focus on Meritocratic accounts of the sort that we have encountered in the NhRP's litigation, which take the capacity for autonomy to be the feature that grounds legal personhood and fundamental rights.[63] To be sure, Meritocratic approaches that focus on a more inclusive set of grounds may fare better with regard to the cases discussed here, but they will run into the same type of problems in other cases, which is why autonomy-based Meritocratic accounts serve as a sufficient illustration for my purposes. In what follows, I will compare the three cases and show that the SMA can provide a more satisfactory solution to them than the Meritocracy, Aristocracy, and, to the extent that one considers it a separate approach, the sentientist rights conception.

3.1 Sesha

Sesha is a human being with a severe mental disability.[64] Now in her early fifties, she was born with cerebral palsy and is completely dependent on others.[65] Sesha is the daughter of philosopher Eva Feder Kittay, who has written

[63] For the sake of the argument, I will also ignore the NhRP's equality argument (see Section 2.3).
[64] Eva Feder Kittay, 'At the Margins of Moral Personhood' (2005) 116 Ethics 100, 127.
[65] Leslie Garisto Pfaff, 'This Mother Knows Best' [2016] *Sarah Lawrence Magazine* <https://web.archive.org/web/20220127151714/https://www.sarahlawrence.edu/magazine/finding-courage/features/this-mother-knows-best.html> accessed 11 June 2023.

extensively on Sesha's life.[66] In philosophical debates, Sesha is sometimes invoked as an example of a human being who lacks the cognitive capacities that some consider relevant for the purpose of moral personhood and rights-holdership.[67] We are interested here not in Sesha's moral personhood or moral rights, but in her legal personhood and legal rights. What is Sesha's legal status under the Meritocracy and Aristocracy, and how does the SMA fare on this point?[68]

Proponents of Meritocratic accounts adopting an autonomy-based approach to legal personhood and fundamental rights would likely object to an extension to Sesha of legal personhood and at least some of the fundamental rights that 'typical' human beings possess. Lacking the capacity for autonomy, these Meritocrats would argue, Sesha should not be conferred the same personhood status and rights that 'typical' humans have. For example, according to Peter Singer, beings who do not have personhood in the philosophical sense lack a right to life, which is why it is 'much less a tragedy to kill that sort of being'.[69] As we saw in Chapter 4, critical disability scholars are highly critical of such Meritocratic arguments. Many of these scholars adopt Aristocratic human rights accounts, which are well-equipped for conferring on Sesha equal status and equal rights. The simple reason for this is that Sesha has what it takes to be an Aristocrat: she was born a member of the human species. Her status and rights are hers simply in virtue of being human.

How does the SMA compare? The SMA is as able as the Aristocratic approach to accommodate Sesha's legal status and fundamental rights. Although Sesha does not possess the same capacities and interests as non-cognitively disabled human beings, she is a member of the human species. This fact alone is sufficient for the SMA to accord Sesha the equal status of legal personhood and equal rights that other human beings possess. In so doing, the SMA manages to accommodate the point—made forcefully by Nussbaum—that a human being 'with severe mental impairments is actually very different from a chimpanzee, though in certain respects some of her capacities may be comparable'.[70] To compare Sesha and her capacities with those of a chimpanzee is to compare

[66] See Eva Feder Kittay, *Love's Labor: Essays on Women, Equality, and Dependency* (Routledge 1999) 147–61. See also Eva Feder Kittay, *Learning from My Daughter: The Value and Care of Disabled Minds* (Oxford University Press 2019).

[67] See Eva Feder Kittay, 'The Personal is Philosophical is Political: A Philosopher and Mother of a Cognitively Disabled Person Sends Notes from the Battlefield' in Eva Feder Kittay and Licia Carlson (eds), *Cognitive Disability and its Challenge to Moral Philosophy* (Wiley-Blackwell 2010) 393.

[68] For Kittay's own approach see ibid. For a similar account see Alice Crary, *Inside Ethics: On the Demands of Moral Thought* (Harvard University Press 2016).

[69] Peter Singer, 'Speciesism and Moral Status' (2009) 40 Metaphilosophy 567, 576.

[70] Nussbaum, *Frontiers of Justice: Disability, Nationality, Species Membership* (n 42) 363.

'atypical' human beings with 'typical' chimpanzees.[71] This is to neglect, however, that Sesha can only flourish as an 'atypical' human being, not as a 'typical' chimpanzee.[72] The SMA can account for this fact because it argues that the way the law should approach Sesha is through the prism of her *own* species, and not that of other species, nor of her individual properties.

3.2 Minnie

Minnie is an Asian elephant held in the Commerford Zoo in Goshen, Connecticut. Born in 1969, Minnie is now in her early fifties.[73] Shortly after she was captured in the wild as a baby elephant, Minnie was imported to the United States and put to work in a travelling petting zoo. In 1976, her then-owners sold Minnie to the Commerford Zoo, which uses and rents her out for 'Indian weddings, film productions, photo shoots, circuses, and fairs'.[74] To train and direct her, staff at the Zoo use bullhooks, which are metal hooks that are slid into the elephant's skin.[75] How does Minnie fit into the different approaches we are considering?

Meritocratic conceptions have no problem with granting fundamental legal rights and legal personhood to Minnie. They point to facts about her capacities and interests and use these to ground the claim that Minnie deserves legal personhood and fundamental rights such as the rights to bodily integrity, liberty, or life. In its *habeas corpus* cases on behalf of Minnie and other elephants, for example, the NhRP provided a series of affidavits from pachyderm experts 'that demonstrate that elephants such as . . . Minnie . . . are autonomous beings'.[76]

Aristocratic human rights approaches, by contrast, have no way of accommodating Minnie's case. Because she is not a human being, Minnie does not have any fundamental rights or legal personhood. As we saw in Chapter 3, this exclusion of all nonhuman beings is the flipside of the Aristocracy's inclusion of all human beings. Minnie's case therefore presents us with a situation that

[71] See David Bilchitz, 'Moving Beyond Arbitrariness: The Legal Personhood and Dignity of Non-Human Animals' (2009) 23 South African Journal on Human Rights 38, 61.

[72] Nussbaum, *Frontiers of Justice: Disability, Nationality, Species Membership* (n 42) 364.

[73] The Elephant Database, 'Minnie (Mignon) at R.W. Commerford and Sons Traveling Petting Zoo (Robert Commerford)' (22 July 2007) <https://www.elephant.se/database2.php?elephant_id=704> accessed 11 June 2023.

[74] Nonhuman Rights Project, 'Beulah, Karen, and Minnie' (*Nonhuman Rights Project*) <https://www.nonhumanrights.org/clients-beulah-karen-minnie/> accessed 11 June 2023.

[75] ibid.

[76] *Nonhuman Rights Project, Inc v Commerford & Sons, Inc et al*, Verified Petition for Common Law Writ of Habeas Corpus (13 November 2017) Superior Court, Judicial District of Litchfield, 2 <https://www.nonhumanrights.org/content/uploads/CT-Petition-11.13.17.pdf> accessed 11 June 2023.

is the exact reverse of Sesha's case. There, Aristocratic accounts could accommodate Sesha's legal personhood and rights, but Meritocratic accounts could not. Here, Meritocratic accounts can accommodate Minnie's personhood and rights, but Aristocratic accounts cannot.

The SMA, by contrast, can accommodate both cases. In contrast to the Aristocracy, the SMA is open to extending fundamental rights to those who do not belong to the human species. For example, it can extend them to all members of the Asian elephant species because 'normal' members of that species can be shown to possess the required capacities such as autonomy. This means that they have the interests relevant to fundamental rights protection, including the protection of life, bodily integrity, and liberty. Because Minnie is a member of that species, she would automatically be eligible for these rights. Importantly, the SMA allows for an extension of these fundamental rights without endangering Sesha's rights and status. Because Sesha is a human being, and not an Asian elephant, she would continue to enjoy the equal status and equal rights of human beings who are not severely cognitively disabled.

3.3 Knuckles

Finally, the SMA is preferable to the Aristocratic and the Meritocratic approaches not only because it can accommodate Sesha's and Minnie's cases—which neither of the other approaches could *for both* on their own—but also because it can accommodate an arguably even more difficult case: the case of Knuckles. Knuckles was a chimpanzee who lived at the Center for Great Apes, a sanctuary for orangutans and chimpanzees in Wauchula, Florida, until he passed away in 2021 at the age of 22.[77] Knuckles was a special chimpanzee because, like Sesha, he was born with cerebral palsy. Due to this condition, Knuckles was at first not able to eat on his own, as his bodily control was limited, and his movement more generally impeded. After years of therapy and care in a special needs habitat at the Center, however, Knuckles 'learned to feed himself, climb up and down steps, and pull himself up on special swings to hang upside down and play'.[78] This allowed him to walk where he wanted to

[77] Center For Great Apes, 'Knuckles' <https://centerforgreatapes.org/chimpanzee/knuckles-2/#:~:text=Knuckles%20was%20a%20true%20inspiration,Knuckles%20had%20serious%20physical%20challenges> accessed 11 June 2023.

[78] Center for Great Apes, 'Knuckles' (*Internet Archive*, 26 January 2021) <https://web.archive.org/web/20210126222813/https://centerforgreatapes.org/meet-apes/chimpanzees/knuckles/> accessed 11 June 2023.

go and to be 'very aware and cognizant of activities around him'.[79] Yet, despite these improvements, Knuckles's mental capacities remained limited.[80]

Knuckles's case is particularly knotty. Assuming he was still alive, neither Aristocratic nor Meritocratic approaches would be capable of granting him the equal status and equal rights of other chimpanzees. This seems problematic for two reasons. First, it would seem wrong to withhold equal status and equal rights from a vulnerable chimpanzee like Knuckles just because he is disabled. Second, even if one did not share that intuition, the fact that neither approach can accommodate Knuckles's case should give cause for concern. This is because, if a disabled being like Knuckles is refused the equal status and equal rights of other chimpanzees on the grounds that he lacks the relevant individual properties, then the same lack of properties could be invoked to justify withholding personhood and rights from humans like Sesha. As we saw in Chapter 4, one of the main worries of critical disability scholars is that humans with disabilities are 'animalised'.[81] The worry is that by allowing comparisons between disabled humans and animals, disabled humans are brought down to the status of animals, rather than the other way around. If one rejects Knuckles's claim to the equal status and equal rights possessed by fellow chimpanzees, then one precisely invites such problematic comparisons.

To be sure, Knuckles would have fared considerably better under Meritocratic accounts, especially Meritocratic accounts that do not focus solely on the capacity for autonomy. For instance, accounts grounding the right to bodily integrity in the capacity to feel pain could have accommodated such a right for Knuckles. However, because Knuckles lacked the capacity for autonomy, he would not have received other fundamental rights that non-cognitively disabled chimpanzees deserve. Nor would Knuckles have deserved to be recognized as a legal person on that approach. He would thus have fallen through at least some of the cracks of the Meritocracy. Meritocrats may not consider this to be a flaw in their conception. A full-blown Meritocratic conception requires excluding those who do not possess the relevant capacities. However, as I have argued in Chapter 4, such full-blown Meritocratic accounts pose a serious threat to human equality that we would do better to avoid or at least mitigate. What is more, as I noted, even if one does not share the intuition that Knuckles should have the equal status and equal rights of other

[79] ibid.
[80] Lori Gruen, *Ethics and Animals: An Introduction* (2nd edn, Cambridge University Press 2021) 78–79.
[81] Licia Carlson, *Faces of Intellectual Disability: Philosophical Reflections* (Indiana University Press 2010) 145 (emphasis removed).

chimpanzees, the fact that his lack of certain individual properties could be used analogically in the human context to deprive humans with disabilities of certain rights or legal personhood should be worrying. While Aristocratic approaches do not suffer from that problem, they fail even more obviously to accommodate Knuckles's case: simply in virtue of being born a chimpanzee, Knuckles was excluded from all the fundamental rights and from the personhood status that human beings enjoy.

This presents us with a problem, as neither the Aristocracy nor the Meritocracy provide a satisfactory solution to Knuckles's case. However, it would seem wrong—or at least politically dangerous because of its implications for beings like Sesha—to allow ownership of Knuckles, or to violate his basic interests, simply because he lacks some of the individual capacities necessary for personhood and fundamental rights.[82]

The SMA overcomes these problems. According to the SMA, fundamental rights and legal personhood would be extended to all members of the chimpanzee species, regardless of their individual capacities.[83] Hence, even a chimpanzee like Knuckles, who would not deserve these legal positions on strictly Meritocratic grounds, could still come to enjoy them. The SMA thus manages to combine as far as possible the insight of the Meritocracy that we should extend rights and personhood to beings who deserve them, with the insight of the Aristocracy that we should not abandon our egalitarian commitments. In other words, the SMA harnesses the strengths of both conceptions, while at the same time minimizing their weaknesses. And as Knuckles's case shows, the SMA is not reducible to either of these conceptions, nor even a conjunction of them. As a result, the SMA is preferable to both the Aristocratic and the Meritocratic conceptions.

But what about the sentientist rights approach? As I explained in Chapter 5, this approach is increasingly influential in animal rights scholarship. For instance, according to Cochrane's theory, which I take to be the most well-developed sentientist rights theory, all sentient individuals have equal value and are deserving of fundamental rights. Can this approach accommodate Sesha's, Minnie's, and Knuckles's cases? After all, because they are all sentient beings, they would have equal moral worth and could be said to deserve equal status as legal persons. Also, they would all deserve certain fundamental rights in virtue of their being sentient and having interests. Does this mean that the sentientist rights approach presents us with an alternative to the SMA, one

[82] See also Crary, *Inside Ethics: On the Demands of Moral Thought* (n 68) 132.
[83] Unless the presumption can be defeated, see Section 2.1.

that is potentially more attractive than the SMA because it is not merely a practical solution?

Let us assume for the sake of argument that the sentientist rights approach was really a third conception, rather than, as I argued in Chapter 5, a more moderate form of the Meritocracy or, at the very least, a non-Meritocratic approach that still lies somewhere on the spectrum between the Aristocracy and the Meritocracy. It is certainly true that the sentientist rights approach is better able to accommodate the three test cases than pure(r) forms of the Meritocracy and the Aristocracy. However, there are two reasons why I believe the SMA is more attractive in practice than the sentientist rights approach. As we saw in Chapter 5, a sentientist rights account like Cochrane's runs into two main problems that potentially endanger beings like Sesha and Knuckles.[84]

The first is the *Spectrum Problem*: if, as seems possible, sentience is not a binary threshold but comes in degrees, then it is not an ideal ground for equal status. For if an adult human being turned out to have more sentience than Sesha, then that human would deserve a higher status than her. And this would undermine the equal status and potentially the equal rights of disabled beings like her. The SMA does not run into this problem because, as a practical approach inspired by Aristocratic defences of equality, it does not make equality contingent on empirical properties such as sentience. Rather, it simply presupposes that all beings of the same species are to be treated as equals.[85]

Second, even if the sentientist rights approach can overcome this problem, it still faces the *Indifference Problem*: theories such as Cochrane's do not pay attention to the species a being belongs to and therefore in principle allow, among other things, for some animals' rights to outweigh some humans' rights. While this may be viewed as a strength in their book, it would be viewed as a problem by many human rights proponents, especially Aristocratic ones. The SMA can avoid this problem because it does not reject the idea of using species membership as a criterion for status and rights. Although the SMA could be implemented in a way that allows for some animal rights to outweigh human rights, it need not be. As a practical proposal, the SMA is open to being used differently in different jurisdictions. As I will show in the next section, one way of operationalizing the SMA, attractive perhaps in a transitionary period,

[84] Another problem that the sentientist rights approach faces is that it would require judges to investigate whether individual animals before them are actually sentient. However, as I argued above in Section 2.1, this is undesirable based on considerations of judicial competence, administrability, economy, and prudence. I am grateful to John Adenitire for drawing my attention to this.

[85] To be sure, as I argued in Chapter 5, sentientist rights accounts can follow the same Aristocratic path and decide or assume that sentience is binary. However, in so doing, sentientist rights accounts would effectively align themselves with the SMA, not become an alternative to it.

would be to allow for some human rights to automatically outweigh certain animal rights in cases of inevitable conflicts.

4 Operationalizing the SMA

The general case for the SMA and its illustration with Sesha, Minnie, and Knuckles have not addressed in any detail how the SMA could be put into practice. This final section will remedy this by showing how the SMA can be operationalized and how it can respond to practical challenges that might arise from its implementation. These issues go well beyond the scope of this book, which is why this section will not attempt to address them in an exhaustive or conclusive way. Rather, my aim here is to sketch a domain of possible answers, and to gesture towards some future directions for research.[86] I will focus on four main questions: which species ought to get rights first (and which last); who counts (and who does not count) as a member of a species; who gets to decide on these questions; and, finally, how should we deal with concerns about how to prioritize rights claims in a world in which many human beings *de facto* lack fundamental rights protection.

4.1 Who comes first (and who last)?

Let us start with the question of which nonhuman species should get fundamental rights and other legal entitlements first, and which last. When determining the order in which such entitlements should be extended using the SMA, two criteria will have to be taken into account: merit and feasibility.

First, a decision to grant fundamental rights to an animal species will be contingent on its *merit*, that is, on whether members of that species possesses the relevant capacities for particular fundamental rights (such as the right to bodily integrity and the right to life). This, in turn, will depend upon the availability of scientific evidence about the existence of corresponding rights-grounding properties (such as sentience and an interest in continued existence).[87] The higher the level of desert, the more reason for extending rights

[86] I say more about possible future avenues for research in the book's Conclusion.

[87] Of course, what is considered a relevant rights-grounding property or interest and who can have it are not settled matters: see Chapter 4, Section 4.1. However, like any analysis, mine is limited in its scope, which is why I cannot address this issue here.

to that species. Take the example of the great apes. In their case, the existence of rights-grounding interests in life, bodily integrity, and liberty is today supported by a strong body of scientific evidence.[88] This evidence is stronger than that for certain species of insects, where the data on their potential sentience and other capacities seem less clear.[89] It is therefore arguable that the desert of great apes of rights to life, integrity, and liberty is greater than that of these species of insects. As a result, great ape species would compare favourably in terms of merit. It is important to note, however, that not only the great apes can deserve fundamental rights. Any species—regardless of its proximity to the human species—can in principle deserve fundamental rights based on the relevant characteristics of the species. Of course, we need to be careful when relying on science to decide who qualifies for rights. As discussed in Chapters 4 and 6, invocations of scientific studies have a problematic history in the context of disability and race, among others. However, as I have pointed out, this problem is not a reason to abandon reliance on scientific evidence. Instead, it is a reason to be cautious when determining merit on scientific grounds.

As mentioned above, legal animal rights are not free from political and practical constraints in the way moral rights are. Hence, *feasibility* considerations are a second element that must be factored into the decision-making process. Some species may be easier targets than others for rights-extension because humans have fewer economic or cultural interests in them. The higher the practical and political feasibility of extending rights to a particular species, the stronger the case for applying the SMA to it. In principle, this means that it is possible that an animal species which is more deserving of rights-extension than another may have to wait longer, because applying the SMA is less feasible. Although the variables involved are complex and cannot be determined here in any final way, it seems reasonable to suggest that great apes should be among the first beneficiaries of the SMA. This is because there is ample scientific evidence that they have interests in basic rights, and because humans have few vested interests in them, for example as a source of food (as compared to, say, chickens). The great apes thus also score high on feasibility.

These considerations will undoubtedly appear arbitrary to some: why should great apes be privileged over chickens, or any other sentient animal

[88] See eg Nonhuman Rights Project, 'Hercules and Leo' (*Nonhuman Rights Project*) <https://www.nonhumanrights.org/hercules-leo/> accessed 11 June 2023.

[89] See eg Andrew B Barron and Colin Klein, 'What Insects Can Tell Us about the Origins of Consciousness' (2016) 113 Proceedings of the National Academy of Sciences of the United States of America 4900; Shelley Anne Adamo, 'Do Insects Feel Pain? A Question at the Intersection of Animal Behaviour, Philosophy and Robotics' (2016) 118 Animal Behaviour 75.

for that matter? Does that not amount to prioritizing 'elite species'[90] or 'charismatic megafauna'[91] at the expense of less well-known and less charismatic species? Is the SMA therefore not guilty of exactly the same kind of arbitrary line-drawing of which it accuses the Aristocracy—a line-drawing that bears no meaningful connection to reality? The first thing to recall here is that the SMA's aim is to provide a practically viable—not a morally ideal—way forward. It simply aims to serve as a useful guide for political decisions that Meritocratize the Aristocracy. To put that point differently, the SMA embraces the insight—ignored by some—that legal norms are bound to be arbitrary to some extent, and that, rather than trying to eradicate arbitrariness, we ought to strive to make laws that are *less arbitrary*. The SMA aims to achieve no more, but also no less, than that.

We should note, too, that feasibility considerations could recommend the extension of a *bundle* of rights to a *set* of species, all of whom share the relevant capacities. This could be useful, for example, in the drafting of a bill of animal rights, where it would be cumbersome to differentiate between the rights of numerous individual species. In other contexts, such as those of judicial extension of rights, it may be likelier that only individual species will become beneficiaries of the SMA, because it is generally individual animals whose cases are brought before court. Irrespective of context, the SMA only proposes that species membership should be the basic unit for rights extensions; it does not rule out the combining of different species for practical purposes.

4.2 Who counts?

This leads to the second question: Who exactly should count as a member of a particular species for the purposes of the SMA? I shall try to elucidate this issue by concentrating on two hard cases: foetuses and hybrids.

A foetus of any given species is biologically a member of that species—but is it also a member *as far as the SMA is concerned*? Put differently, is a foetus a member that should receive the equal status and equal rights of other members of that species? The first thing to note in this respect is that the conceptual problem foetuses pose is not new. There is an abundance of scholarship

[90] See Raffael N Fasel and Sean C Butler, *Animal Rights Law* (Hart Publishing 2023) 161–62.

[91] Ray C Anderson, 'Charismatic Megafauna' in *Berkshire Encyclopedia of Sustainability* (Berkshire Publishing Group 2010) <https://www.oxfordreference.com/display/10.1093/acref/9780190622664.001.0001/acref-9780190622664> accessed 18 December 2023.

and case law on issues surrounding the legality of human abortion.[92] In this domain, too, the question of who is considered a human being for the purpose of rights-holdership and legal personhood is not just a biological question. It is also a political question, decided differently in different jurisdictions. As with the question of which species should benefit from the SMA, the answer to the question of what status and rights are accorded to animal foetuses depends both on the biological evidence that exists for sufficiently developed rights-grounding properties, such as sentience, and on the practical and political limits of extending rights to beings in this state.[93]

While the matter is too complex to be resolved here, it appears likely that political decision-makers might adopt term-based solutions for nascent non-human animals as they have for human foetuses.[94] To be sure, such term-based solutions and abortion more generally are the subject of ongoing controversy.[95] But that does not change the fact that term-based solutions have been adopted in many jurisdictions.[96] Taking into account the gestational state of the foetus has become a way of balancing women's rights and the interests of the developing foetus.[97] In England, Wales, and Scotland for example, abortions of human foetuses are governed by the Abortion Act 1967 whose section 1(1)(a) provides that the termination of a pregnancy is legal when two doctors confirm that it has 'not exceeded its twenty-fourth week and that the continuance of the pregnancy would involve risk, greater than if the pregnancy were terminated, of injury to the physical or mental health of the pregnant woman or any existing children of her family'. After twenty-four weeks, abortions are legal only in special circumstances, such as if the mother's life would be at risk or

[92] See for an overview Marge Berer, 'Abortion Law and Policy Around the World' (2017) 19 Health and Human Rights 13.

[93] The requirement of a correspondence between empirical facts and political considerations ensures that political convenience cannot be (ab)used as an excuse to validate an unjust status quo.

[94] This is not to say that the reasons for adopting term-based solutions are identical in both cases. Also, because of the developmental differences in the foetuses of different species, terms may need to vary depending on the species in question. See eg on the difference between altricial and precocial species Donald M Broom, *Sentience and Animal Welfare* (CABI 2014) 109, 115.

[95] See eg Christopher Kaczor, *The Ethics of Abortion: Women's Rights, Human Life, and the Question of Justice* (3rd edn, Routledge 2023); Kate Greasley and Christopher Kaczor, *Abortion Rights: For and Against* (Cambridge University Press 2018); Kate Greasley, *Arguments about Abortion: Personhood, Morality, and Law* (Oxford University Press 2017).

[96] See 'The World's Abortion Laws' (*Center for Reproductive Rights*) <https://reproductiverights.org/maps/worlds-abortion-laws/> accessed 11 June 2023 (click on 'On Request [Gestational Limits Vary]'); 'Law and Policy Guide: Gestational Limits' (*Center for Reproductive Rights*) <https://reproductiverights.org/maps/worlds-abortion-laws/law-and-policy-guide-gestational-limits/> accessed 11 June 2023. See also Rebecca J Cook, Joanna N Erdman, and Bernard M Dickens (eds), *Abortion Law in Transnational Perspective: Cases and Controversies* (University of Pennsylvania Press 2014).

[97] See eg Ruth Rubio-Marín, 'Abortion in Portugal: New Trends in European Constitutionalism' in Rebecca J Cook, Joanna N Erdman, and Bernard M Dickens (eds), *Abortion Law in Transnational Perspective: Cases and Controversies* (University of Pennsylvania Press 2014) 48.

if the child would be born with severe physical or mental disabilities (subsections 1(1)(b)–(d)). Beyond that period, section 58 of the Offences Against the Person Act 1861 considers ending a foetus's life to be a crime punishable, in principle, with 'penal servitude for life'.[98] This compares with the punishment for manslaughter or murder of an adult human being.[99]

While it would of course not be necessary to adopt the same punishments for terminations of nonhuman foetuses, legal systems could enact similar term-based solutions to mark the start of 'life' as far as the SMA is concerned. In other words, while an animal foetus would already belong to their respective species before the passing of (say) twenty-four weeks, they would only count as a member of that species for the sake of the SMA after its passing.

The second group of beings to which it may be difficult to attribute a certain species are hybrids. By contrast to foetuses, the issue with hybrids is not that they are unborn. Even as fully developed beings, hybrids pose a conceptual problem because they share the characteristics of more than one species. Hybridization can be the result of artificial creation, as is the case of cyborgs. A *cyborg* (short for cybernetic organism) is a being that has both organic and mechanical body parts. A human being who is part robot in virtue of having, for example, an in-built antenna extending that person's visible spectrum, would be considered a cyborg.[100] Hybridization can however also be the outcome of natural processes. The bat species *Artibeus schwartzi*, for example, was found to have a genome containing DNA from at least three other bat species.[101] Both artificial and natural hybrids raise the following dilemma: if, according to the SMA, a being's species characteristics are supposed to determine its legal status and entitlements, then what do we do if it has characteristics of more than one species?

In the case of natural hybrids such as *Artibeus schwartzi*, the solution appears to be relatively obvious: we should try to identify the special characteristics that distinguish members of *Artibeus schwartzi* from members of other species, including the three species that formed these hybrids. In other

[98] Sally Sheldon, 'The Decriminalisation of Abortion: An Argument for Modernisation' (2016) 36 Oxford Journal of Legal Studies 334, 339.

[99] Sentencing Council, 'Manslaughter: Definitive Guideline' (2018) 3 <https://www.sentencingcouncil.org.uk/wp-content/uploads/Manslaughter-definitive-guideline-Web.pdf> accessed 11 June 2023; Sentencing Council, 'Life Sentences' (2023) <https://www.sentencingcouncil.org.uk/sentencing-and-the-council/types-of-sentence/life-sentences> accessed 11 June 2023.

[100] See Michelle Z Donahue, 'How a Color-Blind Artist Became the World's First Cyborg' (*National Geographic*, 3 April 2017) <https://www.nationalgeographic.com/news/2017/04/worlds-first-cyborg-human-evolution-science/> accessed 11 June 2023.

[101] See Peter A Larsen, María R Marchán-Rivadeneira, and Robert J Baker, 'Natural Hybridization Generates Mammalian Lineage with Species Characteristics' (2010) 107 Proceedings of the National Academy of Sciences of the United States of America 11447.

words, regardless of whether members of *Artibeus schwartzi* form a species or some other group, we should determine the special qualities that distinguish that group from other groups, including the species that gave rise to *Artibeus schwartzi*. It is quite likely that there will be numerous features that members of the group *Artibeus schwartzi* share with members of these other species, but *Artibeus schwartzi* may also have some of its own features.

The case of artificial hybrids like cyborgs is more difficult, because it gets us into less explored territory. While more research is needed on this issue, a similar solution to the one I proposed for natural hybrids may be suitable in the context of artificial beings who share the characteristics of more than one species. That solution lies in identifying common features of the relevant beings—features which, although not amounting to species membership in the biological sense, distinguish such artificial beings from other beings in a way that can itself not be further subdivided. Such groups, which possess a set of characteristics that distinguishes them from other (non-species) groups, could be referred to as 'quasi-species'.

For the purposes of our discussion here, it will be sufficient to note that even though foetuses and hybrids are not straightforward candidates for extensions of legal entitlements based on the SMA, they do not constitute insurmountable obstacles to determining who should count under the SMA.

4.3 Who decides?

This brings us to the issue of decision-makers. Who decides on the respective merit and feasibility of rights for a certain species? The answer to this question is both simple and complex at the same time. It is simple because, as the decision to apply the SMA is a *political* decision, it should in principle be made by political decision-makers. But it is also complex because not every political decision-maker may be equally suited to making such decisions. The difficulty thus lies in identifying the political decision-makers who are best placed to apply the SMA. I should clarify that I define 'political decision-maker' in a broad sense here. As I use the term, it includes both lawmakers in the traditional sense (ie parliamentary bodies) and lawmakers in the wider sense, including courts in their adjudicative capacity and governmental agencies which create laws that implement parliamentary legislation. However, I do not limit the term to the national context: political decision-makers also exist on an international and supranational level, in bodies like the United Nations (UN), the African Union (AU), or the European Union (EU).

There is a burgeoning literature on the need to protect animals' interests with a transnational approach, that is, an approach that works on multiple levels simultaneously—local, state, regional, and international.[102] This is sometimes referred to as 'Global Animal Law'. Anne Peters, one of the founders of this approach, explains that, today, 'food production and distribution, working animals, animal use in research, [and] breeding and keeping of pets . . . possess a transboundary dimension',[103] and therefore need to be regulated globally. Following this insight, attempts at extending fundamental legal rights and similar entitlements to animals through the SMA would ideally take a global approach that aims to harmonize protection across boundaries. This could follow the example set by international human rights treaties, such as the International Covenant on Civil and Political Rights (ICCPR) or the United Nations Convention on the Rights of the Child (CRC),[104] as well as that of regional human rights conventions, such as the European Convention on Human Rights (ECHR).[105] For instance, political leaders could develop an international agreement on the fundamental rights of animals that distributes these rights on the basis of species membership. This agreement could do so for example by listing the different species whose right to bodily integrity should be protected, the species whose right to life should be protected, and so on. As is the case with human rights law, state and local actors would then have the duty to implement and concretize these international rights in the domestic context.

While such a global approach to nonhuman rights would have the advantage of promoting the same level of rights protection for animals regardless of the jurisdiction they are in, it is arguably an unrealistic scenario in the near future.[106] In the main, states are still the primary *loci* for political decision-making. This primacy of states is manifested, for instance, in the fact that a treaty on animal rights would only be binding on a state if it ratifies it (or does not object to its becoming customary international law).[107] For these reasons,

[102] See Anne Peters, 'Global Animal Law: What It Is and Why We Need It' (2016) 5 Transnational Environmental Law 9, 20.

[103] ibid 16.

[104] International Covenant on Civil and Political Rights (1966, ICCPR) <http://www.ohchr.org/en/professionalinterest/pages/ccpr.aspx> accessed 11 June 2023; Convention on the Rights of the Child (1989, CRC) <https://www.ohchr.org/en/professionalinterest/pages/crc.aspx> accessed 11 June 2023.

[105] European Convention on Human Rights (1950, ECHR) <https://www.echr.coe.int/documents/convention_eng.pdf> accessed 11 June 2023.

[106] What is more, a global approach runs the risk of watering down standards to the lowest common denominator: Charlotte E Blattner, *Protecting Animals Within and Across Borders: Extraterritorial Jurisdiction and the Challenges of Globalization* (Oxford University Press 2019) 81.

[107] Anthony Aust, *Handbook of International Law* (Cambridge University Press 2005) 7, 16.

it is to be expected that, at least for the time being, it will be national or state parliaments that will decide upon the extension of fundamental rights to other species. An example for a proposed extension of fundamental rights to animals on the state level is the citizens' initiative in the Swiss Canton of Basel-Stadt, which I mentioned in the previous chapter.[108] According to this initiative, all nonhuman primate species should be granted constitutional rights to life and to bodily and mental integrity. On the national level, parliaments could decide to amend the national constitution by adding species-based rights to existing bills of rights. In the United Kingdom, for instance, this could take the shape of a Nonhuman Rights Act, enacted by Parliament following the model of the Human Rights Act (HRA).[109]

As indicated above, courts may play a similarly important role in extensions of rights to animals using the SMA. This is particularly the case in common law jurisdictions where the judiciary is considered to have more expansive lawmaking powers.[110] In civil law jurisdictions, where judges tend to have less room for lawmaking, it seems likely that their role in deciding to apply the SMA to animals will be smaller than in common law countries. That does not exclude the possibility, however, that they could find other legal arguments for applying the SMA. For instance, while writs of *habeas corpus* are traditionally seen as a common law instrument, some civil law jurisdictions also provide for that instrument. As we saw in the previous chapter, the case of Cecilia the chimpanzee—the first animal to have benefitted from *habeas corpus*—was decided by a court in Argentina, which is a civil law jurisdiction. *Habeas corpus* proceedings such as the ones in the Cecilia decision are a case in point for judges' ability to decide to extend rights to suitable nonhumans. Regardless of which instrument they use, or are petitioned to use, in making the decision to extend rights to animals, I propose that judges should adopt the SMA and grant the extension for all animals of the same species—except where this presumption can be rebutted to prevent harm to the animal or others.[111]

Distinct from the question of who the decision-makers are or should be is the question of the process by which decisions to apply the SMA should be made. This issue is too complex to discuss here. For what it is worth, however, we can note that, while further study on this question is required, there

[108] Chapter 6, Section 3.2.

[109] See eg Raffael N Fasel, 'Quelle place pour le royaume animal au Royaume-Uni? Les animaux comme sujets du droit britannique' (2020) 43 Société de législation comparée 119, 128.

[110] See eg the speech delivered by Lord Hodge of the Supreme Court of the United Kingdom, 'The Scope of Judicial Law-Making in the Common Law Tradition' (2019) <https://www.supremecourt.uk/docs/speech-191028.pdf> 11 June 2023.

[111] See Section 2.1.

is promising research suggesting that inclusive democratic institutions may be particularly well-suited, not only for determining which species ought to receive which rights, but also for deciding the more concrete policy questions that arise as a result of these abstract rights.[112]

4.4 How to deal with conflicts?

Finally, we need to address the question of whether the SMA would lead to a conflict with the fundamental rights of human beings, and how such conflicts ought to be resolved. This is a particularly pressing matter, because scarce resources are one of the reasons behind the current *de facto* neglect of many human rights. If we add animal rights to the mix, a sceptic might object, we risk lowering the protection of human rights even more. We thus need to ask if the rights of animals (once extended through the SMA) would have to be withdrawn or suspended in cases where they conflict with the rights of humans.

The prospect of such conflicts is real and should not be ignored. For instance, if all chimpanzees were given fundamental rights to life, liberty, and integrity, then those rights could collide with humans' rights to property, to economic freedom, and to scientific freedom, among others. This is because the sale of chimpanzees and their exhibition in zoos and circuses would likely have to be severely limited, if not prohibited, to protect their rights. Likewise, invasive scientific research on chimpanzees would probably have to stop. Or take the example of cows. If they were granted a right to life, then the human rights to property and to economic freedom could no longer be exercised in the ways they are now for the production of milk and meat.

How, according to the SMA, should such conflicts be resolved? The answer to this depends on how the SMA is operationalized in practice. Broadly speaking, it can be operationalized either in more Meritocratic ways that allow in principle for animal rights to outweigh human rights in cases of conflicts, or in more Aristocratic ways which give priority to human rights.

If a more Meritocratic approach is chosen, how are conflicts between human and animal rights to be resolved? There is, in fact, a tried and tested tool for resolving rights conflicts: the proportionality test. This test involves the balancing of the weights of the different interests that are at stake, and requires that

[112] See Cochrane, *Sentientist Politics: A Theory of Global Inter-Species Justice* (n 10) 36–61.

the right that is based on the weightier interests wins out in any given case.[113] 'The greater the degree of non-satisfaction of, or detriment to, one [right]', the legal theorist Robert Alexy explains, 'the greater must be the importance of satisfying the other.'[114] For instance, the interests of a chimpanzee to not be subjected to invasive scientific testing would have to be balanced against the conflicting human interests in scientific freedom. The greater the gravity of the infringement of the chimpanzee's interests, and the smaller the human interest in conducting a particular experiment, the stronger the case that the human right to scientific freedom would lose out.

Importantly, despite what this emphasis on balancing might suggest, the proportionality test does not allow that *any* interests related to a right can be traded off against each other. Rather, as the test is deployed in many jurisdictions, it does not allow for the balancing of what is often called the 'core' or 'essence' of a fundamental right. As Koen Lenaerts puts it in the context of EU fundamental rights, the essence of a fundamental right amounts to a '"hard nucleus" that guarantees to each and every individual a sphere of liberty that must always remain free from interference. That nucleus is . . . absolute in so far as it may not be subject to limitations.'[115] The idea behind the essence of a fundamental right is that protecting the right would be meaningless if that essence was not absolutely protected. That is why proportionality balancing does not allow consequentialist trade-offs on all aspects of a right. The core, in other words, puts a 'limit on the limits'.[116] Take for example freedom of religion. States adopting the proportionality test generally allow for limitations of public manifestations of one's religion, such as limits on the sounding of church bells. However, limits are not allowed when it comes to a person's faith. Hence, attempts to brainwash a person to adopt a different belief would violate the essence of freedom of religion.[117]

Another important aspect of balancing and proportionality more generally is that they do not allow for an *a priori* determination of which of the two clashing rights is stronger than the other. By definition, this has to be established by taking into account all the relevant factors of the concrete case.

[113] Robert Alexy, 'Balancing, Constitutional Review, and Representation' (2005) 3 International Journal of Constitutional Law 572, 574.

[114] Robert Alexy, *A Theory of Constitutional Rights* (Oxford University Press 2010) 102.

[115] Koen Lenaerts, 'Limits on Limitations: The Essence of Fundamental Rights in the EU' (2019) 20 German Law Journal 779, 781.

[116] Sébastien Van Drooghenbroeck and Cecilia Rizcallah, 'The ECHR and the Essence of Fundamental Rights: Searching for Sugar in Hot Milk?' (2019) 20 German Law Journal 904, 907.

[117] See Heiner Bielefeldt, 'Limiting Permissible Limitations: How to Preserve the Substance of Religious Freedom' (2020) 15 Religion and Human Rights 3, 7.

As with human rights conflicts, conflicts between animal and human rights would have to be decided case by case, by taking into account all the relevant interests and weighing them carefully to reach a just outcome.

To be sure, the proportionality test has become the subject of spirited academic debates in recent times.[118] For instance, some have criticized the test for requiring judges to balance incommensurable values, that is, to compare apples and oranges.[119] Others argue that it undermines what is supposed to be special about fundamental rights: their peremptory force that cannot be balanced against other interests.[120] However, despite these criticisms, the proportionality test remains the most widely used test around the world to decide fundamental rights disputes. As Francisco Urbina, one of the test's most ardent critics, observes, '[i]t is the default test for adjudicating human rights disputes in jurisdictions from all five continents, both national and international, and in civil and common law legal traditions'.[121] To critics like him, this is a reason to be sceptical about the test. But for the purposes of the SMA, it is a reason to embrace the test. After all, the SMA is meant to be a tool that works in practice, even if it is not theoretically perfect. The proportionality test, for all its potential flaws, is employed in many countries to resolve rights conflicts. Judges are thus well-experienced in weighing conflicting interests. Applying the proportionality test to the resolution of conflicts between animal rights and human rights thus means requiring judges to use a tool they already use on a daily basis.

Of course, weighing human and nonhuman interests may pose some new difficulties—including that of a potential anthropocentric bias on the part of the judges. This bias could prove problematic considering that, in contrast to the Aristocracy, the SMA itself is not committed to according humans some *a priori* higher status or larger set of rights than any other species. As a result, the SMA does not, in principle, render it necessary to suspend some animal species' rights if they clash with or threaten to undermine the rights of human beings. Animal rights would be put on the scales of the proportionality test in the same way human rights are. This goes to show that the SMA, though more moderate than purely Meritocratic animal rights proposals, is still a radical proposal when compared to the Aristocratic status quo.

[118] See for an overview Grant Huscroft, Bradley W Miller, and Grégoire Webber (eds), *Proportionality and the Rule of Law: Rights, Justification, Reasoning* (Cambridge University Press 2014).

[119] For a comprehensive account, see Francisco J Urbina, *A Critique of Proportionality and Balancing* (Cambridge University Press 2017). For a response to some criticisms, see Kai Möller, 'Proportionality: Challenging the Critics' (2012) 10 International Journal of Constitutional Law 709.

[120] Nigel E Simmonds, 'Constitutional Rights and the Rule of Law' (2016) 16 Analisi e Diritto 251.

[121] Urbina, *A Critique of Proportionality and Balancing* (n 119) 1. See also Matthias Klatt and Moritz Meister, *The Constitutional Structure of Proportionality* (Oxford University Press 2012) 1.

However, as pointed out above, the SMA can also be operationalized in more Aristocratic ways. Because the SMA is sensitive to political concerns and the requirement of feasibility, officials who find themselves applying the SMA or policies arising from it may have reason for according reduced weight to the interests of nonhuman animals when those interests clash with the basic interests of human beings, in particular those who *de facto* already lack protection of their rights.[122] Especially in the early stages of the application of the SMA, there might otherwise be a backlash that could hamper the long-term success of animal rights. For a transitionary period at least, decision-makers may therefore need to consider whether it would be better in specific cases to allocate resources to human beings first, and to allow important human rights to outweigh animals' rights in cases of inevitable conflicts.

The fact that the SMA is open to being implemented in such ways explains why, as I noted above, it may be more attractive in practice than the sentientist rights approach. In contrast to the latter, the SMA can be operationalized in more Aristocratic ways if that is necessary for it to find enough support.[123] Such more Aristocratic operationalizations may prove necessary until societies become more open to viewing human and nonhuman rights as part of the same enterprise. As Jeff Sebo has put it, 'we might need to accept a speciesist double standard between humans and nonhumans to a degree, in the spirit of caring for ourselves enough to make caring for others possible'.[124]

5 Conclusion

This chapter has added an important qualification to the different strategies of Meritocratizing the Aristocratic legal status quo, which Chapter 6 explored. As I have argued here, any extensions of legal entitlements to animals should be carried out by using species membership as a criterion, not individual capacities or interests. Against the commonplace rejection of the species membership

[122] See also Iddo Porat, 'The Starting at Home Principle: On Ritual Animal Slaughter, Male Circumcision and Proportionality' (2021) 41 Oxford Journal of Legal Studies 30.

[123] Note that, even if a society adopts a more Meritocratic operationalization, this does not mean that it has to accord different weight or value to the same right in different beings. For example, in a case involving a conflict between different humans' rights to life, the German Constitutional Court refused to weigh these lives against each other such as by considering whose rights are stronger or have more value. Instead, it argued that '[e]very human life as such has the same value': German Constitutional Court, Judgment of the First Senate of 15 February 2006, 1 BvR 357/05, para 85. Sentientist rights accounts like Cochrane's, by contrast, would allow weighing the different lives against each other. See Cochrane, 'From Human Rights to Sentient Rights' (n 9) 671.

[124] Jeff Sebo, *Saving Animals, Saving Ourselves: Why Animals Matter for Pandemics, Climate Change, and Other Catastrophes* (Oxford University Press 2022) 201.

criterion in the animal rights community, I have joined more recent species-based proposals to advocate the adoption of the Species Membership Approach (SMA) for extending legal entitlements to animals. Animal rights lawyers, I argued, should no longer view the species membership criterion as a bogeyman. Instead, they should understand it as a pragmatically and politically useful framework for extending fundamental legal rights to animals. Using the test cases of Sesha, Minnie, and Knuckles, I demonstrated that the SMA is more attractive than Aristocratic and Meritocratic approaches, as well as the sentientist rights approach. Lastly, I discussed, in broad strokes, how the SMA could be operationalized and how it can respond to challenges that might arise from its implementation.

It is of course possible that, even if the SMA is operationalized in Aristocratic ways, some Aristocratic animal rights sceptics may still find fault with it. For instance, some might take issue with the very idea of extending legal personhood or rights protection beyond the human species. From their perspective, the SMA may seem little better than the sentientist rights approach, which in Chapter 5 I said would not be acceptable to Aristocratic human rights proponents. However, that does not mean that the SMA struggles as much with *Salaville's Challenge* as the sentientist rights approach does. Unlike the latter, the SMA can explain how fundamental rights can be extended to animals without undermining the equal status and rights of human beings. Hence, even if the SMA may be incapable of appeasing every sceptic, it is at least more likely to be palatable to them than the sentientist rights approach.

8
Conclusion

This book began with the *habeas corpus* petitions filed by the Nonhuman Rights Project (NhRP) on behalf of Leo and Hercules, two chimpanzees who were the first—but not the last—nonhuman animals to have a court hearing on their fundamental legal rights.[1] Justice Barbara Jaffe, who granted the hearing, ultimately denied Leo's and Hercules's petitions on the basis that she was bound to follow the decision that a higher court had reached in the case of Tommy, a chimpanzee who was never given a hearing.[2] However, Jaffe noted in her ruling that '[e]fforts to extend legal rights to chimpanzees are . . . understandable; some day they may even succeed'. Citing former US Supreme Court Justice Anthony Kennedy in the famous *Lawrence v Texas* decision (which legalized same-sex activities throughout the United States), Jaffe pointed out that 'times can blind us to certain truths and later generations can see that laws once thought necessary and proper in fact only serve to oppress'.[3] Importantly, Jaffe also pointed to the actors and factors that are decisive in improving the legal status of the oppressed:

> [T]he parameters of legal personhood have long been and will continue to be discussed and debated by legal theorists, commentators, and courts, and will not be focused on semantics or biology, or even philosophy, but on the proper allocation of rights under the law, asking, in effect, who counts under our law.[4]

This book has argued in a similar vein that law and legal practice are distinct from moral philosophy, and that they provide lawyers with a special toolkit

[1] On the pioneering *habeas corpus* petitions that were filed in Brazil as early as 1972 (albeit without securing a hearing), see Tagore Trajano de Almeida Silva, 'Brazilian Animal Law Overview: Balancing Human and Non-Human Interests' (2010) 6 Journal of Animal Law 81, 89–92.

[2] *Nonhuman Rights Project, Inc v Samuel L Stanley et al* [2015] Supreme Court of the State of New York, New York County No 152736/15; on the Tommy decision, see *Nonhuman Rights Project, Inc v Patrick C Lavery et al* [2014] State of New York Supreme Court, Appellate Division, Third Judicial Department No. 518336.

[3] *Nonhuman Rights Project, Inc v Samuel L Stanley* (n 2) 32; *John Geddes Lawrence and Tyron Garner v Texas* [2003] US Supreme Court 539 US 558.

[4] *Nonhuman Rights Project, Inc v Samuel L Stanley* (n 2) 23.

More Equal Than Others. Raffael N Fasel, Oxford University Press. © Raffael N Fasel 2024.
DOI: 10.1093/oso/9780198907435.003.0008

that allows them to think about and apply fundamental rights in ways that philosophers cannot. Concretely, I have proposed that there are good reasons for extending fundamental legal rights and legal personhood to some other deserving animals on the basis of their species membership rather than their individual capacities. This proposal—the Species Membership Approach (SMA)—has been the concrete upshot of a book that has explored neglected intellectual-historical, analytical, and practical territory surrounding the topic of animal rights and its relationship with human rights.

Focusing first on the intellectual history of human and animal rights, I have shown that modern ideas about the rights of humans and animals have been influenced by egalitarianism and naturalism—two conflicting streams of thinking which became prominent in the French Enlightenment. I explained and illustrated the tension between these two streams with the aid of the debate between Jean-Baptiste Salaville and Jean-Claude Delamétherie, revealing not only the prescient ways in which Salaville defended humanity's special status and equality, but also how Delamétherie anticipated many of the central arguments of contemporary animal rights advocates. Hence, even though Salaville and Delamétherie themselves remained largely unknown figures, the views they adopted are commonplace today.

I went on to subject the two fundamental rights conceptions which sprang from these streams to a thorough analysis. I first portrayed the Aristocratic conception, which reflects a good share of contemporary human rights scholarship and practice. That conception, I argued, has two characteristic elements: *Equal Consideration* (according to which humans, and only humans, have equal status and rights simply in virtue of being human) and *Internalism* (which *founds* this status and rights by drawing on normative decisions, stories, or interpretations). I then compared these elements to the two characteristic elements of the Meritocratic conception: *Differential Consideration* (according to which all individuals are considered deserving of rights, in virtue of and to the extent of their individual properties) and *Externalism* (which *grounds* those rights in the capacities and interests of these individuals).

As I pointed out, both the Aristocracy and the Meritocracy are ideal-types that are located on opposite ends of the spectrum of fundamental rights conceptions. This explains why attempts to devise fused theories that combine the advantages of both approaches, while avoiding any of their respective disadvantages, have proven impossible. More specifically, we saw that the strength of the Aristocratic approach (its ability to *found* fundamental rights independently of an individual's capacities and interests) and the strength of the Meritocratic approach (its ability to provide fundamental rights with a solid *grounding* in an individual's capacities and interests) are in inherent tension with each other. I also considered whether the increasingly popular sentientist rights approach (according to which animals have fundamental rights and equal status based on their shared sentience) represents an alternative to the Aristocracy and Meritocracy. Although more attractive than pure instantiations of these ideal-types, I argued that the sentientist rights approach is itself best viewed as a Meritocratic theory. Even if it was not, I showed why it should still be conceived of as being on the spectrum of fundamental rights conceptions rather than outside it. And, finally, even if the sentientist rights approach was viewed as escaping the spectrum, it runs into problems that would make it unpalatable to Aristocratic human rights proponents.

Finally, I took these insights as the starting point for an exploration of the practical consequences of the spectrum of fundamental rights. As I argued, the most viable path forward is a practical middle ground between the Aristocracy and the Meritocracy. This is because such a middle ground allows us to benefit from the virtues of both conceptions, whilst at the same time minimizing their vices. Having found that current legal systems are too wedded to the Aristocracy, I proposed a 'Meritocratization of the Aristocracy' and demonstrated—by focusing on animals' status as property and on fundamental rights—how this could be achieved. To prevent an excessive move to the other, Meritocratic extreme, I emphasized that such attempts at Meritocratizing the Aristocracy should take to heart the Aristocratic insight that group-based approaches avoid the problem of threatening the status of individuals who lack relevant capacities and interests. This was the basis on which I presented the SMA. As the cases of Sesha, Karen, and Knuckles have illustrated, the SMA is a particularly attractive way forward for those wanting to extend rights to animals without undermining the equal status and rights of marginalized humans.

In many respects, the SMA has raised more questions than it could answer. As my focus in this book was on the history and the conceptual structure of the Aristocratic and Meritocratic ideas that pointed us in the direction of the SMA, I could only cast little light on how, concretely, the SMA should be operationalized. More research is needed on this question. Let me highlight four areas which could prove particularly fruitful for future study.

First, additional studies are required on the exact role 'species' plays in determining a being's salient characteristics and its rights-grounding interests. Closely connected to this research is an inquiry into the question of whether there are other group categories than the species criterion which lend themselves to similar purposes. This latter inquiry will become particularly important if and when artificial intelligences (AIs) develop in ways that make them deserving of certain fundamental rights. Here, more research will be needed on whether and under which conditions AIs can ever be said to deserve certain fundamental rights, and to what extent useful groups (such as the 'quasi-species' I proposed in Chapter 7) can be formed on the basis of their different underlying algorithms. To answer these questions, an interdisciplinary perspective will need to be adopted, bringing together not only the expertise of lawyers, but also that of biologists, philosophers of science, and computer scientists.

Second, more scholarship is needed on the question of which species should first—and which last—benefit from the SMA. I argued in Chapter 7 that both merit and feasibility will play a role in this decision, but much more needs to be said about this, and the processes by which such political decisions will be taken must be analysed. On these issues, political scientists and sociologists will be able to contribute at least as much as lawyers.

Third, we need research examining the ways in which the SMA should apply to beings who are not paradigmatic cases of a particular species, because they have only just been conceived (like foetuses have), or because they share only some of the traits of that species *and* possess features of other species (like hybrids or chimeras do). Hybrids and chimeras exist in nature,[5] so a useful starting point could be to interrogate the characteristics of these beings and to transfer these insights to artificially created ones. An exciting body of literature has developed on the question of cyborgs,[6] and further research could try to marry that scholarship with the question of how hybrids and other non-paradigmatic cases fare under species- or similar group-based approaches.

Finally, with the incipient extension of fundamental rights for nonhumans, there is a need for more research on the issue of potential rights inflations and the question of how conflicts between the fundamental rights of animals and humans should be resolved. Existing human rights and constitutional rights literature and case law have already developed refined frameworks for the resolution of conflicts between competing human rights and between human rights and the public interest. In particular, as we saw in Chapter 7, in many jurisdictions the proportionality test has emerged as a useful tool for balancing the different interests that are at stake in such cases of conflict. Further study is

[5] See eg Sindya N Bhanoo, 'Scientists Find Rare Hybrid of Two Other Dolphin Species' *The New York Times* (13 January 2014) <https://www.nytimes.com/2014/01/14/science/scientists-find-rare-hybrid-of-two-other-dolphin-species.html> accessed 11 June 2023; Rachael Rettner, '3 Human Chimeras that Already Exist' *Scientific American* (8 August 2016) <https://www.scientificamerican.com/article/3-human-chimeras-that-already-exist/> accessed 11 June 2023.

[6] For an overview, see Spyros G Tzafestas, 'Roboethics: Fundamental Concepts and Future Prospects' (2018) 9 Information 148.

needed on how this test would work if applied to conflicts between human and animal rights, and on whether (and if so, which) practical limitations militate in favour of a pragmatic prioritization of human interests over the interests of nonhumans, at least in the short term.

Even though more research is required on these questions, I nevertheless hope to have shown that the SMA, and the historical and conceptual analysis on which it is built, advances the discourse on animal and human rights in important ways. This book has revealed that, contrary to what is widely believed, arguments that animals should have fundamental rights are not an invention of the late twentieth century, but go back to the Enlightenment, when they emerged in tandem with human rights arguments. I have also demonstrated that there is an inherent conceptual tension between the Aristocratic conception of fundamental rights, on which much contemporary theory and practice of human rights rests, and the Meritocratic conception, which is particularly popular among animal rights proponents. Awareness of this overlooked tension—along with the fact that the Aristocracy and Meritocracy have opposing strengths and weaknesses—helps us understand why the main arguments put forward by Aristocratic and Meritocratic thinkers today bear close resemblance to those put forward by their Enlightenment predecessors. More importantly, this awareness also helps show that the best practical way forward is a middle ground between the two ideal-types. And that middle ground, I argued, can best be achieved by adopting the SMA: the proposal that, in law, fundamental rights and cognate legal entitlements should be extended based on a being's species, not their individual capacities.

That the SMA is a moderate solution to bridging two extreme conceptions should not hide the fact that it is also an unorthodox and radical proposal. Not only does it refuse to adopt the dominant conviction that species-based approaches are problematic in both philosophy and law. But it also follows in the footsteps of other rights movements, such as the abolitionist movement and the women's rights movement, which have achieved momentous changes in legal practices worldwide. As Christopher Stone observed in a famous law review article from 1972, in the case of each of these other rights movements, the proposal to extend the circle of rights-holders was 'bound to sound odd or frightening or laughable'.[7] He attributed this to the fact that 'there will be resistance to giving the thing "rights" until it can be seen and valued for itself; yet, it is hard to see it and value it for itself until we can bring ourselves

[7] Christopher D Stone, 'Should Trees Have Standing—Toward Legal Rights for Natural Objects' (1972) 45 Southern California Law Review 450, 455.

to give it "rights"—which is almost inevitably going to sound inconceivable to a large group of people'.[8] One of Stone's key contributions was to show that who the law considers to be a potential rights-holder is not set in—well—stone. Instead, complementing Judge Jaffe's point about the importance of legal considerations, Stone highlights how extra-legal considerations, too, influence and change who counts in law: 'We are inclined to suppose the rightlessness of rightless "things" to be a decree of Nature, not a legal convention acting in support of some status quo. It is thus that we defer considering the choices involved in all their moral, social, and economic dimensions.'[9] My aim in this book was to stop deferring those questions, and to consider the extension of fundamental rights to animals in its many different dimensions.

[8] ibid 456.
[9] ibid 453.

Index

For the benefit of digital users, indexed terms that span two pages (e.g., 52–53) may, on occasion, appear on only one of those pages.

Figures are indicated by *f* following the page number

The manufacturer's authorised representative in the EU for product safety is Oxford University Press España S.A. of el Parque Empresarial San Fernando de Henares, Avenida de Castilla, 2 – 28830 Madrid (www.oup.es/en or product.safety@oup.com). OUP España S.A. also acts as importer into Spain of products made by the manufacturer.

www.ingramcontent.com/pod-product-compliance
Lightning Source LLC
Chambersburg PA
CBHW071250180926
51613CB00002B/191

* 9 7 8 0 1 9 8 9 0 7 4 0 4 *